Praise for *Taking Sacred Back*

"Ritual ideas do not always materialize in the same way that we imagine them. The art of ritual design is something that is often underestimated until we find ourselves in a ritual where the energy does not flow and the functionality is stifled. Nels and Judy Linde have created a book that illustrates some of the best practices that they have perfected in their own community rituals. This well organized book gives a lot of depth and support to individuals and communities in designing and executing meaningful, exciting, productive, and memorable rituals."

—Crystal Blanton, author of *Bridging the Gap: Working within the Dynamics of Pagan Groups and Society*

"Pagan paths have proliferated over the past decades. Beginning with small, discrete congregations, we grew to coming together in larger communities. Of necessity, our rituals have had to expand and adapt to those larger numbers. Sometimes this has been well done and sometimes less successfully. Nels and Judy Linde are among those who, over a period of years, have approached larger ritual creatively, always noting, evaluating, and learning what works best and what doesn't. To our benefit, in this volume they've documented what they've learned and their sharing provides us a worthy contribution to a growing corpus of teachings about working magically with larger groups."

—M. Macha NightMare, interfaith activist and author of *The Pagan Book of Living*

"I believe that one of the greatest gifts that Pagans can give each other, and perhaps the world, is the gift of good ritual. I was fortunate enough to see great rituals in my early years as a Pagan and they transformed my life. We have grown fast as a community and the number of trained ritualists has been spread too thin. Good ritual is becoming a rarity. *Taking Sacred Back* is a gift filled with love, reverence, and hope for our communities. *Taking Sacred Back* is a treasure that I hope finds its way into the hands and hearts of all who are called to bear the torch of ritual."

—Ivo Dominguez, Jr., author of *Casting Sacred Space*

"*Taking Sacred Back* is a must-have for the beginner or the advanced ritualist. It is a concise, well-written guide, full of thoughtful work based on many years of actual experience. Nels and Judy have done a superb job of handling a complex subject while at the same time making it easy to understand and even easier to assimilate. It is an amazing book and I recommend it highly!"

—H.E. Rev. Patrick McCollum, President of the Patrick McCollum
Foundation and author of *Courting The Lady* and *The Sacred Path*

"A wonderfully in-depth book. Everything is here for those who want to create community ritual. It is both insightful and educational. We would highly recommend it for both beginner and advanced ritualist."

—Janet Farrar and Gavin Bone, authors of *A Witches' Bible,*
The Witches' Goddess, The Inner Mysteries, and *Lifting The Veil*

TAKING
SACRED
BACK

About the Authors

Nels and Judy Linde are ceramic artists, drum builders, jewelry scupltors, and thing makers. Together they have eighty years of creative exeeprience and bring the highest standards of craftsmanship and love to each piece they make. They sometimes collaborate in design, or help each other in production, or just support each of their own individual creative processes. *Taking Sacred Back* is their first published work with Llewellyn and incorporates their love for crafts as well as their experience performing and organzing group rituals. Find them online at www.hawkdancing.com.

To Write to the Authors

If you wish to contact the authors or would like more information about this book, please write to the authors in care of Llewellyn Worldwide, Ltd. and we will forward your request. The authors and publisher appreciate hearing from you and learning of your enjoyment of this book and how it has helped you. Llewellyn Worldwide, Ltd. cannot guarantee that every letter written to the authors can be answered, but all will be forwarded. Please write to:

Nels & Judy Linde
℅ Llewellyn Worldwide
2143 Wooddale Drive
Woodbury, MN 55125-2989

Please enclose a self-addressed stamped envelope for reply,
or $1.00 to cover costs. If outside the USA, enclose
an international postal reply coupon.

NELS & JUDY LINDE

TAKING SACRED BACK

The Complete Guide to Designing & Sharing Group Rituals

Llewellyn Publications
Woodbury, Minnesota

First Edition
First Printing, 2016

The meditative approaches in this book are not a substitute for psychotherapy or counseling, nor are they a substitute for medical treatment. They are intended to provide clients with information about their inner workings that can add another helpful dimension to treatment with a trained medical or mental health professional, as their circumstances may warrant.

Book design by Bob Gaul
Cover design by Kevin R. Brown
Cover image by Shutterstock/144847312/©Anna Jurkovska
Editing by Lunaea Weatherstone
Interior illustrations on pages 12–13, 266, 269, 274, 278, 280, 283, 286, 288, 291, 294, 296, 300 by Mickie Mueller
Interior illustrations on pages 122, 143, 223, 239, 318, 322 by Llewellyn art department
Photos on pages 82, 84, 87, 130, 141, 194, 268 by Jenna Touchette
Photos on pages 54, 72, 290, 321 by Harmony Tribe Photo Archives
Photo on page 101 by Kim Brady
All other photos by Nels and Judy Linde

Library of Congress Cataloging-in-Publication Data
Names: Linde, Nels, 1953– author.
Title: Taking sacred back : the complete guide to designing and sharing group ritual / Nels and Judy Linde.
Description: First Edition. | Woodbury : Llewellyn Worldwide, Ltd, 2016. | Includes bibliographical references and index.
Identifiers: LCCN 2016000929 (print) | LCCN 2016004592 (ebook) | ISBN 9780738748917 | ISBN 9780738749662 ()
Subjects: LCSH: Neopaganism. | Ritual. | Rites and ceremonies.
Classification: LCC BP605.N46 L56 2016 (print) | LCC BP605.N46 (ebook) | DDC
   299/.94—dc23
LC record available at http://lccn.loc.gov/2016000929

Llewellyn Worldwide Ltd. does not participate in, endorse, or have any authority or responsibility concerning private business transactions between our authors and the public.

All mail addressed to the author is forwarded, but the publisher cannot, unless specifically instructed by the author, give out an address or phone number.

Any Internet references contained in this work are current at publication time, but the publisher cannot guarantee that a specific location will continue to be maintained. Please refer to the publisher's website for links to authors' websites and other sources.

Llewellyn Publications
A Division of Llewellyn Worldwide Ltd.
2143 Wooddale Drive
Woodbury, MN 55125-2989
www.llewellyn.com

Printed in the United States of America

Contents

Part Two: Your Ritual Toolbox

....

Introduction

We watched as the male shape, covered in feathers and matches, and the female shape, wrapped in clay snakes, each burned, to reveal the opposite-gendered image hidden beneath. Then, when they were joined, we knew that together they forged our strength of spirit. Seeing the participant reaction to this transformation, and experiencing a ritual devoid of words of instruction, helped set us on this path to Take Sacred Back!

The Union of the Elements ritual

Neopagan religions are among the fastest growing in the world, in part because they empower a personal relationship with the sacred. The resurrection of engaged ritual has inspired and introduced a whole new generation of seekers to embrace the sacred experiences possible in a group setting. Ritual can be a safe and creative method of fulfilling our spiritual needs regardless of personal belief or religious affiliation.

In the years since we first came to the Pagan community much has changed. Knowledge in ritual organization, engagement, and theater is passed informally and by regional cross-fertilization among ritual facilitators. These lessons and principles can be used to avoid many common mistakes and jump right to offering the inspired expression you have within. The purpose of this book is to give you the benefit of years of ritual experience and help you overcome the fear of learning leadership skills. We all have our special talents, and whatever yours are, this book will help you form a team that can take your community on the journey you envision!

In the following pages, we will share principles and techniques of developing and presenting successful large-group community rituals. These are drawn from our own observations, personal experiences, and presentations over the course of the last twenty-five years. Large group rituals are designed to engage a broad audience and feel inclusive and welcoming for whoever chooses to attend. Our goal is to help you develop your own ritual toolbox, filled with suggestions and methods to design and increase the impact of your rituals.

Who we are, our personal story, is unique because we each were creating ritual when we met, and then we married, becoming life partners and a team designing and presenting rituals for our community. We speak in this book mainly from the "we" voice. We each also have had personal experiences in ritual, and when we speak from that personal perspective, we will identify ourselves as such.

Nels: *I first experienced ritual with my introduction to Paganism. In 1986 I was convinced by a friend to attend Circle Sanctuary's Pagan Spirit Gathering (PSG). The day after my arrival I went to the co-created men's ritual, and as luck had it I ended up perfectly in the South of the circle of men. During the walk to the site I had met the ritual priest, and at the appropriate time he said, "Nels, please invite the fire of the South to join us." I have no idea what I said as I turned, raised my arms, and spoke, but it was good enough for the magic to touch me that day. Several times that week in ritual I danced, sang, chanted, and cried. After five days of ritual I went back home with my head spinning! I became an "eclectic Pagan" and started reading. I had no coven or group, and those first few years my Pagan "practice" became a yearly journey to PSG and participation in the festival's co-created rituals. As an artist and creative thinker, for 51 weeks a year my head would fill with ideas to include in ritual. Then for a week each year I became a ritualist. After a few years of contributing I figured out that no one else could create the ritual I envisioned. If it was going to happen, I would have to organize and lead it; no one else could do it for me. I began sponsoring Samhain rituals at my home that involved large effigy figures set aflame. I eventually contributed this prop-building skill to the main rituals at PSG and three times was priest for the men's ritual there. My vending as a craftsman took me to many festivals around the country, where I always participated in and deconstructed their rituals. And then at one festival I met Judy.*

Judy: *My fascination with ritual began early, as a child raised in a very traditional, pre–Vatican II Catholic church. The doctrines and dogma never made much sense to me, but the ritual experience—the mystery, incense, chiming bells, burning candles, and chanting which flooded my senses—that is where the magic was. Later as a young artist I began to study symbology, which led me to tarot, which led to Qabalah, Hermeticism, Ceremonial Magic (and yes, even through the doors of the Gnostica Bookstore), and on from there to the Pagan community in the Twin Cities, where I found a home in the Craft. The Wiccan teaching circle I was working with at the time celebrated every Sabbat with ritual. These were commonly attended by anywhere from 20 to 60 people. Here again I found the burning candles, incense, chanting, and chiming, and now the dogma matched the intent. Not only could I attend, as I had when I was a child, now I could also present ritual. By the time I met Nels I was surprised to find that I was good at it.*

We both began contributing to the ritual committee at Sacred Harvest Festival in 2001. In 2003 as a team we wrote and led an arc of rituals on elemental magic. This series of four rituals worked together and built upon a theme over the span of a festival. In the first ritual, we were using wet clay to cover a prop. We were at the ritual site mixing clay in buckets and had doffed our white costumes to keep them clean. The procession from the gathering point was approaching, and we realized we did not have enough time left to get ourselves clean. We looked at each other and said, "In for a penny…" and proceeded to cover our naked bodies in clay slip. We facilitated the whole ritual nude, covered in clay. After you have been naked in front of 150 people you no longer worry about making mistakes. Besides cementing our relationship as a ritual team, it verified an oft-spoken piece of Pagan folk wisdom about ritual: If you want a powerful ritual, either include a nude person or burn something. Do both and you are guaranteed success. In this one we did both.

At the festival's end people came to us in tears, saying the experience had changed their lives. We witnessed the magic that is community, and our audience of participants grew. We became engaged and committed to ritual, offering at least four major festival rituals each year, large-scale Sabbat celebrations at our home, and guest rituals at other events over the next dozen years.

Working together we found that what one of us lacked at any point in time, the other could often provide. When one got fanciful in concept, the other brought us back to earth. When one had a mental block, the other had a swell of creative inspiration. Judy came to excel at movement, blocking, voice, memorization, and flair. Nels found he was the skilled organizer, percussionist, prop builder, and problem solver, and was good at speaking from the heart. We are both master craftspeople (Judy a goldsmith and Nels a ceramic artist), so creative thinking and expression were the assets at our core. We discovered the joyful challenge of working within limits. Our best rituals came from being forced to present many aspects of a single theme. When we started we were both shy and with limited talent in the theatrical arts. Until we took the risk to offer what we saw a need for, we had no idea we could be ritualistas.

We had a major role in the creative development, production, and facilitation of all the rituals presented in this book. Some we wrote exclusively as a two-person team, others included the input of a ritual committee or team in their development. Every community ritual is made possible by the contributions of many people, and every hand helps it evolve as it takes form. Although we include the originally written words in these rituals, there were some situations where others adapted performance words in their own style. To the many people who participated in creating these rituals, we offer a profound acknowledgment and thank-you.

Permission is granted to directly use these rituals as written. We ask that credit be given in any promotional literature if used or only slightly modified. We offer them as reference for your own creativity and adaption to your circumstance and community. We hope you will use these examples as inspiration to create rituals or make them your own!

Community ritual can transform your participants and, most amazingly, will certainly change anyone who works to offer it. Taking on a leadership role in creating community ritual may seem daunting, but as it was for us, you may find it is your task to claim, and for no one else. When you do this work, you are in effect taking sacred back into your own hands and in turn, giving it as a gift to those you care about, whether you call them family, community, tribe, or clan.

We want you to succeed, to take on the challenge of offering ritual, and to create the joy it can bring to others and yourself. We structured this book to help firmly set you on that path. It begins with Part One: Your Ritual Plan. These four chapters give you a framework to consider the nature, community context, and various types, purposes, and styles of ritual available to you. To become a ritualista you will need to see all the possibilities before you. Part One will help you envision and translate your ideas and concepts into your first group ritual.

Part Two: Your Ritual Toolbox dives into every specific aspect to consider and provides the tools you need to be confident and successful with even your first ritual. It covers how to get organized and stay on track with your plan. You will learn what you might include in your ritual and why and how to do it. Engaging your audience in the ritual process is essential, and you will discover the techniques that will make your group eagerly await your next ritual. Chapters 11 through 13 contain ritual tips and props to refine your ritual to the highest level of engagement, and adapt what you have planned to different-size audiences.

Each chapter has specific examples and exercises for you to work with. As you move through the book, try them out, and by all means, write! Every idea that comes to you, every list you create, will be an asset as you grow, so begin with the ritualista's first rule: save everything! At the end of this book are resources to further explore group ritual and to find the idea, story, song, or chant that is just what you need. A good ritual experience is like love. If it is sincere and engaging and touches another, there can't be too much of it. You can do it, and every community needs you to. Now get started taking sacred back!

We offer a brief anecdote at the start of each chapter, and the complete context and script of a ritual at each chapter's end. They are a good way to practice visioning a ritual. The following ritual describes our real introduction to self-identifying as "ritualistas."

Ritual: The Union of the Elements

••••••••••••••••••

Location: Moonspirit Festival, 2006
© Judith Olson Linde and Nels Linde

Ritual context

This ritual was originally offered as three separate rituals for audiences of more than 150 each. As invited ritualists for the Moonspirit Festival, we rewrote those rituals into one combined ritual, which was more effective for a smaller audience. This ritual represents our first experience as co-facilitating ritualistas. Originally written in 2003, it betrays our Wiccan foundations and is notable for the many familiar elements we include. We created sacred space without a word of direction, danced and told relevant stories from many cultures, and included a transforming prop element that helped participants look at their gender aspects from a new perspective.

Ritual intent

Deepen your experience and understanding of the power, symbology, and connection between the masculine elements of Fire and Air and the feminine elements of Water and Earth, and their intimate relationship with each other.

Ritual description

Consider which masculine aspects need enhancing within and prepare to charge a feather symbol with them. Which feminine aspects within need recognition as you add your snake of renewal? Masculine and feminine conjoined create magic.

Ritual setup and supplies

- Four directional altars, each with tiki torch, lighter, and a small table with the following: a bowl of sand for North, a sage smudge stick and holder for East, a sparkler for South, and a bowl of water for West

- A central fire, with a shovel for spreading fire to sculptures

- A glow stick pentacle, hidden nearby

- Two straw-covered steel sculptures. One was male, with an exterior female straw "skin"; this was placed in the Northwest, along with a tub of wet clay, a bucket of wash water, and a towel. One was female, with a male straw "skin"; this was placed in the Southeast, along with a basket of feathers and stick matches.

- Smudge stick and red clay slip anointing bowl at gate

- Bell, drum, flute, chime, didgeridoo

Team members

Co-facilitators Ritualista 1 and Ritualista 2 with bell; four people as elementals; four dancers, one at each direction; percussion core (four people) in place: drummer for North, flute for East, chime for South, didgeridoo for West.

Ritual script

The circle was silently banished (cleared of negativity) and blessed by ritualistas together, as a drum-led procession arrived. The East and West elemental team members formed a gate in the East. As festivants entered through the gate, the East elemental briefly smudged each participant, the West marked their foreheads with a dot of red clay slip, and they were silently directed to form a circle. The ritual opening was without words.

Having completed the entrance, the directional elementals sat at their respective altars. The ritualistas were near the center fire. The bell was chimed by Ritualista 2, and the North/Earth elemental rose and with an exaggerated flourish took the hand of the person to her left, who took the hand of the next person and so on (hand-to-hand circle casting with no words). As the hand-to-hand circle approached the East altar, the bell was chimed again and the East/Air elemental repeated the action. The bell chimed as each elemental continued the action around the circle until the circle was completed in the North.

Ritualista 2 rang the bell, and the Air elemental faced East and with a large exaggerated flourish made an air-invoking pentacle using a smoking smudge stick. He lit his tiki torch, and a flute played as the East/Air spirit dancer welcomed the element.

Ritualista 2 rang the bell, and the Fire elemental faced South and with a large exaggerated flourish made a fire-invoking pentacle in the air using a lit sparkler. He lit his tiki torch, and a chime played as the South/Fire spirit dancer welcomed the element with movement.

Ritualista 2 rang the bell, and the Water elemental faced West and with a large exaggerated flourish made a water-invoking pentacle in the air with water flung from the bowl. She lit her tiki torch, and a didgeridoo played as the West/Water spirit dancer welcomed the element.

Ritualista 2 rang the bell, and the Earth elemental faced North and with a large exaggerated flourish made an earth-invoking pentacle in the air using sand spray from a bowl. She lit her torch, and a drumbeat played as the North/Earth spirit dancer welcomed the element.

Ritualista 2 rang the bell, and all the instruments began a rhythm, then the elementals and helpers added in a clapping beat. When all had joined in clapping, Ritualista 1 (as the Spirit dancer) began at the North and danced around the circle, making eye contact with each participant in turn. Ritualista 2 stoked the ritual fire.

At the Southeast (between the participant circle and the center fire) stood one of the metal frame sculptures, supported by a pipe in the ground and standing about three feet tall. It contained a hidden feminine image covered with a masculine shape formed of straw.

Ritualista 2 rang the bell, signaling the elementals to begin speaking Air and Fire myths in turn:

1. (Greek) *"Daedalus conceived to escape from the labyrinth on Crete with his son Icarus by constructing wings and then flying to safety. He built the wings from feathers and wax, and before the two set off he warned Icarus not to fly too low lest his wings touch the waves and get wet, and not too high lest the sun melt the wax. But the young Icarus, overwhelmed by the thrill of flying, did not heed his father's warning, and flew too close to the sun, whereupon the wax in his wings melted and he fell into the sea."*

2. (Australian Aboriginal) *"A man went to put another log on the fire, and found it light to the touch, for it was hollow. He noticed the entire length was covered with termites, and he could not throw the branch*

into the fire, because it would kill the termites. He carefully removed all the termites from the outside of the log by scooping them into his hand, and he deposited them inside the branch. Then he raised the branch to his lips and blew the termites into the air, and the termites blown into the air became the stars, and the first didgeridoo was created."

3. (Native American) *"Coyote went East to the fire people to dance, play, and gamble, and came wearing a pitch-and-cedar-bark headdress. He complained he could not see well enough, until the fire people stoked the ritual fire high. He danced, leaning in, until his headdress caught fire, and then he ran out the lodge door swift as the wind. As the people approached to catch and kill him, he ducked behind a tree and gave the fire to the tree. Since then the people have been able to draw fire from wood with fire sticks."*

4. (North European) *"Tales of Santa Claus were inspired by flights of Laplandish shamans and tales of Odin, who flew through the air with his Howling Host on the night of the birth of the new year. He delivered gifts to his worshipers and fiery punishments to those who were not."*

Ritualista 1 said:
"In ancient times the thunder's breath, lightning, began fire, and the people hid as the wind carried it with devastation across the land. With the magic of community, these elements of Air and Fire were tamed to serve our tribe for heat and cooking and magic."

The East and South elementals joined Ritualista 1 as he took a basket from below the masculine straw sculpture and demonstrated taking a feather and a match from the basket, inserting each into the masculine straw sculpture. Ritualista 1 said, *"Such is the transformative nature of Fire and Air."*

The hidden masculine steel sculpture in the Northwest had been bound tightly with straw and string in the rough shape of a feminine figure. Ritualista 2 rang the bell, signaling all elementals to begin speaking Water and Earth myths in turn:

1. (Egypt) *"The people were created on a potter's wheel, from clay and straw, by the god Khnum. However, to be fully alive they had to be animated with the ankh, the symbol of life, by the goddess Hathor. Khnum created humans after heaven and earth were established and the battle with the water monster was won. Then Khnum made the breath of life for their nostrils. They who have issued from his body are his images."*

2. (Ojibwa) *"Manabozho climbed the tree of life as the flood waters grew until they abated, and when all was covered except his chin. The loon came and he asked it to dive down and bring back earth. It tried but floated back dead. Then the muskrat came and he promised it the ability to live on both land and water if it succeeded, so it dove and came back senseless. Manabozho breathed life back into it and begged it try again. This time it returned with the tiniest bit of earth, but that combined with the dead loon carcass allowed Manabozho to recreate the earth with all the animals, plants, and birds."*

3. (Sumerian) *"The first people were fashioned from clay by Enki, who then decreed their fate. This creation was so successful that deities celebrated with too much beer. Ninmah, who was assisting Enki in the process of making the first humans, wanted to be even more involved. Because she had drunk too much, her creations were different: One was blind, one had paralyzed feet, one lacked sexual organs, and one woman could not give birth. They are all divine creations whose dignified place in society was granted by the creators themselves."*

4. (Australian Aboriginal) *"In the beginning there was only sky and earth. In the earth was Ungud in the form of a great snake and in the sky was Wallaganda, the Milky Way. Wallaganda threw water on the earth and Ungud made it deep. In the night they dreamed and life arose from the watered earth in the forms of their dreams."*

Ritualista 2 rang the bell and said:

"Since awakened consciousness, our ancestors lived in the comfort of the earth, their homes always near water. With the deepened connection of community these elements of Water and Earth were combined like bricks to build the magic tribal village."

The Earth elemental gave Ritualista 2 a grape-sized clay blob (she had a larger one for the demo). Ritualista 2 made a clay snake by rolling it in her hands and with exaggerated gestures demonstrated wrapping it onto the straw feminine form. She washed her hands and said, *"Such is the transformative nature of Water and Earth."*

Ritualista 2 rang the bell and Ritualista 1 took the hand of a participant and drew the whole circle into a line to the masculine sculpture so they could each insert a feather and stick match onto the male straw shape. Then Ritualista 1 continued on to the feminine straw form, made a snake by hand-rolling, and pressed the snake onto the feminine straw sculpture, and then returned to the circle edge. Ritualista 2 acted as wrangler and guide as the participants repeated these actions. The East and South elementals gathered to help participants place the feather and match. The West and North elementals helped participants make a clay snake and place it on the figure, and wash up.

All sang "Earth My Body" (author unknown) during this process:
"Earth my body, Water my blood, Air my breath, and Fire my spirit,"
with a descant of *"I am born of the elements"* (four times).

Ritualista 2 rang the bell on completion of the process, and the re-formation of the circle signaled the ending of the song. Ritualista 1 and Ritualista 2 spread fire coals with the shovel to light both figures and burn off the straw. A bell cued the song by all of the ritual team when the figures were alight: "Behold (There Is Magic)," by Abbi Spinner McBride.

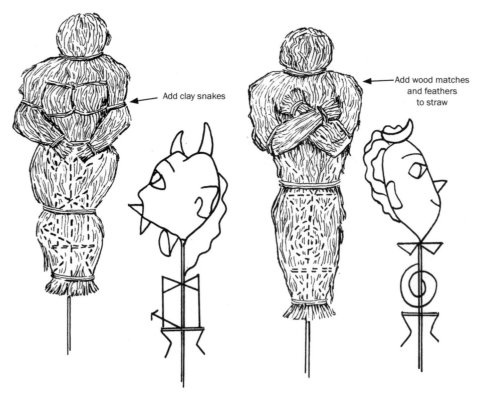

Add clay snakes

Add wood matches
and feathers
to straw

Feminine sculpture covered in straw to display a masculine profile (left).
Masculine sculpture covered in straw to display a feminine profile (right).

The song continued as the transformation of the elemental sculptures to their opposite gender by fire took place, and was recognized as magically creating our god and goddess figures. The elementals each removed their sculpture to a frame in the central area and held it as helpers joined the two sculptures together at the base and top, creating a pentacle shape where they joined. A glow stick pentacle was taped on to accent it. Ritualista 2 rang the bell for the song to end.

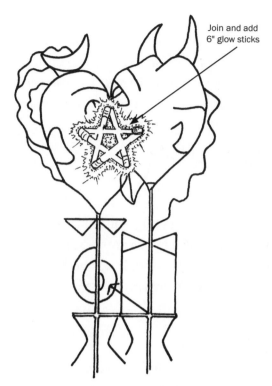

Join and add
6" glow sticks

Joined sculpture creates a pentacle,
outlined in glow sticks.

The Elementals now spoke in turn:

"Ireland had five great roads, five provinces, and five paths of the law."

"The fairy folk counted by fives."

"We note five stages in our lives: birth, adolescence, lovers, parenthood, and death."

"We have five senses: hearing, smell, sight, touch, and taste."

"We have five fingers or toes on each extremity."

"There are five knightly virtues: generosity, courtesy, chastity, chivalry, and piety."

"The Wiccan Kiss is a fivefold salute: feet, knees, womb, breasts, and lips."

Ritualista 1 said:

"Magic of five, breath of life, in mathematics and magic in many cultures. Alchemy of community, the matrix upon which the layers of existence and reality are woven, like cloth on a loom, our spirit. And at the root (the center of the pentacle) is implied a sixth element, love and free will, with which we gain control from within ourselves. With free will, we rule matter and the spirit."

Ritualista 2 said:

"As above, so below."

The ritual team started a closing song: "Air I Am," by Andras Corban Arthen (1982).

The joined sculpture was walked once around the circle by Ritualista 2, displaying the pentacle to all. For the second round, it was held at the center for a moment and then carried to each direction, starting with East. Ritualista 2 and Ritualista 1 led a farewell closing song (author unknown):

"The circle is open, but unbroken.
May the love of the Goddess be ever in your heart.
Merry meet, and merry part, and merry meet again!"

A farewell pentacle was made by Ritualista 1 while the song continued. The sculpture was then put back in its holder. Ritualista 2 rang the bell to end the song.

PART ONE

Your Ritual Plan

ONE

·········

What Is Ritual?

The 28-foot-tall effigy figure of the Corn King was swept into flames, and the result of many days of effort by scores of people was soon engulfed, sending sparks high into the dark sky above us. We who experienced the journey to this moment had created a bond. It was a connection that would sustain us through the dark time of the year, and bind us to again join in this gift to our collective spiritual expression as a community for years to come.

ANCESTOR CHAIR RITUAL

Ritual is being defined right now as we speak. In city parks, community centers, farm fields, meeting rooms, libraries, condo party rooms, and church basements, large group rituals are taking place. People are joining together to bless a new baby, welcome the return of spring, support a family whose house burned down, or just to celebrate the blessing of making fresh apple cider. The prescribed order of the ceremony, its liturgy and visual impact, are uniquely created just for the moment, much like performance art. Similar to the use of the word "ritual" to describe an oft-repeated habit, today people are assembling to share their feelings, vision, sorrows, and joys as a growing reoccurrence. We call it community ritual.

Photo by Nels and Judy Linde

The Corn King burning.

Describing ritual is like this parable common across many Eastern cultures: What is the true nature of an elephant? Six blind men feel different parts of the elephant's body:

- The man who feels the trunk says the elephant is like a tree branch.

- The man who feels the tusk says the elephant is like a pipe.

- The man who feels the ear says the elephant is like a hand fan.

- The man who feels a leg says the elephant is like a pillar.

- The man who feels the belly says the elephant is like a wall.

- The man who feels the tail says the elephant is like a rope.

Ritual is as clear in its nature as our experience of the elephant. It is defined by what we feel and perceive, and then we transcend our first impression of that elephant, and the "truth" becomes different every time!

Ritual can be an honoring or devotional ceremony. It can be a practical method to accomplish a goal. It can be a set of actions designed to create change or influence a situation. A ritual can be a spiritual event to open a pathway between oneself and the unseen. Ritual is sacred theater, evoking the principles of belief or faith, reenacting tales of the gods or of myths. Participation in ritual is a commitment to set aside time to explore our world and ourselves from a new perspective, and share that experience with others.

Rituals send signals directly to our subconscious. Mythologist Joseph Campbell believed that "by participating in a ritual, you are participating in a myth."[1] Ritual is one method for the subconscious to communicate with our waking selves. We can think we know a thing, and speak about it, but until our subconscious embraces it, it remains superficial to us. To enlist the cooperation of the subconscious we need to show it, in a sensate manner, that it can absorb the essence of the information presented in a structured time and space. Ritual is a tool that helps us take the experience and processes of living and understand and integrate them.

Rituals are a feature of all human societies. Each historical and regional culture has defined its own specific priorities through how it has shaped its rituals. How did they establish their status as adults, leaders, elders, warriors, or in spiritual leadership? How did they promote their group welfare or survival? How did they deal with loss and tragedy? The rituals a society practices are the key defining feature in understanding a culture, past or present.

We demonstrate our need for ritual all through our lives at births, spiritual dedications, entry into adulthood, pairing unions, graduations, anniversaries, and even at

---

1   Joseph Campbell, *The Power of Myth* (New York: Anchor, 1991), p. 82.

death. Ritual can be for just a few people to conduct in private, or it can be for an experience for a specific or large community.

Ritual is a response to our questioning the existence of magic or deity. When we doubt, ritual comforts that uncertainty.

Nels: *I recently attended a sumbel ceremony, which involves three rounds of individual toasts offered by participants.[2] In the first round we each toasted to our own deities, and the participants were instructed that they could answer with "All hail [deity name]!" if they felt they had a relationship to that deity. When it came to be my turn, I raised the drinking horn and said, "I honor the un-named Horned God who is my patron," since he had not revealed his name to me. I had no idea how others would react to him. At that instant the heavens cracked open with lightning striking directly behind me. Those assembled responded immediately with "All hail the Un-Named God!" All knew he was present.*

Judy: *Years ago, at a friend's coming-of-age ritual for her teen daughter, I took the role of ritualista. Just as I started my incantation to the Goddess, it began softly raining. As I finished, maybe a minute later, the rain stopped. She was certainly there, and tears were shed.*

In ritual we experience the supernatural, unseen forces that shape the present and future. To speak to the power within nature, or the supernatural embodied as deity, requires a special time set aside from normal life. These events occurring within ceremony confirm that forces are at work in our lives and reassure us spirituality is real. In this way, the experience of ritual offers healing for recurring feelings of doubt.

Ritual is not synonymous with theater. Not all ritual involves theatrical principles and skills. Neither is a theatrical performance inherently a ritual. There is a lot of overlap between the two, and the tools and techniques of each can be used enhance the effectiveness of the other. Theater almost always defines its audience as spectators in something performed *for* them. It is rare in theater for the audience to be meaningfully drawn into the story and experience it at the same depth as a ritual can offer.

---

2   Norse ritual toasting celebration.

Ritual offers a way to acknowledge and meet our specific needs, and be free of the control of religion within the experience. Rituals outside the context of religious tradition are by nature ephemeral—they tend to be different each time they occur and can change rapidly even when repeated. This uniqueness does not define the potential of their impact upon us nor their importance to our well-being.

Why Create Community Ritual?

We embrace this definition of community ritual: "*A community ritual is a set of actions, gestures, and words offered within a large group to benefit its shared spiritual and emotional needs or interests.*"

Why would you offer community ritual? The prime motivation must always be to offer it as a sacred gift of service. It is not about ourselves, our message, or our ego. It is about a community, their needs and desires, and how we can help to fill them. In ritual we connect with the sacred, and that experience is of benefit to ourselves and our audience. Many of us live in isolation, even when surrounded by people. Ritual creates a mutual intimacy that draws solitary people out to dare to reveal themselves.

You will personally experience the benefits of the community you build through ritual. You will make new friends and find people similar to yourself. If you are a spiritual seeker, you might find a teacher, or if you are a teacher, you may find students. You will certainly create a base of people who have a common interest in exploring their spirituality and establish a network of people who can offer each other support.

Creating ritual will expand your perspective about people and their feelings. Humans respond to the ritual experience in very individual and sometimes surprising ways. You may find a reserved person speaking deeply from their heart in ritual, or a seemingly unemotional person awash in tears. You will also learn so much about yourself. What emotionally moves you? How do you express your own spiritual nature and share it with others?

You will grow from the experience. You will learn how to share yourself with others authentically. You will learn how to work with a team, how to ask for what you need and offer what you can give. The skills of working with others come easily for some of us, but putting together a ritual involves knowing both when to step up and knowing when to step back and let someone else shine. A ritual team is made up of volunteers, and working with and guiding a group of volunteers requires patience, finesse, polite firmness, and compassionate understanding.

You will observe the effects of authentic rites of passage upon people. Most of us have experienced life passage rituals that had little meaning to us, other than we survived them. You may discover you haven't had meaningful rituals that were needed to move past and integrate your life experience.

You can create ritual! The creation and offering of this gift of service requires some learned skills. In our larger society we too often relegate the skills we can benefit from learning ourselves to professionals or clergy. Today most couples are intensely involved in making their wedding ritual relevant to what they particularly want. They are taking a hand in creating a ritual that is sacred to them.

Ritual validates and affirms what we already know as we move through our lives. We need ritual! We crave it and suffer from its absence. The created ritual experience, in its diversity of types, forms, and purposes, can be of great benefit for both individuals and communities. The lasting ritual tradition of the future will be one created by all of us and for our benefit.

How to Use This Book

Most people who pick up this book have had a significant or life-changing experience or realization in a group ritual. Until you have felt that sacred jolt or heartfelt joy, all these words are a bunch of interesting concepts. It takes time for this kind of motivation to come to you through observing the real difference ritual can make in people's lives. Offering ritual to others can be a very heady ego boost, and you need to remain aware of that possibility. Those who commit to it and keep at it will connect to ritual's true nature. It is a vehicle for improving the human condition and making us all more whole.

Creating and offering a ritual involves many different skills. Especially as the numbers of participants in a ceremony increase, the skill level needed and the complexity of the many factors affecting the ritual experience also increase. By starting with smaller communities (fewer than 25 people) and offering basic and focused rituals, you can develop your skills and confidence to overcome any doubts you might have in your abilities. The power of ritual to create change will be felt within you as you seek to make your gift the most meaningful it can be.

Creating ritual involves a lot of list-making and brainstorming. This is a great time to start a ritual resource notebook or folder. As you move through this book there is a lot of information to absorb. Start keeping notes of those concepts and ideas that resonate with you. Judy keeps a small voice recorder with her at all times for preserving thoughts while driving. This book contains exercises to help you develop your ritual skills. Take the time to try them and add them to your notebook, even if they feel premature. The information you add now will be invaluable to review and include again later as your skills develop.

We have included stories of ritual experiences we have offered to different communities. While most could be used as presented, they were designed for a specific time, place, and community. Use them to get your imagination and creative juices flowing. Once you begin working with ritual you will find ideas, songs, concepts for props, and hands-on activities start coming to you. Jot every idea down; you will probably use it at some later time. We have held on to ideas for years and it is so gratifying to pull them out when we need a solution.

All that is essentially required to start creating ritual is a vision and the desire: knowing you want to help people, groups, and communities be better friends, be closer, and share the joy of being human. With some tools to guide you, the rest will fall into place.

Ritual: Ancestor Chair
• • • • • • • • • • • • • • • •

Location: Home Samhain Ritual, 2003
© Nels Linde and Judith Olson Linde

Ritual context

Every year for the last 20 years we have provided a Samhain celebration for our extended community and family of choice. This has always included a corn-covered brush effigy figure, from 20 to 35 feet tall, constructed over the two weekends before Samhain. On the weekend nearest October 31, more than a hundred people come out to our rural home, decorate, and make final preparations of the ritual circle and effigy centerpiece. Our ritual is different each year but has evolved to include similar elements. We cast sacred space surrounding our whole property at dusk. We all gather in our home for a potluck spirit supper at which a mysterious figure joins us, and then follow a path-working experiential journey in the darkness to our ritual circle, where within the ritual the Corn King is set aflame.

Ritual intent

We embrace the time of our ancestors when they are nearest and can hear our pleas. We offer sacrifice to them that they will help and guide us.

Ritual description

Prepare your offering, a symbol of your sacrifices, and hear the words of Charon. Journey to the river Styx and pass over to death or plant the seeds of rebirth. Your card holds the key to the year ahead.

Ritual setup and supplies

We instructed participants ahead of time to bring a dollar bill with them to the ritual.

- House: Spirit chair, ancestor altar curtain, ancestor silhouette, dollar bill basket and instructions, a red marker, hemp rope, lamp oil

- Along path: Luminaria, Hecate setup with scissors and bag of fava beans, hot-glue gun with cord, bowl of pomegranate seeds, bowl of apple stars, tarot deck

- River: Four-foot planter box hung on metal posts at river edge, oar for Charon

Team members

- Two guides to select people to send down the path from the house

- Hecate

- Maiden with glue gun

- Pomegranate giver

- Apple giver

- Charon

- Death Dancer

- Several keeners at the river

- Card reader at the final circle path

- Choir in circle

- Ritual tasks:
  - » Pairs for calling the directions
  - » God caller
  - » Goddess caller
  - » River path regulator

Ritual script

The ancestor altar was set up all day Saturday in the house: two main tables and the spirit chair between them at the west wall of the living room. A colored-paper silhouette of a person was behind the chair, and there was a curtain for privacy. There was a board in front of the chair with two candles, the dollar bill basket, and instructions: "Close the curtain and mark your bill in a manner you will recognize. Place in the basket for the ancestors, and spend some time imagining the sacrifices made to allow you to progress to this point. When you are done, open the curtain."

Food for the spirit supper was fully prepared to serve when the ritual began at 7:15. The ancestor curtain was removed. The ritual area was blessed privately at dusk. The circle was defined by a teen carrying a torch, encompassing the whole property. The directions were called by pairs who were spotlighted as the moving torch reached their direction, then the male/female deity was called in the front yard. All returned to the house, where we filled and offered the ancestor plate.

There was a knock at the door and Charon entered. He was dressed as Death and offered his advice: honor and respect the ancestors, and know and appreciate all the sacrifices that were asked of them to bring you to this day. Dinner began with his departure.

When dinner was finished, the team prepared the ritual area. They lit all the torches and altar candles and the small drummers' fire at the ritual area, as well as luminaria along the path. The glue gun was plugged in. The fruit givers, Charon, and the path characters and guides took their places.

Two keeners in white face came into the house and removed the spirit chair outside to Hecate's path station. Then guides began selecting guests to give the "start card" to. This was a card that said to ready themselves, go to the basket and retrieve their marked sacrifice (dollar bill), and make their way to the back door. So the team got the full experience as well as the guests, the guides selected people in this order: Hecate, glue maiden, basket givers, regulator, keeners, Death Dancer, Charon, card reader, drummers, and choir. They each traveled the path to their station, and finished their experience when all guests had passed by.

The path to the ritual led first to Hecate, where she took the sacrifice (dollar bill), folded it, and cut it in the center with scissors. She passed a fava bean through it to the guest, saying:

"The seed of life always resides within death. Plant it in its time… when the dead dance for you." She then offered her tarot deck and told each guest, *"Draw a card to find your key this night."*

Hecate handed the participant's dollar bill to the glue maiden, who folded it decoratively and hot-glued it to the ancestor chair. A helper guide sent the guest down the river path. Next the guest met an apple server at the crossroads, who offered a piece and said, *"Eat of the fruit of Life that is Death."*

The guest proceeded onward to meet the pomegranate server, who offered a piece and said, *"Eat of the fruit of Death that is Life."*

Approaching the river, each guest was stopped by the regulator, who timed the progress of the guests so that each went forward to the river alone. Charon was at the river's edge, with a keener on each side of him, walking upstream and downstream making sorrowful sounds. The Death Dancer was across the river in a black leotard painted as a skeleton, and front-lit by three candles.

The Corn King, 2011.

Charon introduced himself and asked, *"Is it your time to cross over?"*

The planter filled with earth was nearby, and the guest was left to meditate and commune with the dead until their bean had been planted (if they didn't figure it out, Charon chided the guest to plant it). A keener moved each guest down the path, where they encountered the card reader.

The card reader looked at the tarot card each participant had been given and handed the guest a candle to light, saying:

"Light this from the torch of the [East, South, West, or North by type of minor arcana card]," or *"Light this where the ancestors call to you [for major arcana cards]."*

The card reader noted who had the Magus and Empress cards and told Hecate their names when she arrived.

As the last person down the path, Hecate walked the circle, saying:
*"You have all tread the path, tasted the fruit, and planted your seed at the edge of
the underworld. Your sacrifice has been accepted here, upon the seat of our ancestors.
Two of you have been called this night to open the gate. Hold out your cards now so I
may find you!"*

The guests held up their cards and Hecate quickly found them (Magus and Empress) by the advance tip from the card reader. She took them to the ancestor chair, now covered in dollar bills. Hemp rope, which had been dowsed with lamp oil, was fastened down the back. A torch was passed to Hecate, who lit the chair that was covered with the sacrifice (dollar bills). The Magus and Empress carried the chair once around the circle and placed it between the legs of the corn effigy figure. Hecate and the guests, using their candles, lit the circumference of the effigy.

The choir began the song "Hecate," by Seridina. The song continued until a bell was rung at the fire's crescendo, followed by a silent elemental release by Hecate … and drumming and dancing continued on into the night.

TWO

·········

Getting Started

A hundred people were gathered tightly around our sacred fire, declaring we were
now "walking in the way of gratitude." It was a difficult road to get here, to make
acknowledging our collective and individual blessings the primary force now
moving us forward. As participants added their own verses declaring their personal
blessings, what became clear was that our collective reverence for the earth and
the opportunity to share our diverse spiritual selves were at the heart of our
gratitude. We were all together in this moment, ecstatic and blessed.

GRATITUDE RITUAL

To be successful at creating sacred experience for others you need to bring some commitments to the process. You must be willing to develop techniques for working with people. Learning and using all the skills needed for groups to work together as a team and increase their unity is as important and sacred as the ritual you offer. You need to accept that you may create ritual and attend to every detail, provide every symbol and clue as to what the intended experience will be like, but once the ritual starts, the best you can do is offer your gift and let each person define what is shared and what meaning they will take from it. You have no control over another person's individual experience and how they accept the opportunity that sharing ritual in groups offers.

The purposes of rituals for groups are as varied and diverse as people are. Celebration of relationship with deity and the expression of our spirituality remains a primary purpose. The satisfaction of physical or emotional needs, strengthening of social bonds of support, moral education, demonstrations of respect, and obtaining acceptance have all become common themes within ritual.

Helping another ritualista or group is the best way to jump into learning. You can see how people think, share, and work together. Establishing a mentoring relationship with someone more experienced gives you a chance to learn some basic skills and observe the whole process from beginning to end. However, you may have no access to creative group ritual or a mentoring relationship.

If you are working as an individual, a rite of passage for another person or a celebration ritual is a good place to start. These have a clear purpose, hone your skills at meeting the needs of others, and have history to draw upon for inspiration. The purpose of the ritual inherently sets the tone, and participants are usually already prepared for what to expect. They are attending because they support the sharing that will take place and will be happy to be included. These rituals have an expectation that there will be a clear leader, a master of ceremonies, and are some of the few rituals that can be offered for fairly large groups by an individual.

As the ritual purpose becomes more complex or participant numbers grow, there are drawbacks to working alone. You have all the decisions to make and no one to bounce your ideas off of. You have the benefit of complete control over the script and execution, but one person can only do one thing at a time. Your plan must be very basic, something you can handle alone. You may be able to ask for specific help as your audience arrives, but be prepared to fill every role you plan for. Starting out, it is helpful to present your outline to someone you trust to give honest feedback before you finish planning. When you work alone, it is much easier for your vision of the event to get sidetracked into areas that may not be essential.

Many people have had some experience in a small group or coven participating in ritual as part of a tradition or as a guest. Any group in which you already work spiritually is a natural place to look for team members to join you in offering a ritual with a broader appeal. If you are offering a ritual for a more public or expanded group for the first time, be wary of using those familiar tradition methods without adapting them for your larger audience.

Everyone brings their own interests, skills, and biases to the ritual table. You may have a dominating love for theater, song, or dance. Costumes, pageantry, or constructing things might be a strong interest you want to share. You may only see ritual as meant for a deeply spiritual or transformational experience. Not every person who is willing to help will have the same commitment, and that is okay. It's easy to think we know the best or right way to think about something, but at this point you are casting a wide net for people to work with!

Find and Assess Your Community

Who is your community? You may think it is just the group of your friends, but it can include most of the people you interact with. A casual assembly at an annual festival can create a community. With use of the Internet, people who have never met in person can interact and become a community. The amount of time spent together limits what a community shares but not necessarily the depth possible within it. In a mobile and fragmented society, place is not such a primary factor in the formation of communities anymore. Place loses its importance when you don't know your neighbor, the guy upstairs, or the widow down the block.

• • • • • • • • • • • •

Exercise

Make a list of all the connections you have and groups you interact with, then classify what characteristics each group has using the questions below. Add this to your ritual notebook.

- *What groups are place-based?* School, work, home, neighborhood, city, and larger areas.

- *What groups share your interests?* Hobbies, sports, vocation, spiritual beliefs, political or social issues, intellectual pursuits, volunteer work.

- *What groups share a particular characteristic you have?* Your gender, sexual orientation, age group, social status, ethnicity, or history.

- *What groups focus on personal improvement?* Recovery groups, exercise clubs, diet and other food groups, social skill groups.

It may be difficult to imagine engaging many of your groups to participate in a community ritual, but individuals from any of them may be interested in attending. The more the group shares in common, the more successful you will be. Most importantly, it should include people who are willing to explore their spiritual nature. Those groups we call your *core* ritual community, the best ones to create ritual for.

Many people who pick up this book will not have a community ready-made to work within. You may be new to your area, or in a place where a conservative mindset or a religious group dominates. You will need to find or create the community that will embrace sharing ritual together. Any group meeting to connect with the power within us becomes a community.[3] For groups large or small, intimate or public, community forms around the ritual experience.

We work mainly in the Neopagan community, a diverse audience. Some follow specific religious beliefs; others have a vague sense of the divine in their lives. Most have a connection with the natural world, which includes people focused on environmental concerns without a strong spiritual component. Some are oriented toward promoting health, nourishment, and techniques to heal or help others.

How do you find Pagans or others in the alternative spirituality movement? You may have to search in your area to find this community or gather one up. Social media groups are the place to start. Use Facebook, Yahoo groups, Meetup.com, and other social networks online to look for alternative spirituality groups in your area. Try searching with many different words to find the diversity of people in your area exploring spirituality. The Pagan Pride Project has groups in every major city, and the Covenant of Unitarian Universalist Pagans (CUUPS) has many chapters around the country. Check Witchvox for groups or events to contact.[4]

---

3   Malidoma Patrice Somé, *Ritual: Power, Healing, and Community* (London: Penguin Books, 1997), p. 49.

4   Pagan Pride Project, www.paganpride.org; CUUPS, www.cuups.org; Witches' Voice, Inc., www.witchvox.com.

....

Exercise

Write down descriptive search terms, words and phrases that describe where you might find your community. Later, use the resources above to search online for groups and activities that you can network with. Add this to your ritual notebook.

Many types of groups, events, and activities could benefit from sharing a sacred experience together. Don't overlook more general groups and communities that may welcome adding a spiritual component for their members. You may also find friends and potential team members by researching, participating, and volunteering with these groups:

- Food: Community Supported Agriculture Farms (CSAs), food co-ops, or organic food groups

- Growth and education: Spiritual groups, dance, choir, drumming, exercise, yoga, or meditation groups

- Change: Environmental, political, social justice, or transformational groups

- Empowerment: Twelve-step, public speaking, fellowship, or groups responding to a crisis

- Crafts and interests: Book, study, knitting, hunting, or sports groups

Take care in how you present yourself when forming or looking for a community to work with. If you use words that are too specifically Pagan or "Wicca-centric" you may frighten off people who could be a part of your potential community or team. Even the word "ritual" can be off-putting if you don't explain exactly what you mean in describing the event you want to plan. "I want to find others to help create a ritual ceremony in a park to honor and celebrate the bounty of the harvest" will resonate with a broad group of people. "I need help casting a Mabon circle to the Gods in a park" will draw a more limited response, even in the Pagan community.

The Audience

You have made observations about your community in your notes and have some idea of whom you are working with. Now you need to identify with them as an aspect of yourself or you will be helpless to design a ritual to meet their needs. It is easy to make superficial assumptions and apply them to a whole group of people. In ritual design, you will need to experience the ritual you imagine though their eyes.

What is the demographic information about your specific audience? Are they predominately young or old? What stage of life? Are they single? Do they have small children? Are they experienced in ritual or new spiritual seekers? What factors or interests do they have in common? Here is where you must rely on relationships already forged within that community; call, chat, and network until you have the information you need. Do your best to get accurate data.

You will also need to decide which parts of your potential audience you will accommodate. Adults are easy, but children and teens may need special consideration in your planning to keep them engaged and participating. Elders and many others may have limited mobility or may not be able to stand for extended periods. Will you provide or allow chairs for those who need them or a shortened distance to move within the ritual? Sight- and hearing-impaired people will often attend if they know they are welcomed and accommodated. How you integrate portraying and speaking in regards to gender can either empower or offend participants. Being sensitive and aware of the biases you bring to ritual is crucial if you want to reach the full range of diversity your community may include. In these important areas it is wise to ask for help reviewing your ritual plan from people who work with impaired or marginalized populations.

You may not have the resources to fully fund the event you envision. For some participants even a small fee may inhibit their attendance. Will you provide the budget yourself, fundraise, solicit private donations, or ask a fee of your audience?

·············
Exercise
Write down all the different types of people, ritual experience, spiritual beliefs, and limitations you want to be sure to accommodate in your ritual. This may change with subject and circumstance, but make a record now of who you generally want to adapt

for in your planning to ensure they are welcomed and can participate. Add this to your ritual notebook.

At some point in your planning, projected attendance will have to be addressed. If there is history with a community or event, that is a good place to start. If it is a new venture, look at similar events and their first-time attendance to get a reasonable estimate. Start with an estimate of the total of your likely audience pool, then consider any scheduled competing events that may draw some of that audience away.

Outdoor events can be completely dependent on weather for attendance, and even indoor rituals will be limited if travel is affected by weather. If outdoors, is there an alternate location? Can the ritual go onward in a light rain? Will you need to cancel in strong wind or rain, and if so, is rescheduling a possibility? How would rescheduling affect attendance?

Rites of passage and small group events (between 15 and 40) usually have a well-defined invitation list. Planning is much easier in this case. The difference between the number of people expected and those who actually attend is small enough that planning and ritual design need not be critically changed. The difference between 20 and 40 is much easier to accommodate than between 150 and 300!

For a large-group community ritual, you should be able to start with a "reasonable expectation" of attendance, say 75 people. This should be a just slightly optimistic estimate. Then add about 50 percent to that number (35, or 110 total) and be sure to have supplies to accommodate that many. Imagine the ritual's ability to function well with that maximum number. Plan in advance for likely problems in the ritual design if attendance reaches this point. Have a few alternate changes to make on the fly to resolve these problems if you are blessed with overwhelming participation!

A peer ritual audience can be one of the best and easiest groups to design an effective and intimate ritual for. As their peer, you know their issues, likes, backgrounds, and have a common base of knowledge. You should be able to speak easily to their perspective and life insights. At times a unique interpretation of what a group has in common will touch peers more effectively than incorporating their obvious similarities. Here a brainstorming group can aid in expanding your ritual perspective in the early planning stages of ritual development. Even in this most homogeneous group a written definition elaborating the nature of their similarity will be helpful in your ritual description.

A shared experience may serve to define an audience. A traumatic event or cultural tradition may bond a group together. Recent conflict, resignation, death, or a reason to celebrate can be powerful elements to consider. An interview with a group elder may reveal more about this audience than other information available.

Public rituals can be some of the most difficult to design. In public rituals anyone who wishes to attend is welcomed. A public ritual outdoors may include anyone who happens by, the curious, or a casual participant. Indoors, a public ritual is usually limited at least to those who made the conscious choice to attend in advance. The tendency is to develop public rituals with a mind toward the lowest common denominator. This is usually a mistake that leads to the most unmemorable rituals! Rarely is your audience truly a simple societal cross-section. They may have a common interest in spirituality and spiritual matters. They may be generally familiar with Pagan, New Age, and occult concepts. They may have cultural, ethnic, or class similarities to draw upon. Advance research on your locality, advertising target, and likely audience draw will help narrow down which "public" you will likely be working with.

Sometimes the best method to really engage a public audience with an intimate ritual is to make your best assessment of unifying factors and work from there. The concepts you present and tools you use may seem old hat to some of your audience, but may be perfect for a majority of them. For instance, many people may have experienced the use of mirrors in ritual to promote self-examination, but for others it will be a totally new concept.

However you assess your public audience and choose to approach the ritual, you will probably need a larger ritual team. You won't be able to presume a basis of ritual experience, and so will require more facilitators for key movement or action parts of the ritual. If you are using songs and chants you will need both a larger "choir" and a printed handout. These are good ideas for any ritual, but with this audience you need to plan on more of everything. Keep to a solid and simple ritual design, with a well-practiced team.

Children and Youth
Children are generally welcomed within community ritual. Your ritual should be clearly enough defined so parents know whether it will be suitable for any child, particularly if

children are to attend the ritual unaccompanied by a parent, as is sometimes the case with teens. As parents, we always tried to consider whether we were bringing our children because we felt they would get something out of it, or because we could not secure other care for them. Children's actions during ritual can be disruptive, but with a fully engaged ritual audience they often become invisible to participants, or even better, bring a blessed lightness to the proceedings. The effort to provide for participation of children will expand the audience of your ritual and help it become a shared family experience.

Parents, embarrassed by a child's behavior, can be more disruptive with scolding and attempts at containment than the children themselves. A child's attention span varies wildly with age and experience. Parents are the best judge of the length of time and the experiences their children can handle. A fiercely screaming or out-of-control child should probably be removed, at least to the margins of a ritual, but only by their parent.

A child's reaction during your ritual is not within your control as a ritual team. The best you can do is clearly inform parents of the details, timing, and nature of the ritual in advance, and let them make wise choices. There are some ritual experiences that are not suitable for children. Direct sexual or death references, even when framed carefully, are not appropriate. It is so much easier to exclude and say "not appropriate for children" if you are offering controversial content. Most young children have a fairly short attention span, so long speeches or somber guided meditations are not recommended.

Rituals designed specifically for youth demand special attention to age-appropriate themes and content. Many would experiment with the tender sensibilities of youth in ritual, to offer what they believe they may have been moved by as a child. We believe the opposite approach is warranted. The best way to design rituals for youth is to find what issues and themes concern them most and then aid them in the development of their own rituals. Parents should be included in planning and reviewing the ritual intent. Lighthearted rituals and fun, even "crafty," activities work the best for younger children. Clarity of ritual intent is particularly important for older youth rituals. They can easily lose sight of the purpose and focus on props or theater. Older youth have a tendency to organize rituals mimicking adult rituals, replacing content with what they find more relevant. Work with teens by reviewing the elements of ritual and then let them suggest methods and processes that they find meaningful to accomplish the main parts of a ritual. There are several published resources specifically for rituals for children and teens.[5]

Rites of passage for youth can be the most profound of experiences for young people and their parents. We don't advise youth presenting their own rites of passage or creating one for their peers. The whole point is for the wise ones of the community to provide this event. The best results occur when both youth and parents are consulted in their desires and expectations for these rites, and then experienced ritualistas offer the actual ritual. These are not appropriate times to experiment.

The Ritual Team

What if you have a grand ritual vision for a large group of people? This is the time to start forming a team. A team is not the answer to a lack of experience, or a way to avoid responsibility by spreading out the leadership role. We have worked in purely co-created ritual, where many people collectively create by consensus. We have found over the years that working with a team to refine details and production is great, but having just a couple people at most with the overall guiding vision for the finished ritual usually generates the strongest result. Occasionally one can assemble a team of people with previous ritual production experience who can also effectively share leadership and co-create a ritual. This is a thing of beauty and reflects a community with significant ritual experience.

Being a leader is a scary thought! Responsibility is expected, personal risks must be taken, and demands are made upon you. No one starts out a leader. Sometimes you may find that you have stepped up because no one else will. Dare to take small risks, push yourself, and then bang! You get called a leader. Whether you are working alone or with others, it is time to start learning this skill.

Leadership is needed to recruit members, encourage team enthusiasm, develop talent, and make sure the essential decisions are made. Leadership styles that solicit member input, listen attentively, and respectfully direct the final choices for the team function best. The theatrical model of a director may work well for a specific vision with paid actors, but has some inherent obstacles to building the real team feeling of co-creation needed for creating an effective ritual.

---

5   David Salisbury, *Teen Spirit Wicca* (Soul Rocks Books, 2014).

In any group process, the leader needs the ability to sort through the personal dynamics and relationships involved in communication. This can be more important than the talent of the team or any other factor in creating ritual. Ritual team members want to feel appreciated and respected for their gifts. Being able to accurately assess people's strengths and weaknesses is an ability that will serve well in the long run. Your leadership style will need to acknowledge and praise each person at every step of the process to keep your volunteers intact and happily involved. Often team brainstorming can produce enough good ideas to flesh out five rituals, and we all tend to invest ourselves into our ideas. Your job will be to sort through these ideas and decide which are most appropriate for your intent without offending team members.

To assemble a team, first look to the community for which the ritual is intended. Community members already have an investment and know their help will be appreciated by the ritual participants. To reach out to a larger community, the team leader will need to personally appeal to and inspire members to contribute. As in politics, a leader's ability to translate personal capital (the goodwill accumulated by past acts and relations with others) into a ritual team volunteer becomes paramount. We as ritualistas have been compared to Tom Sawyer finding help to whitewash the fence.[6] You may need to develop the ability to cajole ritual service from community members!

Ritual teams for smaller rituals usually function as a "committee of the whole." They make plans and most decisions together. The more egalitarian a ritual team becomes, however, the harder it can be to assert the leadership needed to focus on the intention of the ritual. With larger ritual teams, organizing smaller groups by the type of ritual role works well. Team members who help wrangle or move people, or have isolated or uncomplicated roles, can be integrated and rehearsed without the same time commitment as major action role players. Often a large ritual will have a choir, and they can certainly meet separately and be integrated with cueing. Volunteers appreciate attention to limiting their time commitment. No one likes to stand around at meetings or rehearsals that don't engage the majority of the team.

---

6   Mark Twain, *The Adventures of Tom Sawyer* (San Francisco: The American Publishing Company, 1876), Ch. 2.

Team Roles

For teams large or small, produce a list of ritual roles that you need to fill. In looking for members, try to fill the most challenging action roles first. Understand, you as team leader may need to take one of these roles, to inspire others to participate. Then cast the net wide in your community and follow up by personally contacting those who seem promising. This will be the most likely method to entice someone to join you.

Most community rituals will need someone to look to for cues and direction. These roles can be taken on by individuals willing to act as a priest and/or priestess or spirit worker. They represent a channel through which the energy of the ritual is distributed toward its intended result. Traditionally, and in many small groups, they may take the active role in directing nearly all facets of the ritual action.

Make sure it is clear who will be giving cues, and which action or activity follows each part. Designate at least one of your team as the handler or wrangler, the person responsible for dealing with issues that arise that may affect the success of the ritual. You need someone in this handler role so the whole team doesn't stop to resolve any issues that come up. If your ritual is organized without a distinct leader, or the action leader is required to remain acting in character, a handler is essential.

One of the beauties of community ritual is the diversity of talents and limitations that your team will bring to your rituals. Some people will be natural thespians, able to speak loudly and act without inhibition. Others will avoid the limelight but may have a great sense of pacing or attention to detail. Some may be able to write words but not to speak them. You may have people willing to help who could dance, sing, or prepare costumes or props. Adapt your ritual to the team you gather to produce it. Most of your team will voluntarily gravitate toward roles that suit them.

More important than individual talents is the team members' commitment to working well together. A cooperative and problem-solving attitude allows the joy of ritual team participation to dominate the experience. If a person can't control their ego or treat every member with respect, their participation will be detrimental to the team no matter their amount of talent.

Community ritual is also a place for the team to grow as individuals. Encourage everyone to stretch their abilities, find and offer their creative expression, and expand their comfort zone. It is necessary to be flexible in the execution of your vision when working with other people. Don't plan a ritual based on long, flowery, memorized lines with a team that does not have the time to memorize and rehearse or the skills to carry it off!

One of our first experiences as part of a ritual team presented this situation. A community ritual had been written with elaborate words to be spoken by many characters. When the team was presented with the actual text at rehearsal, just hours before the ritual, it became apparent that the team could never memorize their lines in the time available. We talked as a team about each character reading the words from cards, or if simplifying the words could work. Feeling these options would not be able to convey the ritual intent, we got creative. We assigned the loudest and best voice to speak for all the ritual characters. The team was able to focus on their actions as their character while the reader delivered all their lines standing off to the side. It was not a perfect solution, but in this case it was a success.

Assemble your team as early as possible and assess their capabilities. It is not necessary to have a group of experienced actors for a successful ritual, only to adapt your plan to fit the skills they offer. A simple act, such as inviting and acknowledging the qualities of a cardinal direction, can be done in many ways. A thespian can use elaborate words and actions. A dancer can welcome the East with movement. A singer can use a song. A speaker can use a few sincere words from their heart. A shy person can fan a smudge stick with a feather or bow silently in that direction. It is more important to have your team act with sincerity and confidence than to try to follow the details of the ritual vision but do so with inhibition.

Not everyone will want an action role in the ritual. For those who wish to help out but not have a starring role, consider whether their abilities and the ritual's needs would make them an asset in these types of roles:

- **Narrators** can be an option when you have an intricate story to tell. That role is difficult to integrate into your ritual as they set a level of separation you may not wish to have. A narrator is neither a participant nor an active ritual presenter. Before you commit to the use of a narrator, take a look at your ritual story. Determine if a better script or action can convey its essence. A narrator role being included often defines your participants as an audience, and they may be more reluctant to change to being a full participant later. When verbally telling a story, a ritual takes on a theatrical character. Carefully review how the narrator influences and contributes to the basic intent of your ritual when you include one!

• **Greeters** put people at ease and make them feel welcome. People who attend a public ritual may not know anyone else there. The fact that someone greeted them, smiled at them, and made a connection with them establishes a positive feeling that is transferred to the ritual right from the start. As the ritual is introduced, if there is any doubt about the experience, the greeter is the obvious resource to turn to with questions. They need to prepare to accept feedback and answer questions as well. Your greeter will ensure that each attendee has had a personal connection with someone from the ritual team.

• **Guides** are essential, especially in rituals involving more than 50 people or where much movement or action takes place. Even for simple tasks like directing people to form a circle, or evenly distributing participants around a ritual stage, they are an asset. Far better to have the participants' direction accomplished by silent example than by someone shouting, "Okay, form a circle and spread yourselves about evenly." Words of direction work in conflict to the feelings and mood you will want to generate in most rituals. We often like to include a personal individual experience for each participant in a ritual. Here guides are needed for leading participants through a path of experience or into smaller groups, or for isolating them from a larger group during that personal experience. The role of guide is a good introduction to the experience of participating in a ritual team. Guides get to experience the ritual from the presenter's point of view, and observe the profound effects ritual can have on participants, with a minimum of personal risk.

- **Invisible guides** appear to be a part of your audience and by their example begin modeling an action that you wish everyone to follow along with. In the carnival world, they are called shills. A good ritual plan should make most actions expected of your participants pretty obvious. Even when actions are obvious, these invisible guides stepping forward to begin an action will stimulate in your participants the natural desire to fully engage in whatever the ritual has to offer. Just a few people, seemingly on their own volition, stepping up to light their candle is far more effective than a verbal direction by a visible member of your team to do so.

- **A guardian** is sometimes a necessary role in community rituals. This person protects a community ritual from interruption once it has started. They might integrate latecomers into the ritual stage. Rituals of high emotional intensity may need guardians to surround the area and be available to participants who become emotionally overwhelmed. Guardians should not be casually chosen. They should have experience and skills dealing with people in distress. A good candidate is able to sense people and their energy well, and to generate an atmosphere of calm and centeredness under stress. If the work and intent of your ritual is so intense that you feel it needs to be heavily guarded, you might reconsider whether the ritual as written is suitable for the audience you are working with.

A major requirement for all members of your ritual team, in whatever role they take, is to overcome the fear of being real and authentic in their person. Ritualistas need to set aside any alienating or caustic traits they may have absorbed to cope with the world. Drop any sarcasm, ridicule, mockery, contempt, disparagement, or cynicism that you might normally allow to creep into your personal expression. Ritualistas offer themselves, their essence, to create a ritual. They evoke a sense of intimacy from their innate ability to recognize the heart of a human being shining through any action. A thespian relies on exact language or a stunning performance to convince us to believe something. Even so, we are only convinced for a moment. When a ritualista misses a line or trips or makes any mistake while offering himself or herself honestly, most folks will not notice. Our failings can even have the opposite effect. They demonstrate that the ritualista is fallible and human. When handled with confidence, this can help erode participants' defenses and create a feeling of shared vulnerability.

Ritual: Gratitude

· · · · · · · · · · · · · · · · ·

Location: Sacred Harvest Festival, 2014
© Judith Olson Linde and Nels Linde

Ritual context

We assessed the community we had been deeply a part of for over a dozen years, and it was weary. We had together, in recent years, suffered betrayal, discord, and the loss of members. Those who remained had faced circumstances head on, facilitating a process of restorative justice to both acknowledge the harm and pain that had occurred and to reinvigorate the trust and values that had drawn us together originally. Our community needed something, a ritual theme that elevated us past our sorrow to a new state of grace. This ritual incorporated the words and wishes, and appreciation for our blessings, developed over a week of engagement with the theme of gratitude.

Ritual intent

To fully know and embrace the state of grace where gratitude lives. Move past our challenges and enter a new world that our gratitude creates and makes flourish. Bathe in the positive outpouring of well-being and good intention.

Ritual description

Gather and process from the Heart Chakra to the Sacred Circle. We live in this moment and graciously meet our future with each step. Share your heart and embark on the way of gratitude. Feast to the blessings and delight of the Gods. The rewards of our generosity of spirit return tenfold.

Ritual setup and supplies

All week the festivants had been writing words of gratitude on five muslin banners using black-light pens. Each banner had a unique theme: one for our ancestors, one for heroes or people who inspire us, one dedicated to life's pleasures, one for challenges that help us grow, and one for the mysteries of the natural world. On the ritual night, the banners surrounded the sacred space, evenly spaced, displayed by team members in turn at the proper time. The path to the sacred space had five sheer veil gateways spaced along it, and a large veil at the deity pair.

We came together at Heart Chakra (the gathering place) and taught a procession song: "There Is No Time but Now," by Veronica Appolonia. Five different-colored veils were set up along the woods path with two whisperers at each. At the path exit to enter the sacred space were two cots with veiled male and female deity figures lying in state, each holding a bowl of grapes.

Team members

Path regulator, 10 whisperers (5 pairs) at the veils, one male and one female deity, Ritualista 1, Ritualista 2.

Ritual script

A procession led participants to the entry of a brief path-working experience where they were sent in pairs about 10 seconds apart through the woods toward the ritual space. As each pair reached a veil, the veil was named, and words were offered by the whisperers, alternating lines as participants were greeted by one and passed through by the other.

At the green veil:
Whisperer 1: *"The Veil…"*
Whisperer 2: *"…of Challenges."*
Whisperer 1: *"With no expectations, what can possibly stand in your way?"*
Whisperer 2: *"Can you offer generosity of your spirit to those who wrong you?"*

At the blue veil:

Whisperer 3: (kissing the back of each participant's hand) *"The Veil…"*

Whisperer 4: *"…of Pleasures."*

Whisperer 3: *"What joy will move you to tears?"*

Whisperer 4: *"Whom do you remind of simple gifts each day?"*

At the red veil:

Whisperer 5: (pressing each person with an open palm on their heart) *"The Veil…"*

Whisperer 6: *"…of Heroes."*

Whisperer 5: *"Who reflects to you your highest self without obligation?"*

Whisperer 6: *"Who recognizes your worth whether you deserve it or not?"*

At the orange veil:

Whisperer 7: (asperging their feet with water and a branch) *"The Veil…"*

Whisperer 8: *"…of Ancestors."*

Whisperer 7: *"When we feel lost, who knows the way?"*

Whisperer 8: *"Connected to our roots, what can stop us?"*

At the yellow veil:

Whisperer 9: (sweeping the earth before them) *"The Veil…"*

Whisperer 10: *"…of Life."*

Whisperer 9: *"What glorious vision of nature awaits us?"*

Whisperer 10: *"What moment of beauty is laid before us?"*

At the woods path end was the purple veil:

Whisperer 11: (opening the veil) *"The Veil…"*

Whisperer 12: *"…of the Gods."*

Whisperer 11: *"What blessings flow from the gods of your hearth?"*

Whisperer 12: "What harm can befall us when we honor the gods?"

The male and female deity figures, with bowls of grapes, were veiled and lying in state. As participants passed by the deities, they were greeted by Ritualista 1 and Ritualista 2.

Ritualista 1: (anointing them)
"Enter and know divine protection."

Ritualista 2: (waving toward the bowl of grapes)
"Eat of the blessing of fruit, that the gods know your devotion."

Participants were directed to form a circle just inside the five black-light-sensitive banners evenly spaced around the circle, still rolled up and so hidden. When all were assembled, Ritualista 1 created sacred space, saying:

"In a clearing on a moonlit night, illuminated by firelight,
Assembled here we circle round, to see what blessings can be found,
In the company of other folk, to see what magic we may invoke."

Ritualista 1 then welcomed the directional forces, saying:
(To East) *"Where the moon rises and dawn breaks the day,*
on scented breeze newness comes wafting our way."
(To South) *"To the South lie the sands of fire, choices made, the loin's desire."*
(To West) *"In the West, the misty shore, the rainbows' end, the oceans' roar."*
(To North) *"To the North, the mountains of stone, caves of our ancestors; antler, bone."*
(To Spirit, center) *"The Lord and the Lady are present here too, and spirit,*
as always, within each of you."

The male and female deity figures rose up and began passing grapes around the circle, as Ritualista 1 and Ritualista 2 spoke of gratitude:

Ritualista 2:
"An attitude of gratitude can't grow within blame or fear or entitlement."

Ritualista 1:
"Opposite from entitlement, gratitude is not getting what you deserve; it is appreciating what you have."

Ritualista 2:

"The reward of gratitude is that it reinforces generosity of spirit. We realize it is safe to give."

Ritualista 1:

"Living in the way of gratitude is a state of being; every single thing is a blessing."

Ritualista 2:

"People who experience gratitude have more positive thoughts, have a powerful sense of well-being, and are happier."

Ritualista 1:

"Gratitude takes an awareness and appreciation that but for the grace of the gods, it could be another way!"

Ritualista 2:

"Gratitude is a state of optimism that never ends. The more gracious you are, the more you have to be grateful for."

Ritualista 1:

"Rather than looking at life as a glass half empty or full, gratitude is being happy there is a glass, and that you have it!"

Ritualista 2:

"Gratitude is the perception of being showered with blessings and divinely protected."

Ritualista 1:

"Life can be a frantic lust for money, love, acquisitions, and happiness. Gratitude creates happiness; you appreciate and find joy in whatever you have been given."

Team members revealed the five gratitude banners by unrolling them as Ritualista 1 and Ritualista 2 walked the circle with the deities. The deities shone black lights upon each banner in turn.

Ritualista 1:
"This week we have expressed gratitude to our challenges, our pleasures, our heroes, our ancestors, and for the Great Mystery of all we see."

Ritualista 2:
"Tonight we recognize devotion to deity as another veil of gratitude to embrace."

Ritualista 1 cued the deities to join them and began the spiral dance. All sang "Gratitude," by Judith Olson Linde:

Walk in the way of gratitude, walk in the way of gratitude,
Walk in the way of gratitude, walk in the way of gratitude.
All around me, open my eyes, see
Blessings aplenty, give it freely.
Walk in the way of gratitude, walk in the way of gratitude,
Walk in the way of gratitude, walk in the way of gratitude.

Ritualista 1:
"Shout your blessings!" (inviting personal ad lib verse additions)

Ritualista 1 modeled the additions:
Nels and Joby (drumbeat, drumbeat), *Max and Marty* (drumbeat, drumbeat), *smoke and campfires* (drumbeat, drumbeat), *these are my blessings* (drumbeat, drumbeat).

Call-and-response singing with drumbeats continued throughout the duration of the spiral dance.

Ritualista 2 gathered limited-mobility participants and drummers in the center as Ritualista 1 made the second turn in the spiral dance to gather participants toward the center.

He changed to an energy-raising song:
"Gratitude—Gratitude—Gratitude!" (Crescendo!)

Ritualista 1, as participants ground:
"Take a moment and catch the gaze of everyone here present and know gratitude,
for in an instant, this moment is gone!"

Starting in the East, Ritualista 1 moved to each direction and danced a goodbye. He then joined Ritualista 2, and they bowed to the deities, took their hands, and led all from the circle.

THREE

·········

Ritual Conception

Theseus and the Minotaur battle their way through the sacred space and out into the woods where we can all hear the fight still raging. A bellow echoes through the grove, and we hear the rattling of bones and then there is silence. Theseus returns carrying the head of the Minotaur, its mane draped with our deepest, darkest fears. He mounts it on a stake near the fire. We watch as he exchanges his sword for a torch and the mane catches fire. We sing for our cleansing and our future, our words building in intensity. Finally in a thundering crescendo we all shout, "I release and I let go!" The shadow we carried is gone!

Naming and Claiming the Shadow ritual

What is your motivation to create a ritual? Every ritualista needs to periodically reassess and examine their motives for creating ritual; they will not always be pure and altruistic. We cannot help but bring our life perspective to whatever we create. Knowing oneself and what drives us to create ritual is invaluable to keeping our intentions focused and our ritual content objectively assessed.

Photo from Harmony Tribe Photo Archives

The Minotaur mask added to the fire.

Framing your ritual to relate to a specific and defined community is a great way to keep your motives and ego in check. Ritual driven from our creativity alone can too easily lose relevancy within a community. It is easy to work with our own inspiration and then try to impose our feelings where they are not appropriate. You must be sure that your offering is what your community really needs.

Style

We use the term "ritual style" to describe the ways your participants experience ritual. Rarely is a ritual able to be categorized as all one style. Usually rituals will combine two or more. You will naturally fall into a style that your past experience, history, and personality direct you to. Part of the beauty of creating ritual is that the process will stretch your experience and abilities as much as it does for the ritual participants. A good way to consider what ritual style to begin with is to compare the skills and talents you (and your team) have, and ones you could benefit from more experience to develop.

Exercise

Brainstorm a list to document your personal skills and resources and the skills to improve upon. Use the example below. Add this to your ritual notebook.

I can create a ritual with:	I can grow my skills to:
• Memorized speeches	• Lead songs
• Costumes	• Speak spontaneously from my heart
• A separated audience	
• Leading a small team	• Make well-crafted props
• Guided movement	• Add wild dancing
• Me being myself authentically	• Add percussion
	• Share intimacy
• Ceremonial actions	• Create an ecstatic crescendo
• A procession	• Get everyone participating

When starting out as a ritualista it is best to use the skills and resources you already have. Rely on any past experience or participation in ritual and expect your ritual style will reflect that. As you gain experience it is rewarding to pick a few things from your skill set, and add a few skills you need to grow to put into your next ritual. You will make mistakes and learn to understand what makes different ritual techniques successful.

Theatrical style is used to describe a ritual if there is a clear separation between ritualistas and attendees. Participants are expected to invest their energy into the activity, but from a distance. Often the participants are seated in a horseshoe arrangement and only interact with the performers at the culmination of the ritual. This style can be effective for telling a story or demonstrating an extraordinary skill, such as music or dance. The more the drama that is offered has a mythic resonance that it draws upon, the easier it will be for the audience to experience it as a ritual and not simply entertainment. Theatrical style can be very effective in highlighting the actions, costumes, and words of the ritual players. One of the advantages of a theatrical style is you can thoroughly vision, script, plan, and rehearse your ritual in advance. Elements of this style are often incorporated into other styles as well.

Experiential style describes a ritual where all who enter the space are invited to contribute to the energy and the activity that takes place. Often this style manifests as a circle of participants with the presenters moving about inside the circle. In this arrangement most of those attending can see and hear not only the ritualistas but each other. Words, gestures, items, or energetic opportunities can be passed from person to person easily. This style of ritual presentation is very effective for making those who attend feel valued as contributors and included in the community.

Path-work style describes a ritual experienced while moving through a space—think of a candlelit labyrinth on midsummer night. When using this style you might arrange a journey passing by stations in the woods with different experiences at each one, or a series of mini-meditations spoken by guides as participants walk from one place to the next. This style of ritual gives each person a feeling of individual intimacy. It is easy to integrate this style with other styles.

Intimate style describes a ritual that involves as much one-on-one interaction with members of your ritual team and other participants as is practical. This ritual style requires the utmost in authenticity by your team to be successful. An intimate ritual demands we act, speak, and react from our sacred core at all times. When the ritual is structured carefully, participants can be confronted with deep emotions and observations that lead them to engage your ritual purpose. However you express this style in ritual, consider multiple "tracks" for participants to follow. You don't want to rush the offering of intimacy, and it may be better to divide the experience into several groups to keep the ritual moving.

In chapter 2, you learned the importance of and some of the factors in assessing the ritual needs of your community. What we begin now is the process of sorting through all the factors you are facing to engage your community through ritual.

To clarify the ritual purpose we will be working with, we review a whole list of verbs and adjectives that can describe how our proposed ritual might affect our community. Make your own list and keep it as a reference. We look to words like bonding, building, informing, uplifting, honoring, acknowledging, enriching, or engaging. Most rituals will incorporate more than one purpose, but they should have a primary one that becomes woven into every aspect of the ritual vision. When you develop your ritual this way, your "honoring" ritual will probably also end up a very "bonding" event.

··········

Exercise

Write down as many descriptive action verbs and adjectives that describe what you see your community benefiting from, experiencing, or feeling in ritual. Add this to your ritual notebook.

Both purpose and style help define what type of ritual you are creating. We often use descriptive style words like these to describe what the ritual experience will be like: experiential, theatrical, spiritual, transformative, celebratory, ecstatic, devotional, or meditative. Here you will use every bit of information you have gathered. What is the ritual purpose? What methods of ritual style will your community likely respond to best?

Who are your ritual team members and what are their abilities and desires? A ritual is a gift, and like any gift it is more important that it comes from your heart than what exactly it contains. How the gift is received is often more important than what the gift is. A highly spiritual ritual will not be received well by a group that does not share spiritual beliefs. In many cases, though, you will have a wide range of choices to make in what to offer any specific community.

Inspiration

Ritualistas find inspiration all around them, in nature, in spirituality, in people, and in their interactions. We got you started in observing by looking at your community, noting all the things that make each community unique. Before we can have anything to say we need to quiet ourselves and listen. Place yourself in the imagined essence of your working community and feel, hear, and imagine what is filling that community consciousness. We can observe the thoughts, circumstances, and issues that are current in the many individuals of our community. They show up in our ideas or images of what our community *is*—in a small sense, this is a vision.

Ritual is spoken in the language of symbols. To find the inspiration that fits a community, you need to take your most objective observations and translate them into the language of symbols. You might observe anger, frustration, pride, or accomplishment in individuals and gain some insight into what is most influencing of the individual experience. Sometimes we avoid the most obvious symbols because they seem, well, so obvious. A sprout, seed, or egg will always resonate as a symbol for new life or a beginning. This is the nature of symbol in ritual: sometimes the most direct symbol will be the most effective, no matter how obvious.

Just as you should have a primary ritual purpose, you should have primary symbology that will support your purpose. Even when you include several thoughts into your ritual intent, a single strong symbolism to demonstrate the primary purpose will usually make a stronger ritual. Keep it simple!

Be educated in the events that are affecting individual lives in your audience community. A birth in a community of a hundred may not seem like much of an influence. One significant experience can affect a small subgroup profoundly but then also ripple outward, causing many to think about or be touched be the nature of an event like a birth or death. Drawing upon what is current and evident in the life of your community for your ritual purpose will often lead to incorporating the most effective ritual symbology for that moment.

A great prop or trick of sleight-of-hand magic has inspired many a ritualista to then develop a deeper purpose as the ritual is defined. Anything that evokes a sense of awe in us opens a channel to our subconscious, making the experience memorable. The yearly calendar, the seasonal changes, even weather trends create a shared impact on a community. Our region's local specifics, from a high pollen count to an invasion of cockle burr or a shortage of woodpeckers, all can inspire a symbolic examination of our world through ritual.

Our collective or individual stories are an account of an event or experience. These words that describe our experience help translate our ideas, our observations, into a symbolic form others can hear in their subconscious. Since they arose from the here and now, they will always reflect something current. These personal stories can be difficult to work with directly; we are too close to them to recognize the symbology. In ritual, the telling of personal stories to others can transform them into tales with mythic status.

Beyond these specific stories, we have the stories of hundreds of cultures to draw upon, to reflect the symbology demonstrated through our community experience. Native people from the poles to equatorial regions have culturally based tales, often animist or shamanic in origin. They are a ritual resource that offers a story for every ritual purpose. Anthropological studies of indigenous peoples are another rich source of story and myth. As we move outside our own ancestral heritage we must be careful in the use of culturally based stories. Starhawk advises: "But when we take over the symbols or practices of another tradition without permission, acknowledgment, training, or commitment to the real-life struggles of the people, we are in effect appropriating their culture..."[7]

Children's stories, parables, and folktales can work well when adapted to your ritual inspiration and symbology. Children's classics, from the brothers Grimm to the tales of the Turkish trickster Nasreddin Hodja and even modern children's books, can provide source material for the story needed for your ritual.

"Stone Soup" is an old folk story in which a hungry stranger persuades local people of a town to give him food. A traveler arrives with an empty cooking pot. The villagers are unwilling to share their food. He goes to a stream and fills the pot with water, dropping a large stone in it, and builds a fire under it. One of the villagers becomes curious and asks what he's doing. The traveler answers, "Making stone soup." He says it tastes great, it just needs a garnish to improve it. The villager adds a few potatoes to the soup. More and more villagers each add to the pot until a delicious soup is complete and eaten by them all. Now imagine that story as part of a ritual, where the contributions from the community are symbols of health, prosperity, and healing. (See the chapter 12 ritual, "Stone Soup.")

Most tales and myths are already written using the language of symbols and symbolic acts. They are meant to inspire the reader, and can guide the ritualista to think within the language of symbols when seeking inspiration from them. Myths already have a resonance with our collective psyche. Even when they are altered for a ritual purpose we are predisposed to find their content compelling.

---

7   Starhawk, "Creating Community Ritual," *Communities* magazine, Issue 154, www.ic.org
    /creating-community-ritual.

Find the Story

Think of ritual as the framing of a story. An opening statement sets the stage, there is development of the storyline, the empowerment of action, and then the grounding conclusion. Nearly every effective ritual will follow this outline. Each part is an important aspect in the development of the story, and yet each part can take a myriad number of forms.

Essential to your ritual is the relevance and type of storyline. To discern from the many types of stories, these definitions from Donna Rosenberg will help us sort out some story types:

- "A myth is a sacred story from the past."

- "A folktale is a story that, in its plot, is pure fiction and that has no particular location in either time or space."

- "A legend is a story from the past about a subject that was, or is believed to have been, historical."[8]

American mythologist Joseph Campbell wrote the most complete works of comparative mythology available. Study of his research, writings, and thought is inspiring training for the ritualista. "Myth is the secret opening through which the inexhaustible energies of the cosmos pour into human manifestation."[9]

Myths to inspire you may come from cultures all over the world, including Norse, Celtic, East Indian, Chinese, Sumerian, Egyptian, and African. Many indigenous cultures have stories and myths passed by oral tradition that now are available through research, including Aboriginal, Native American, South American, and Inuit. Myths follow a familiar format. They have strong, usually godlike characters who are confronted with a problem to solve or quest to complete. There is usually a twist in the story that results in a resolution unique to the context. Key to the nature of myth is that somehow the story's resolution can be applied to our common human experience.

---

8   Donna Rosenberg, *Folklore, Myth, and Legends: A World Perspective* (Columbus, OH: Glencoe /McGraw-Hill, 2001), pp. xiv–xxv.

9   Joseph Campbell, *The Hero with a Thousand Faces* (Novato, CA: New World Library, 3rd edition, 2008), p. 1.

Most familiar are the Greco-Roman stories, as they are some of the earliest myths that are fully documented. Their relevance to human psychology is evidenced by their use in clinical terminology, from Oedipus to Psyche. Greco-Roman stories contain most human archetypes and describe every aspect of the human condition. These myths should be a familiar reference for anyone serious about community ritual. They can be a primary source of inspiration and are easily accessible. Having been active in the Western consciousness for thousands of years, they contain a subconscious, symbolic connection with us, whether in exact retelling or by subtle reference. Their powerful messages can be used as they arose within the classic myth or to support a different or derivative ritual vision.

....

EXAMPLE

In the myth of Icarus, Daedalus (his father) built two pairs of wings out of wax and feathers for himself and his son. Before taking off, Daedalus warned his son to follow his path and not fly too close to the sun. Overcome by the thrill of flight, Icarus soared higher into the sky. He rose higher, too close to the sun, which melted the wax. Soon Icarus had no wings left and fell into the sea and drowned.

This myth could be used in ritual as a metaphor to symbolically connect to:

- A youth not heeding an elder's wisdom

- A person not knowing restraint

- A person filled with ego meeting calamity

- A community reaching for heights outside their capability

- Being blinded by excitement after initial success

If you have never read mythology texts and want to get a simplified overview, look for resources adapted for children.[10] They contain the essence of many stories, and once you find one that can support your ritual idea, you can read more deeply for the context and details that defines it.

---

10   For example, "Myths, Legends, Fables and Folklore," at www.planetozkids.com/oban /legends.htm.

Adaptive Myth

Ancient myths that have entered into our common psyche carry the power of the archetypical characters and story inside them, even when we modify the story to suit our ritual purpose. Mythic reference can prepare us to experience spiritual mystery. Even with a different storyline the strength of the original myth can empower the presented symbology. As an example, we have used the Greek myth of Theseus and the Minotaur effectively in ritual.

In this myth, the hero, Theseus, responds to the injustice of Greek children being offered as sacrifice to the monster Minotaur on the isle of Crete every seven years to appease the threats of war from King Minos. Theseus takes the place of one of the children, and on arrival conspires with King Minos's daughter, the spoiled and bored Princess Ariadne. She gives him a ball of string to mark a path back through the labyrinth maze and a sword to slay the Minotaur. All she asks is to be taken away so others may adore her for her beauty. Theseus succeeds, and on a stop while sailing home, the princess falls asleep on a remote island, the island villagers adore her, and Theseus then sails away.

This myth has many levels to it: the hero righting injustice, conspiring with one of questionable stature and ethics, a trick to gain advantage against insurmountable odds, the hero's success, and then the bargainer getting what she deserves. These elements speak to classic human confrontations, and even if we extract a small portion of the myth for our ritual, our story will resonate with the power of the whole.

In this adaptive myth, "Naming and Claiming the Shadow," ritual participants wore an adhesive name tag, randomly received, with a negative personality trait written on it. They followed a maze and passed by the Minotaur, who read the tags and insulted them about their written failing. Theseus approached and the confrontation ensued with the Minotaur. As they worked around the circle battling, participants released these traits by sticking them to the Minotaur's mane. The fight then carried the battling pair outside the circle, and Theseus returned with the head and mane of the Minotaur, which was burned, disposing of the unwanted traits.

Here is how the ritual intent and description were offered to participants:

Naming and Claiming the Shadow

Ritual intent

Using the myth of Theseus and the Minotaur, identify and become intimate with the diversity of our shadow names. Discard our unclaimed shadow elements.

Ritual description

Carry the shadows of your community in the walk of sacrifice to the Minotaur. The way has twists and turns, but the psyche always follows the thread to guide the way back. What hero can save you and offer your own time of choice? Confront and embrace the monster as is your fate. Take the piece that ties it all together.

This ritual theme was about self-awareness and symbolically releasing negative personal traits from our shadow selves. We confronted the Minotaur, transferred the traits to him, and then vanquished him and these unwanted elements. Even though we took liberties with the myth, participants recognized the analogy between our hero confronting a seemingly invincible foe and each of us facing our inner dark side as similar and heroic acts.

The direct involvement of the participants in this adaptation brought that deeply embedded archetypical relationship into each person's ritual experience. While the actual myth of Theseus and the Minotaur was not accurately presented, they witnessed and aided the hero in victory against impossible circumstances. This demonstrates the power of adapted myth included in your ritual story to carry forward your ritual intent. In researching myths or stories, you may not be looking for the complete ritual story-line. Most often you are looking for archetypical analogies that can be made through reference or inference to the main theme of the myth. Also consider any myth or story from a different perspective. How would Ariadne tell the tale of Theseus? How would the sun relate the story of Icarus?

Brainstorming

Everyone has experienced brainstorming—being asked to come up with ideas for some project. Learning to be effective when generating ritual ideas is more difficult. In 2014, we needed to create a series of rituals around the festival theme, gratitude (see chapter 2's ritual). We did what we usually do, a brainstorming session while traveling by car.

We taped the discussion and realized it was a great way to demonstrate how to use brainstorming to inspire ritual. Here are some notes from that session:

How do you show gratitude? Does the object of gratitude need to know or feel gratitude for you to express it? No one needs know that you feel gratitude; it is about the feeling. It doesn't need to be validated by anyone.

What is gratitude? Gratitude is a state of being and a way of life. First, learn to be aware of the blessings in your life. Understand that but for the grace of a higher power or fortune, things could have gone another way. Don't look at the world as a glass half full or half empty, but with pure joy just knowing there is a glass waiting for you.

What does one look like when living in a state of gratitude? Gratitude is a state of awe and optimism that never ends. The more gracious you are, the more things you have to be grateful for. When you adopt an "attitude of gratitude," life begins to give you additional blessings. Happiness is simply appreciating all you have no matter what it is. Gratitude is the opposite of feeling entitled.

What does gratitude look like? Making you feel thankful because you feel like you are special, to live in gratitude. A ritual about gratitude might be about making people feel special.

What makes a person feel special? Which actions best reflect gratitude? People getting noticed for something that may not be obvious as a quality, being attentive to others' qualities. Ritual might include the careful observation of others, and then a reflection on what is observed.

Graciousness is from gratitude? We rely on the benefit of the doubt, assume the best of everyone. A presumption of good intention makes gratitude authentic. We are grateful for kind acts, but not that another did it. We presume that they sincerely wanted to be kind without thought for themselves.

To translate gratitude to ritual, how do we engage participants, what do they do? What do we learn from gratitude? To be humble? To appreciate others? We learn that it is safe to give. When people show gratitude for what you offer it makes you want to do it again. It reinforces a behavior of Generosity of Spirit (GOS): a good concept to use to model what gratitude is in ritual. It is listening to others, being polite, eliciting feelings from others, making others comfortable and at ease. GOS is what it takes to offer gratitude and appreciation for the contributions of those who may have slapped you in the face in the past. Acknowledge all who built the festival, even in absentia and after a harmful leaving. Read all the names in ritual. Appreciate those attending, those who have left, those who have passed, those who can't attend now. Honor all categories in stages: guests, workshops, kids, etc.

How does gratitude make you feel? Like crying, emotional relief, a momentary reprieve from self-doubt. It is a recognition of self-worth, and worth in general. You feel pride. Gratified means well thanked. It affirms a choice another has made, implies value within another's choice.

Why is it hard to express gratitude? It is at the core of prayer and devotion. An expression of gratitude to deity. If gratitude isn't a core element of your spirituality, how can you express it to each other?

Can gratitude grow in an atmosphere of blame? Gratitude cannot exist when you are blaming someone else for your problems. Maintain an "attitude of gratitude." The need to blame makes a difficult human medium for gratitude to grow in. Blame is not accepting responsibility for your circumstances. Disempowered people are stingy with gratitude. Empowered people don't blame. People who do not fear empowering others can offer gratitude.

Summary of ideas to integrate in gratitude rituals:

- Display levels of thankfulness in gratitude.

- Cosmos, universes, solar systems, planets that sustain life.

- Forces of nature, the elements, seasons, moon cycles.

- Humans are unique life forms, connected in a moment.

- Our gods and their roles for us.

- Ancestry, lineage, and lifelong influences and happenstance.

- Wonder, beauty, lovers, children, work.

- Occasions, times of challenge, despair, take risks and opportunity, find resources needed.

- Being here, now, all together, by choice.

- All who contributed, large and small, teaching, acts, crafts.

- Bring participants through all the levels of thankfulness. Ask them to draw forward into their consciousness one example of thankfulness at each level.

- Focus on an experience that makes each individual feel special in some way.

- Develop techniques to demonstrate and encourage an "attitude of gratitude."

- Develop exercises to experience being attentive to others' qualities.

- Model a Generosity of Spirit attitude: listening to others, being polite, eliciting feelings from others, making others comfortable and at ease.

- Develop personal pride, empowerment over blame. Acknowledge with gratitude even those who have harmed us.

- Include humble prayer and devotion to deity.

Essential to productive brainstorming is asking creative and relevant questions that explore a topic, and then documenting the answers you discover. All this material then becomes a resource when we create ritual.

Visioning

Visioning is a special type of experiential brainstorming that is intuitive and creative. Considered by some to be a natural talent, we believe a serious will to understand and employ all the tools presented here can allow anyone to learn to envision the ritual experience. Visioning is that part of ritual development that requires the most practice. It helps to know your audience and learn their issues.

Visioning includes every aspect affecting the environment of your audience. It is very much like guided meditation. Imagine all the details, the blocking, sounds, and smells. Be aware of thoughts or emotions that bubble to the surface as you create a complete model of a participant's experience in ritual. When you have a significant personal experience, you may relive it in your memory, slowly adding in all the layers of what was sensed and felt as it occurred. Using ritual visioning, create what you imagine the ritual experience to be, and then add layers of sensory "tracks." Each track is another stimulus refining, adding to, and moving the participant toward the ritual purpose. We live in an era where we are sensually bombarded with media telling a story. In ritual visioning, your mind is the camera used to place yourself in a realistic "movie" of how your ritual will unfold. As you "live" the ritual experience, note which areas seem inauthentic, or which don't have enough action or sensory experience to support the results you expect. You will vision your ritual many, many times as the outline and plan develop. With each visioning, the details become clearer, and also what may be missing or incomplete will start to appear for you. When working in a team it is very effective to lead each other through this process.

Once you have some experience designing ritual this process becomes second nature. To get started, having a general outline of ritual organization to refer to is helpful to make sure you cover all the things a participant would encounter. A written format is the first major tool in your ritual toolbox.

Review the results of your ritual team's initial brainstorming of the whole ritual experience. Try to see it through the eyes of the participant. Does it flow from one part to another? Imagine what a person without any expectation or preconceived notion of this ritual would feel. Make a mental space for questions to bubble up into your consciousness. Where should I be standing? How will I know what to do? Will I understand what I see? Will the action distract me from feeling the emotions of the intent? Is there something missing? The deeper you are able to create a mental experience of your ritual, the more precise your assessment can be.

Your sense of the audience's direction, community issues, current events, and even economic conditions may shape the direction of this process. Look at the broadest limits imposed by the shared experience of your audience, and seek areas where you see relevance and an impact in people's lives. Placing limitations on the scope of your ritual can be beneficial in shaping that initial canvas of ideas. A ritual designed to truly develop or effectively explore a simpler vision often outshines one with too broad a scope. Starhawk describes the three levels of impact within effective ritual: "Ritual is most powerful when it works on multiple levels: the cosmic, the community, and the personal, giving us each a stake in the outcome."[11]

Working Within Limits

Much of our challenge in developing community ritual has been in creating large group rituals for festivals. As both blessing and curse, we were charged with the limitation of developing specific ritual experiences that explored the theme for that year. It was a curse because writing a single ritual specific to a subject can be difficult enough. Writing a series of rituals to express various approaches to a theme was even more demanding. Writing within this limitation was a blessing because we were forced to dig deeper and probe the sometimes subtle aspects of a larger motif.

Theme work in ritual can be a most difficult limitation. We all tend to find inspiration within our daily, personal, and community life. These are limiting factors for us. You may have to reach out to others with more experience if the theme is beyond your scope. No one can be expected to have complete experience in all areas of life. In these cases, much like an author, "go to the source."

The limitations of a theme can also be liberating. You may collect many great ritual ideas through brainstorming relating to a topic. Using the limitation of theme as a filter, you can quickly sort through to find the ones better left for another ritual. Most devotional or seasonal celebration rituals have themes, so whatever ideas emerge, they will never be wasted.

Ritual: Naming and Claiming the Shadow

· · · · · · · · · · · · · · · · ·

Location: Sacred Harvest Festival, 2004
© Judith Olson Linde and Nels Linde

Ritual context

This ritual was written for participants to work with their shadow selves, those parts of ourselves we are not so proud of. To do this effectively, participants were only asked to "carry" those traits, which were then ritually destroyed through this adaption of a Greek

---

11   Starhawk, "Creating Community Ritual."

myth. This is a wonderful example of an adaptive myth that was used to confront negative emotions but from a positive perspective.

Ritual intent

Using the myth of Theseus and the Minotaur, identify and become intimate with the diversity of our shadow names. Discard our unclaimed shadow elements.

Ritual description

Carry the shadows of your community in the walk of sacrifice to the Minotaur. The way has twists and turns, but the psyche always follows the thread to guide the way back. What hero can save you and offer your own time of choice? Confront and embrace the monster as is your fate. Take the piece that ties it all together.

Ritual setup and supplies

A simple, three-turn labyrinth was defined in the circle with barn lime and lit with tea light candles on the ground. The Minotaur wore an elaborate mask and a long, flowing mane of twine, foam hooves, a sword, and a cloak. He sat at the center near the fire. The Priest and shadows acted as guides. A pole was set upright in a cardboard tube for the mask to be placed on near the conclusion of the ritual. A papier-mâché openable Moon Egg sculpture and a soft snake sculpture were used as props. The "golden thread" used was yellow mason's line, later cut and distributed with a small moon bead to be added to a tribal bead necklace gifted in a prior ritual. Adhesive name tags were marked with shadow traits (see the list following).

Photo by Nels and Judy Linde

The Moon Egg bead added to the Dark Moon year necklace.

Team members

- 4–6 shadow assistants dressed in all black with black face paint and black hats. These also acted as the choir.

- Priest (lead spirit worker)

- Theseus with sword

- Minotaur with mask, mane, tail, sword, cloak, and foam hooves

- Ariadne as a young goddess

- Three Fates characters

Ritual script

Participants entered the woods and moved through an induction path to get to the circle. They encountered shadow guides along that path who chant-whispered as they walked by, washing them with a cacophony of thoughtful sound:

> *"Conceal myself... reveal myself... heal myself,*
> *know myself... find myself... free myself."*

Ariadne was waiting at the ritual circle entrance and asked all participants to pause and aid the community by carrying whatever shadow burden the gods may decree. Participants then chose a shadow tag (adhesive name tag) at random, affixed it on their chest, and entered the circle area. They were taken around by the Priest to form a circle. There was a brief sacred space setup by the Priest, who began casting with the staff, saying:

> *"With this bone that is her essence, with ocher her blood, I chant into being the*
> *magick circle. From the void of Khaos, the self, protected by Nyx, and encased as*
> *are the stars within the shell of moonless night, grows the embryo of consciousness.*
> *This circle is between the worlds where all is possible. Time waits for Luna as she*
> *hides. Like the snake swallowing the cosmic egg the moon has been swallowed*
> *into the womb of space.... It is done."*

The Priest was preceded around the inside of the circle by a shadow who smudged with sacred smoke. Behind the participants, outside the circle, were two shadows with antler rattles that sounded like bones. They stayed even with the smudger but varied their rattling in height as they moved. A fourth shadow started the Moon Egg passing hand to hand around the circle of participants, and then picked up the soft snake and followed the egg around the circle, symbolically "chasing" it. At completion, the snake was coiled around the egg back at the West.

> The quarters were called simply by the Priest:
> *"Blessed is the sacred air, for breath is life."*
> *"Blessed is the sacred fire, which warms the hearth."*
> *"Blessed is the sacred water, which washes away."*
> *"Blessed is the sacred earth, which renews us."*

The Priest, with help from the shadows, now guided the circle of participants into the labyrinth while unraveling a spool of golden thread onto the ground. As the participants reversed upon themselves in the turns of the labyrinth, the shadows made chiding, mocking introductions among facing participants:

"Repression, meet Envy here, the great distracter. And Self-Pity, I'm sure Addiction can help you out!"

The Minotaur awaits the ritual participants.

Once the Priest reached the center, he left the rest of the golden thread at the Minotaur. As the participants got to the center and faced the Minotaur, he greeted and confronted their carried shadow tags, threatening to claim them (ad-libbing):

"Welcome, Anger—I can hold you!... Shame, let me mix you with Guilt and make a wash for my mane.... Addiction, when will you have enough?"

The participants then circled around the central fire and reversed in the labyrinth to follow the golden thread back out to re-form the circle. The shadows began the song "Cauldron of Changes," by Lindie Lila.

Theseus now emerged from the woods with a sword and slowly followed the golden thread into and through the labyrinth slowly and deliberately. After he passed, a shadow followed him and removed the golden thread and collected the labyrinth candles into a basket so the circle was cleared.

The song ended as Theseus confronted the Minotaur. They battled with swords, moving outward to the edge of circle. As Theseus backed the Minotaur around close to the circle of participants, the shadows followed and encouraged participants to add their shadow tags to the Minotaur's mane, saying, *"Take your chance!! Unburden yourself now!!"*

The shadows facilitated getting all tags from participants and onto the mane. When this was complete, the battling pair backed out into the woods where the battle raged out of sight, and then there was silence.

Enter the three Fates, who spoke in turn to each person:
"What speaks to you?"
"What must you release?"
"What makes you whole?"

And they held, cut, and gave a piece of golden thread to each participant. A shadow followed, handing out moon beads from the opened Moon Egg prop, and the other shadows helped participants tie the moon bead onto the golden thread. This Moon Egg necklace was a symbol of their personal path back from the shadow confrontation with the Minotaur.

The sound of the Minotaur roaring and swords clanking could be heard every little while, but they were still out of sight in the woods. The Priest kept Theseus and the Minotaur updated on the Fates' progress handing out the golden thread. As the Fates finished, there was one last huge bellow and then silence. After a pause and some bone rattling, Theseus returned with the mask/head of the Minotaur with tags stuck to its mane and placed it on the center pole.

A Pagan variation of a song was started: "I Release," by Rickie Byars Beckwith and Michael Beckwith.

Theseus exchanged his sword for a torch and circled to the building energy of the song. As the energy was near climax, Theseus set fire to the Minotaur's mane with the shadow name tags on it. The energy climaxed with the mane completely burning up to the mask. After a pause the entire ritual team squatted and modeled placing their hands on the earth and lowering their heads in an action of grounding in silence.

The Priest entered and gave Theseus his new Moon Egg necklace. He circled once with it as Priest said:

> *"As at the time of rebirth, I accept no negative thoughts, words, or deeds from*
> *others. I flesh my own bones and bring my own shadow fresh to this world.*
> *Knowing the shadow within I transform, and remember, and find balance."*

The Priest donned his own new Moon Egg necklace and thanked the four directions, rattling at each quarter. The shadows followed the Priest outside the circle, rattling the antlers. The Moon Egg and snake, each carried by a shadow, slowly chased each other once around circle. The Priest said to Theseus:

> *"Come, let us carry the mask of our shadow to the celebration, and there bind*
> *our knowledge lest we forget. The circle is open."*

The drums began for the procession back to the gathering location. The Priest took the hand of the first person Northwest of West and peeled the circle back on itself deosil and outward, then back around to West and past, and back out the gate, leading the exit procession.

Shadow traits for tags

Abuse, addiction, alienation, anger, apathy, argumentativeness, arrogance, bigotry, blame, compulsiveness, confusion, cynicism, deceit, denial, depression, despair, detachment, disdain, disowned, domination, envy, fear, greed, guilt, hate, ignorance, indifference, intimidation, intolerance, insecurity, irresponsibility, isolation, jealousy, judgmental, lies, manipulative, narrow-mindedness, opportunism, over-indulgence, pain, pessimism, pro-crastination, purposelessness, racism, repression, resentment, rigidity, self-centeredness, self-consciousness, self-doubt, selfishness, self-pity, sexism, shame, short-sightedness, spite, stubbornness, violence.

FOUR

·········

Your Purpose

On Saturday, February 24, 2007, facing stiff winds and biting sleet, more than 150 bundled, excited Pagan activists of all ages braved a travel advisory to converge on the front steps of the Minnesota State Capitol. Our circle was banished (cleared of negativity) with five brooms, blessed by the hoop of community, and then these were assembled into our pentacle symbol. The color guard, flags blowing horizontally, began its cast in formal cadence. As their colors were presented, and our veterans and families came forward to be honored, emotions were high. The words of area groups and our priest and priestess came forth easily, but it was so cold they were immediately frozen in time and memory. Voices were raised in song, and our community's cry for justice was solidified as individuals charged their ribbons, and then joined them to our pentacle symbol. People danced, and cried, and hugged, and then sang again as the color guard ended our rite. Only a few gathered to watch, but it made no difference because we were there, together, in public and demanding our soldiers' rights.

We took our memories of strength and union and ran for the warmth of the hearth. We had nearly a foot of snow that night. It felt like the weather was a test of our commitment, and we had been offered a pause to complete our work. Our ritual intention carried through in the following weeks to active support for the call to add individual comments in opposition to the new VA rules proposed for symbols of belief. The pentacle symbol we created has been displayed in area stores since then, with many others adding their magical intention to it.

Veterans' Pentacle Rights Ritual

We have a working definition of community ritual, but it is still very broad. There are many purposes, styles, and techniques that define and describe any particular ritual. The boundaries between these differences are often just a perception. A ritual can include many different styles and goals, and blend several purposes together. A ritual can have a specific theme or focus, and be adapted using most ritual techniques. By looking at the different purposes for community ritual you can learn about them individually, and get familiar with some of the descriptive terms and techniques we will be using. This information and the principles in this book can be applied to most ritual, but we will keep our focus on rituals for large groups and communities.

Celebration

A celebration is a time of remembering or acknowledging, of festivity or joy. As a purpose in ritual it is an opportunity to empower or to glorify playful merriment. Humans need to celebrate, to cut loose, and to collectively mark holidays, special occasions, and life events that don't involve a change of status (these we consider rites of passage). We all have experienced celebrations without a ritual, so why not include a ritual within a celebration?

A celebration ritual can include a solemn structured ceremony or a time to boisterously share our joy, and be either or both. A farcical, ironic, or absurd ritual theme can offer a way to encourage a look at ourselves from a different viewpoint. Rituals of celebration can also include a fool or jester-like character or characters. The mummery of these roles sets a mood of festivity and encourages us all to release ourselves from the norms of behavior we tightly hold to. Many traditional celebrations have events, stories, or short dramas to do just this, and we can create them for our own celebrations.

Seasonal Celebrations

We live in a world marked by many units of time, season, and regular natural events. Many religions set the day of celebration not by the calendar but by the cycles of the earth in the solar system, such as on the first full moon following the vernal equinox. Reliance on the earth's cycles helps celebrations to stay *relatively* on the same day whatever cultural calendar is used. These astronomically defined times affect humans, as directly as the full moon affects the ocean tides. What associations we bring to a ritual purpose marking these celestial events will reflect our spiritual bent, a historical reference, or correspondences we define for ourselves.

The day of the full moon has obvious associations with the moon's full visibility, its closeness to Earth, and the ocean tides. You can draw from our examples for a full moon celebration, or you can create your own. You just need to fully spell out the reasons within the course of your ritual. The full moon and new moon are often contrasted in qualities and characterized for appropriate ritual purposes. A full moon can represent completion or abundance, and a new or dark moon can represent beginnings and introspection, but these are only examples among many possible ritual purposes at these times.

Each of the 13 moons of the year has many names based on the culture that places them in sequential order throughout the seasons of the year. This list from the *Farmer's Almanac* has names that can offer a ritual theme and help define how to celebrate any particular moon celebration.[12]

- Full Wolf Moon—January

- Full Snow Moon—February

- Full Worm Moon—March

- Full Pink Moon—April

- Full Flower Moon—May

- Full Strawberry Moon—June

- Full Buck Moon—July

- Full Sturgeon Moon—August

- Full Harvest Moon—September

- Full Hunter's Moon—October

- Full Beaver Moon—November

- Full Long Nights Moon—December

---

12 *Farmer's Almanac*, "Full Moon Names and Their Meanings," www.farmersalmanac.com /full-moon-names.

The passage of the earth around the sun has four clear demarcations. The two equinoxes are days when the hours of light and dark are equal in the spring and fall. The two solstices occur when the earth's tilt is directly opposed to the sun, either giving us the most hours of daylight (summer solstice) or the least amount of light (winter solstice). These are the earliest days recognized and acknowledged with celebration and ritual in recorded history, and can be positively determined by simple observation. They were ritually immortalized by prehistoric cultures with the orientation of temples. Places like Stonehenge and even older Egyptian temples[13] are aligned to mark these dates with sunlight. In northern climates, the winter solstice—the return of the life-giving warmth of increased sunlight—is always an important seasonal celebration. Many Celtic, New Age, and Pagan spiritual systems also celebrate the cross-quarters. These are the dates that further divide the calendar year (between the equinoxes and solstices) into four more divisions, making eight relatively equal portions. Between the number of full and new moons per year (26) and the four seasonal division days and the cross-quarters, there is a lot to celebrate!

Fellowship

The shared experience in almost any type of group ritual naturally creates a feeling of fellowship. The benefits of just not feeling alone justify this as a ritual purpose. When the focus and form of the ritual are designed to encourage these feelings, very strong bonds within a group are formed. Individuals come away from a fellowship ritual with renewed self-confidence. Most of the rituals we have created for festivals we consider transformational fellowship rituals with an experiential, path-working, or eclectic style.

A fellowship ritual uses techniques to enhance those factors that contribute to feeling a part of something greater than oneself. This type of ritual will often include parts where participants interact directly with each other, and the group, with some increased level of intimacy. Fellowship rituals usually involve some trust-building techniques to prepare the participants.

---

13   David Furlong, "Astronomical Alignment in the Temples of Egypt," www.davidfurlong.co.uk /egyptarticle_temple_orient2.html.

EXERCISE

Practice this with your team and then adapt it to include as a trust-building gateway in a fellowship ritual. Your group forms two rows in an alternating pattern with their arms extended, fingertips and elbows apart from each other. As a person walks between the two rows, people raise their arms just before and drop them back down just after the passing.

Participants in a fellowship ritual might be asked to speak, toast, or honor one another. They might speak about people who inspire them, their ancestors, leaders, or the group as a whole. A few strong and sincere voices opening the process of participant speaking goes a long way toward establishing an atmosphere where verbal sharing expands in intimacy as the ritual progresses. The sumbel is a ritual drinking ceremony of Heathens in the Northern European tradition. The entire ritual may be three rounds of toasts—one to the gods, the second round to ancestors, and the third round may be to whatever or whomever an individual chooses. This ritual has a spiritual component and is also a great source of fellowship.

Physical actions that demonstrate a need to share dependence, vulnerability, commonality, and support for each other build a bonding relationship. The more all participants are encouraged by the design of the ritual to engage and feel safe contributing in these ritual actions, the more sincere and unanimous involvement will become, and the greater the feeling of fellowship as a result. Including actual physical actions, such as lifting or carrying a person, helping them navigate a treacherous path, or being guided while blindfolded, demonstrates a level of trust we don't normally encounter.

Fellowship-building activities and components can be included in most rituals. The bonding generated through fellowship creates a lasting growth of closeness between individuals and in their relationship to their community as a whole.

This young woman just finished her coming-of-age ritual.

Rites of Passage

A rite of passage is the acknowledgment, affirmation, and celebration of an important event or milestone in life. Personal emotional history and the highs and lows within it are times of passage. We fight alienation, loneliness, and depression. We celebrate victories in intimacy, in our work lives, and over personal tyrants and demons. Each of these times of intense emotion, transition, and transformation can become the story and purpose of ritual. Rites of passage mark times that we have now moved past, and once the passage is made there is no return. We each have a unique path in life and we may completely miss some experiences that others find of paramount importance to mark with ritual. People often need a ceremony to mark the passing of a revered pet, for example. If you don't have the experience of pet ownership you may not understand how important it is to acknowledge this grief with ritual. You will need to determine if your idea for a rite of passage transcends the personal and is suitable as a community ritual.

Think of all the times of change in a person's life that could be marked with a rite of passage. Birth, naming, starting kindergarten, riding a bike, starting middle school, religious dedication—all these occur in the early years of life. In many families, these take a very prescribed form within a religious context or family tradition. Some rites of passage in these tender years are mainly for the other participants, such as for godparents to bond with their godchild.

As young people mature, a new set of passages occurs. Rites of puberty for young men and women are often missing but clearly important to most youth. Personal events acknowledging sexual orientation or gender identity can be a rite of passage. The changes we experience from ages 12 to 21 are many and varied. Attainments like getting a driver's license, receiving an award or scholarship, and graduations are reasons for rites of passage.

With maturity, rites of passage naturally change. Marriage or commitment is a major change of status. In modern society, many initiations take place later in life, from fraternal lodges to spiritual and unique interest groups. As we age, many experience a sense of invisibility in our youth-focused society because rites of passage enhancing the status of older people are left undone. Each stage of life can have meaningful rites of passage, enough to fill our needs.

Judy: *When I was in my early fifties I realized that I could be defined as a crone. Age, my grown children, my progress through menopause, all defined that about me. It wasn't until my croning celebration that I understood it on that deep subconscious level. I remember the tastes of the crone's luncheon, the smells of incense, the colors worn by those in the moon lodge, the sound of the chant that accompanied my procession, my welcome back by the men of my tribe. I am a crone now in my deepest being. It is within these rituals that the meaning of our lives is made real.*

Photo by Jenna Touchette

Judy Linde at her croning community celebration.

None of us can avoid the inevitable change death represents. Rites surrounding this passage are as important for those passing, the focus of the rite, as for those left behind. Too often we avoid or delay these rites until they only serve the survivors (funeral). A rite of passage for those immanently facing death can be invaluable to help an individual make this final transition while feeling a part of a community.

Like other types of rituals, a rite of passage can be strictly defined by religion or tradition, or it can incorporate a broad range of ritual styles, forms, and techniques. A rite of passage can be the most important day of your life, so why not make it one, or make it one for someone else?

When designing a rite of passage as a community ritual there are several important considerations. An individual's desires should be solicited for the ritual design. A personal loss, such as a miscarriage, is only appropriate as a community ritual if the person of focus is seeking the support of their community. We cannot assume every personal transition is furthered by a community ritual. An intensely emotional passage should allow people the option to speak, but trying to require vocal involvement by all participants may be both impossible and unwise. The ritualista needs to keep an awareness of the focus of the ritual throughout its execution. It is easy to let the desires of parents become the focus of a teen rite of passage, because they may have strong and particular views about what the rite should include. Many rites of passage have at least some of the content withheld from the person of focus so that they encounter something unexpected, similar to how life presents these transitions to us.

Many rites of passage are best offered as a secret initiation or private ceremony, something intimate friends, family, or a worship group prepare and offer. Then later, maybe immediately after, a community ritual can celebrate the passage and effectively sanction the rite that has already taken place, but for the larger community.

Honoring and Blessing

Some rites of passage are a time for honoring an accomplishment. They may still also represent a time of change or transition, and acknowledging that transition is often included within the ritual. As community ritual these can take the form of celebration. These rites of passage are primarily an honoring ceremony:

- Conception

- First steps

- First day of school

- Driver's license

- First job

- First house or apartment

- Becoming grandparents

- Retirement

Sometimes part of honoring an accomplishment is a community blessing of it, using our group focus to empower a path of positive growth in the future. We will cover some techniques to accomplish this once we open our ritual toolbox. These types of rites of passage often have a community blessing included in the rite:

- Birth

- Reaching puberty

- Dedication to the gods

- Graduation

- Betrothal

- Marriage

Nels completes a Saging ritual for Skywolf.

Photo by Jenna Touchette

Healing Rite of Passage

Not all rites of passages acknowledge our positive accomplishments; many significant life changes are devastating to an individual or a family. A ritual purpose for the healing of individuals, groups, or a whole community falls into this type. A healing rite of passage confronts and acknowledges the life-changing event or condition and through community ritual engages our individual connection to the divine to promote a transition to the best outcome.

Typically these rituals are in response to severe illness or injury of individuals, or great personal loss through divorce, miscarriage, abortion, or the death of another. When any individual is suffering greatly, we as a community will feel and be affected by that suffering. Together, a community and a family or individual of focus can move past these events through ritual.

Ritual does not actually create the desired change, but can prepare and energize the participants to do the physical and mental work required for the change to take place. Healing ritual must focus on the outcome we expect for both the individuals and the community. A ritual for healing needs to be structured so it has a positive and affirming intention. The subconscious cannot affirm a negative message in ritual. A ritual to "cure" someone of cancer is less effective in its inherent design. A ritual to empower a return to health has a better chance of a successful outcome.

Rituals of this type can bring up past memories, strong feelings, and even provoke a physical response in participants. Preparing your audience within the ritual description, and again at the start, is essential and a primary responsibility of the ritual team.

Communities themselves can also experience passages. They can acknowledge, create, and empower changes community-wide through ritual. A community betrayal, embezzlement, the loss of leadership or identity for a group, any event that shatters their trust level or ideals can be devastating. Groups can also suffer all the effects of physical and mental trauma from a natural disaster or accident. Moving past these events can be done with community-based healing ritual. Most individuals and groups try to "tough it out" through these occurrences. A community healing rite of passage can be the most effective way to achieve and renew a sense of wholeness and purpose, while acknowledging the pain that has occurred.

Communities suffer from many social ills, including issues such as discrimination, hate, sexism, and poverty. Widespread harmful attitudes, emotions, disrespect, or a climate of fear can be addressed with a ritual of healing. For the group to effectively heal, it must be able to envision a positive future through the actions of the ritual. Again, the subconscious cannot affirm a negative message in ritual. We cannot heal away hate, but we can empower a community of love.

When a community's future looks bleak, a healing rite of passage ritual can also be a way to prepare for danger or a difficult challenge that a community is about to face. Oftentimes an educational ritual purpose gets muddled up with a healing purpose. You may be able to empower a community to grow toward respectfulness with a healing ritual, but often a ritual to "heal the earth" is best presented with an educational purpose. The actual healing sought is way too large and beyond our community control.

A ritual for community healing can include a creative way to inform or educate participants and explore the depth of the causes, methods, and nature of the change needed for healing. That thorough identification with the change and its process is a key part of making a healing ritual successful.

Individuals and communities can suffer tragedies, things that shake them to the core and disrupt lives. Which of these are appropriate for a community ritual of healing will be completely dependent on the individuals affected and the community they are a part of.

Devotional

We believe all ritual, for any purpose, connects people to their sacred nature, and in that sense all ritual is spiritual. The word "devotional" as a noun has a pretty limited dictionary meaning: a short religious service. We like "devotional" as both an adjective and noun describing a type of ritual purpose. Devotion in the spiritual sense is ardent, loyal, selfless affection and dedication to something beyond ourselves, of the spirit. A devotional ritual purpose for a community is one that creates an experience that helps the participants increase their relationship with their spirituality.

A devotional ritual does not automatically define the ritual form, style, or occasion, as the term "religious devotional" implies. Devotional rituals can use symbols drawn from many beliefs or religions, without limiting the focus to a particular religious belief. When you declare your own authority to do this, you are taking sacred back.

A devotional ritual purpose describes rituals that have increasing the connection with spirituality at their core. A devotional might include:

- Developing a relationship to unseen forces or supernatural beings

- Working with specific symbols with spiritual or religious connotations

- A particular method and intention to make the ritual experience sacred

- A place set apart to talk to god forms and express a community's spirituality

All devotionals take care to establish that the space in which the ritual takes place is a sacred one.

Worship Devotional

A worship devotional—a ritual honoring deity, deities, or supernatural forces—is one type of devotional ritual. It is a ritual purpose specifically to express your love, praise, honor, and devotion to a god form. A worship ritual is how people cultivate a bond and relationship with deity. In return, worshipers get a deeper level of awareness of the symbols of (and access to) the strength that the deity represents, as well as the benefits of the shared spiritual experience. You can honor a monotheistic god form (as in Christianity) or an aspect of a particular god form. A worship devotional can be directed very specifically to a named god form from a pantheon, a historical group of gods from a specific culture. A devotional can also be dedicated to a force of nature like the wind or a supernatural force like "the Mighty Dead."

Traditional Devotional

A traditional devotional is a worship ritual that requires some particular religious form and structure be included. There may be a prescribed rite of preparation for participants and for the altar or temple, and very specific acts and words may be included. In some traditional devotionals there can be oaths, commitments, prayers, sacrifices, and specific promises expected to be made by participants to a god form. These rituals involve the manipulation of specific religious symbols through objects, words, and actions, and they may be required to be performed by an accepted religious authority within the tradition. A devotional within a religious tradition may ask more of participants than they are comfortable giving, and may not be suitable for larger groups with a variety of beliefs, unless they are willing to accept the experience simply for its shared spiritual content and are informed in advance about the tradition.

Eclectic Devotional

A devotional ritual can be designed to be suitable for a community with very little in common, including religious belief. One need not be a devotee of a particular deity to participate and be uplifted by a shared ritual dedicated to that deity. God forms can be experienced through their symbols, relationships, aspects, and qualities, and if participants come to know those, they can benefit. An eclectic devotional ritual can include many other ritual styles and purposes within it. It might have god form symbols, their favorite foods, honoring songs, chants, and prayers, even a special dance or activity. An eclectic devotional does not demand a long-term relationship of commitment from participants.

Your ritual purpose might be to work with a community to explore their shared spirituality, and these rituals become eclectic devotionals. You make up the rules as you go along here, following where your inspiration, intention, and experience lead you.

Ecstatic Devotional

An ecstatic devotional ritual purpose is one designed to support an emotional or spiritual frenzy, a trance-like state of euphoria where participants might experience mystic self-transcendence and spiritual awareness. The ecstatic experience is also used to connect directly with divinity and join with them for a time. People invoking deities through ecstatic experience claim a range of experiences from perfect calm to elation, and can often speak and view the world through a deity's persona. Since prehistoric times shamans have used tools of movement, trance, exhaustion, substances, and voice to seek ecstasy. Transcending ordinary consciousness allowed them to connect with the animals needed for survival and the forces of nature that ruled their experience.

With the rise of agriculture and religion, the ecstatic experience was often relegated to mystics and clerics, and eventually, only within their religious traditions. The Christian churches historically had been places that included spiritual dance. By the 14th century, most had banned religious dancing within the church for, as Barbara Ehrenreich documents in her history of ecstatic dance, "if it became ecstatic dancing ordinary people might get the idea that they could approach the deity on their own."[14] When individuals experience a direct link to the divine, they may realize they do not have a need for religious structure.

Each part of an ecstatic ritual is designed to create a separation from normal consciousness and open the mind's doorways to transcendence. Movement, dance, or any physical activity to exhaustion is a common practice. Quieter methods to induce trance states such as meditation, voice, and particularly chanting are also used. A sense of fear at

---

14   Barbara Ehrenreich, *Dancing in the Streets: A History of Collective Joy* (New York: Picador, 2006), p. 84.

the point of losing conscious control and awareness often takes place for participants and must be prepared for by the ritualista. A sacred and safe space must be established for this ritual, with specific tilers (designated guardians) or the whole team available to assist participants. Either a particular god form is invoked or, more commonly for a diverse group, a symbol or object of focus is used related to the nature of the ecstasy that is to occur.

For these rituals with community groups, ecstasy as a shared intention is a prerequisite of success. Even when focused, the ecstatic experience will vary widely and be unique to each individual. The shared ritual experience has distinct advantages over seeking the ecstatic experience alone. The group actions toward the shared goal make this experience contagious, as is often the case within a religious context. Most other ritual purposes can also include an energy-raising piece that seeks to generate the ecstatic experience.

Any ritual, if successful for the participants, will feel sacred. Whether educational, a celebration of fellowship, a rite of passage, or a spiritual sharing of devotion, what the community emerges with is what is important. A sense of having shared the sacred within us all, together as a community, is meeting the intention for any ritual purpose.

Anthropologists, mythologists, and academics in religious and cultural studies all have different ways of defining and classifying rituals by type and purpose. Defining ritual, its types and styles, is difficult. Each type of ritual we talk about can be best understood by looking at the different components included in its structure. When working with rituals for communities, each ritual will evolve as a unique blend of the types and styles we have described. Community ritual will usually have one aspect that is primary. There are no firm and definitive boundaries when trying to classify rituals. The definitions blur between types and forms with wanton creativity. This is the beauty of ritual: we may not know what it exactly is, but we know when we experience it and when it works for us.

Education Within Ritual

Education of a community can be supported and deepened when it occurs within ritual. We don't consider education a purpose for ritual on its own, but it can be integrated as a secondary outcome. As an intellectual process, it draws participants away from the intuitive experience. We integrated the Ogham symbols, colors, and characteristics into a group of rituals we offered.[15] By week's end our community had learned much about the Ogham through ritual participation.

Incorporating an informing, educational aspect into a community ritual is a great way to stimulate a community dialogue around social problems we all see. Homelessness, poverty, or violence can be more effectively confronted with solutions from an educated and informed community. A ritual that explores the experiences and effects of what is easily ignored by individuals will give them an opportunity to see and feel the world as others in their community do, and learn to understand diverse perspectives better.

Including an educational goal for a community ritual needs to be approached with sensitivity and care. Education doesn't take place when participants feel like they are being lectured to or told what to do with the information they receive. Ritual techniques that present information as part of a drama or story allow people to see what they are ready to see and feel what they are moved to feel. We can lecture about the harm that street violence causes, or we can present a ritual that dramatically tells the story of the loss of a child or brother by gunfire and helps us to imagine the feelings involved.

It takes creativity to find a story that is not so simplistic as to be boring, but presents enough for people to realize something about the subject that they may not have seen or known before. Sometimes viewing an issue or concern from a different perspective than is common can create the moment of insight that education really seeks to generate.

---

15   Ogham: An early medieval alphabet in which the names of various trees can be ascribed to individual letters.

The ritually constructed broom pentacle on display in a Minneapolis store.
Shoppers added their prayer ribbons for months after the public ritual.

A community-created prop built or decorated within a ritual can offer a focus for the theme or topic. It is a great way to symbolically (or actually) include all the diverse perspectives and ideas that make a community vibrant. It can join the results together to create an educational tool that lasts beyond the ritual and becomes a community resource. A collectively built symbol connecting the ritual with an existing community center, club, or infrastructure is an ideal way for ritual to be embedded into the social fabric of a community. During the Veterans' Pentacle Rights Ritual at the Minnesota State Capitol, our community built a 4-foot broom pentacle and attached ribbons charged with our individual passion and energy to work to secure rights for our veteran warriors. This symbol then circulated for several months at area shops to both educate those who encountered it and to solicit their additions to it. It was a great way to take the power and energy present that day in ritual and continue it forward through education.[16]

Ritual: Veterans' Pentacle Rights Ritual

· · · · · · · · · · · · · · · · ·

Location: Minnesota State Capitol, 2007
© Judith Olson Linde and Nels Linde

Ritual context

The organization of this ritual was stimulated by a local talk show host's public chiding over the inability of Wiccans to secure Wiccan veterans the right to have the pentacle on their tombstones. Judy and I organized our community to create a public ritual at the state capitol. This brought more than 130 local Pagans together and took place at the end of February in an ice storm. Each participating group was allowed to frame their own spoken words, so this summary reflects the guidelines they were provided, not their actual words. The ritual gained the issue local and national publicity. After the ritual we formed a human pentacle, which was photographed from the capitol rotunda.

Ritual intent

A community working to aid in the securing of Wiccan and Neopagan religious freedom and rights for all (including the rights of fallen soldiers to display the symbol of their faith in national cemeteries) and to support a positive result in the active court cases relating to this issue. Additionally, we seek to enlighten and present a positive face of Wicca and Neopagan religion to the general public, generate press coverage and support for this issue, and provide an opportunity for regional groups to join together in action.

Ritual description

This public ritual will include simple sacred space setup, with sponsoring community groups invoking the elements and spirit in concert with the intent and in relation to the

---

16 "The Story of the Veteran Pentacle Quest," www.circlesanctuary.org/index.php/lady
-liberty-league/the-story-of-the-veteran-pentacle-quest.

points of the pentacle. The community will ritually charge symbols of our intent (ribbons) and add them to our community symbol (broom pentacle). This community symbol will be displayed in public places (billboard, stores, community center) over time to extend the working.

Ritual setup and supplies

A 4-foot hoop wrapped in elemental colors (yellow for Air, red for Fire, blue for Water, green for Earth, white for Spirit), five 5-foot simple besoms (brooms), wire to join them together. Basket of multicolored ribbon. Five elementally colored scarves. Three flags: United States, Minnesota state, All Armed Services. Plywood block flag stands.

Team members

Color guard (three veterans), Besom Brigade (a witches' drill team that does precision unified movement with besom brooms), 13 guides (also acting as security). Two Ritualistas, several team assistants, local area Druids, covens, and groups.

Ritual printed program

A printed program was produced which included a brief ritual outline, a song sheet, and event sponsor recognition. It also included an explanation of the continuation of the magic through the display of the pentacle image and the request for continuing energy and support of the issue.

Ritual script

We gathered at the Minnesota State Capitol at the end of the upper mall. Principal players were held at the circle center, all others were directed toward the capitol by the guides (13 assigned orange vest–wearers).

Gate

A color guard of three veterans formed an honor-guard gate. At 12:30 pm, all participants entered through this gate. Ribbons and programs were passed out to those entering, and they formed a circle. Direction-invoking groups gathered as part of the circle but at their respective direction.

Besom Brigade Banishing

The Besom Brigade (BB) members faced out from the center, surrounding a Druid from the Mists of Stone Forest group, who was holding the hoop. One at a time, they banished negativity from the circle with besom movement and voice, speaking toward the circle (for example, banishing fear, anger, frustration, bitterness, naysaying, negativity, etc.). The Brigade remained in the center with their besoms.

Blessing the Hoop

The hoop was carried around the circle to display to the people, the blessing words spoken spontaneously by the Druid (for example, hoop of the people, cycle of life, from birth to death, ancestors, community of the spirit). A team member assistant and the Druid then crouched with the hoop held horizontally at the center of the circle.

Forming the Pentacle

Five Besom Brigade members declared "Form Pentacle!" and five did so over the hoop, each adding a broom to form the lines (the other BB members dispersed to the circle). The Besom Brigade was now holding the hoop and the pentacle points, as team members began the pentacle assembly with wire. During this, the casting of the circle began with the color guard.

Casting the Circle

The color guard began with the circle casting of their choosing. (Example words: *A warrior perceives a threat to their community's liberty, their spiritual freedom, their family's safety, and rises to meet that challenge. We cast our circle today with freedom and with ashes.*) They moved with their flags around the circle, followed by a symbolic ash spreader. The color guard determined this process and ended back at the gate where they started. They then put the flags in their holders.

When the pentacle had been assembled, five Besom Brigade members held the pentacle horizontally at the color-coded pentacle points in the center of the circle.

Call to the Elements

This included basic characteristics by elemental tradition and ritual intent.

East: The Covenant of Unitarian Universalist Pagans (CUUPS) group entered the circle center, facing outward to the East. One member tied a yellow scarf to the yellow pentacle point, and took over from the Besom Brigade member as a pentacle holder. CUUPS now loudly called to the East as they chose, facing out toward the circle. (Example: Freedom, justice for our fallen warriors, eloquence to those who speak for them, etc.) The call ended as the group chose. All CUUPS members except the pentacle holder then returned to the circle.

South: The Circle of the Phoenix coven entered the circle center and faced outward to the South. One member tied the red scarf to the red pentacle point and remained as a pentacle holder; the Besom Brigade member who had been holding the red pentacle point returned to the circle. The Circle of Phoenix now called to the South as they chose, facing out toward the circle. (Example: Energy for our struggle, passion to maintain an active defense of our liberty, etc.) The call ended as the group chose. All Circle of Phoenix members except the pentacle holder then returned to the circle.

West: The Shades of Grey coven entered the circle center and faced outward to the West. One member tied the blue scarf to the blue pentacle point and remained as a pentacle holder; the Besom Brigade member who had been holding the blue pentacle point returned to the circle. The Shades of Grey now called to the West as they chose, facing out toward the circle. (Example: Empathetic understanding, peaceful resolution, healing of personal loss, end division in our broader community, etc.) The call ended as the group chose. All Shades of Grey members except the pentacle holder then returned to the circle.

North: The Standing Stones coven entered the circle center and faced outward to the North. One member tied the green scarf to the green pentacle point and remained as a pentacle holder; the Besom Brigade member who had been holding the green pentacle point returned to the circle. The Standing Stones now called to the North as they chose, facing out toward the circle. (Example: Manifesting change in the real world, solid foundations, rest at peace in Mother Earth, a supportive home to return to, etc.) The call ended as the group chose. All Standing

Stones members except the pentacle holder then returned to the circle.

Spirit: The Harmony Tribe group entered the circle center and faced outward toward the full circumference. One member tied the white scarf to the white pentacle point and remained as a pentacle holder; the Besom Brigade member who had been holding the white pentacle point returned to the circle. The Harmony Tribe now called to Spirit as they chose, facing out toward the circle. (Example: Apex of the pyramid, hub of the wheel, the still silent point around which creation rotates, etc.) The call ended as the group chose. All Harmony Tribe members except the pentacle holder then returned to the circle.

Lord/Lady Call: Ritualista 1 and Ritualista 2 entered the circle center, facing outward on opposite sides of the circle at East and West. They each did a brief call to no specific deity, evoking qualities of justice, liberty, and protection.

Ritual Working

During this, all the circle guides raised their ribbons with a flourish to model charging them energetically.

Ritualista 1 in the West:
"We come from many paths and are diverse in our worship, yet we call to you in one voice. Aid our efforts to secure our rights and recognition of our fallen. We charge these ribbons with our passion to achieve justice for our warriors." Silent pause for personal charge. *"We ask you accept these ribbons as a symbol of our determined work, and in the healing of our fallen and our community."*

Ritualista 1 and Ritualista 2 added their ribbons to the pentacle with a flourish, then walked away and started clapping, cueing the drums to start the song "Freedom," by Christian Williamson (1997).

The pentacle holders held the pentacle horizontally to allow the participants maximum access as they came forward and tied their ribbons to the pentacle edge, led by the guides' example. The song ended with a drumming break when everyone was finished.

Close the Circle Deosil

The CUUPS pentacle holder, with an exaggerated motion, touched the yellow point, turned and faced East, blew a kiss, and rejoined the large circle. (It's fine to close a circle without words, or you can use "hail and farewell" or another short phrase.)

After a pause, the Circle of the Phoenix pentacle holder, with an exaggerated motion, touched the red point, turned and faced South, blew a kiss, and rejoined the large circle. Ritualistas 1 and 2 replaced the East and South directional people as they left the pentacle.

After a pause, the Shades of Grey pentacle holder, with an exaggerated motion, touched the blue point, turned and faced West, blew a kiss, and rejoined the large circle.

After a pause, the Standing Stones pentacle holder, with an exaggerated motion, touched the green point, turned and faced North, blew a kiss, and rejoined the large circle.

After a pause, the Harmony Tribe pentacle holder, with an exaggerated motion, touched the white point, turned and looked upward, and blew a kiss. The Harmony Tribe person stayed and held the pentacle along with Ritualistas 1 and 2. They lifted up the pentacle and displayed it to the circle participants, rotating around the circle.

Ritual Farewell

Ritualista 1 improvised words of farewell:
*"When all gather in her name to speak with
one voice, positive transformation can begin."*

Ritualista 1 then shouted:
"Can you hear it?" (Silence, no answer)

Ritualista 1 with hand to ear:
"Can you hear it?"

Guides answer in unison:
"Hear what?"

Ritualista 1:
"Can you hear it?"

There was a pause, and then a drum cue (boom, boom, boom), followed by the choir introducing the song "The Sound of Change," by Christian Williamson (1997). The color guard walked the inside of the circle back to the gate and re-formed as the exit gate. The song continued until the color guard formed the gate; then a drum break ended the song. Ritualista 1 spontaneously offered words to open the circle.

Selena Fox accepts the broom pentacle donated to Circle Sanctuary and awards the Pentacle Medal to Nels and Judy Linde during the Pentacle Quest victory celebration at Pagan Spirit Gathering, 2007.

PART TWO

Your Ritual Toolbox

FIVE

·········

Ritual Organization

We had been in the planning stages for months, fleshing out the roles and finding people who would take them on. I spent hours in the thrift store, looking for objects to use for the workings. I had lists of lists. The big unknown was how smoothly it would all go. Would the blocking work? How well had we estimated the timing? Would the activities be engaging? Once the ritual began my role was to stay in the center, watching the hourglass and chiming the cues, so I saw it all unfold. I could hear muttered voices, popcorn popping, children chattering, and everywhere I looked, participation! The only adjustment I had to make was for the popping corn, which took a little longer than expected. When I chimed the cue, groups moved seamlessly from one activity to the next. How did it happen? The mystery of ritual organization had brought us here.

RITUAL OF THE 13 MOONS

You may not realize how far you have come already in your planning. Open your ritual notebook and see what you have in your ritual toolbox. Start by assembling all you have collected about your community and your particular group. Summarize who exactly you expect your audience to be, and what limits and accommodations you need to make for them to all fully participate. Make note of anything that you know for sure will be part of your planning. Will it be indoors, for 30 people, and need to last under an hour? Write down the physical limits you know will exist.

You have some idea of who you can include in your team, or you know that you will be offering this ritual as the sole leader or maybe with a partner. You have made an assessment of your skills and talents, but now you need to include a look at any others and possible roles you will need to fill or the "hats" you will wear.

···········

EXERCISE

Write down all the people who have agreed to join your team. Next to them list any ritual roles you expect to need filled and any talents or limitations they have expressed. Some may have said, "I will help move people or model actions for the team, but I am not prepared to speak." Others may have said they will help with whatever is needed. Label this your "Team Talent Pool" and use this as you continue planning. If no one is willing to sing, don't plan on something based on strong voices! Add this information to your ritual notebook.

You have read about the various purposes, styles, and types of ritual. You may have an idea for the purpose and may be drawn to a particular style. Keep an open mind. As you work through the next section, consider this a trial run at narrowing your focus.

Writing Your Intent

Ritual intent is not simply the ritual's purpose; it is a concise description of the experience and the anticipated outcome that guides all action within the ritual. Writing one seems an easy enough task, but it is deceivingly difficult. A well-written intent, summarizing in words and focusing the action of the ritual to reflect the goal, will cause many a ritualista to lose sleep. The intent is your best guide for bringing your vision to reality and is essential to the creative process. Writing it is important because you can immediately begin to use it in describing the ritual concept to potential members of your ritual team or the host community. Ritual intent is essential to keeping your ritual concept and team on track.

Your vision, the ritual intent, and the ritual itself will develop like a living thing, and will grow with the addition of each new idea and action you include. The acuity to recognize when changes in one aspect are changing the essence of the ritual is of critical importance. Make these changes by choice, not by accident. Don't let your vision be altered by the developing intent, or the intent changed by including an idea or ritual technique without acknowledging the changes you are accepting. Like an artist choosing the tone and shade of each brush stroke, build your ritual first upon the vision, then upon the core intent or purpose defined by the choices your inspiration has led you to.

A well-crafted ritual intent will be broad enough to avoid any appearance of personal lecturing. It should allow each person to imagine the ritual through the filter of their specific beliefs. You cannot presume to have a spiritually homogeneous audience. With sensitivity and advance information, most spiritual viewpoints can be successfully encountered and accommodated in a community ritual.

If your community has a shared history of ritual experience, key words and phrases can be descriptive enough to define your intent. Terms like participatory, formal, introspective, or guided meditation give just enough information to let individuals decide whether to participate. As your audience broadens in diversity, it becomes the ritualista's responsibility to increase the clarity of the ritual intent that is communicated.

• • • • • • • • • • •
EXERCISE

Write a concise ritual intent for what you and your team envision. In this first draft just include the purpose and nature of the ceremony in affirmative terms and who it is for. As you begin writing an outline, return to this draft and strengthen it by connecting it to the larger cosmos, our spiritual nature, and describing what effect it will have on participants. Add this to your ritual notebook.

Take, for example, "Celebrate the legalization of universal marriage rights with supporters of freedom." Later, as your vision develops, this might become: "Feel the sunlight of sacred love intensify as we celebrate with honoring and dance our freedom to form sacred union with those of our choosing."

Writing a clear ritual intent is a lot like writing an organization's mission statement. You want to be clear, concise, and thorough. One or two sentences is an ideal length. Do not stray too far from your vision. Think of the major questions: who, what, where, how, and why. Take your basic ritual idea and purpose and create a draft ritual intent. Start with simple words that affirmatively and positively declare what participants will do, feel, experience, or create. In ritual we never "try" to do something. That leaves room to be absent from engaging in the ritual or to fail to attain the ritual purpose.

The balance sought is to offer enough information to allow your community an informed choice, without defining each individual's ritual experience in advance. Revealing all the aspects of a ritual's elements in an intent or description removes the power of surprise and discovery from the moment. Ideally, your community has ritual experience to build upon, and your written intent can just be a short summary or a poetic description.

Intent Example: Rite of Passage

There is a special type of ritual that celebrates individual life passages: births, dedications, transitions to adulthood, marriage, special status, aging, and death. Although it is common for these important occasions to be celebrated on an intimate level, with the close support of kin, they can also be very successfully shared as public rituals. Common experience or achievement is acknowledged, shared, and celebrated and the community is enriched. These rituals are most often custom tailored to an individual's history, experience, needs, and desires. Community-attended rites of passage can also allow for significant creativity in design.

These rituals most importantly serve the individual need, and limitations are often already in place based on local, family, or individual tradition. Here the primary obligation for defining the ritual intent is in communication between the ritualista, ritual team, and subject individual. Participants attend because of their relationship to the individual of focus.

Let's say a friend has completed a nursing degree and wishes to be recognized and empowered to transition into the work world as a healer. He asks you to create a community ritual for this life transition. You meet and ask him questions, such as:

- Do you want the sacred nature of becoming a healer emphasized?

- Who do you want included? Close friends and family? Anyone who may know you? Do you want an open and public event?

- Do you want people to speak directly to you or about you, and if so, who? Would you like an opportunity to speak to the group?

- Do you want the attendees to have an active role in the ceremony?

- Do you want to be surprised by the ritual experience or firmly know what it will contain?

- Tell me what effects you think this transition will have on you. What are your hopes, needs, and expectations?

- Do you want you and/or your guests to come away from this with memorabilia of the event?

- Do you want a defined ending, or will this ceremony transition into a meal or other type of group sharing?

- Do you have any music, pictures, or props that would be meaningful for you?

- Do you want to be the center of attention or will that make you uncomfortable?

- What kind of seating or staging would work best for you?

These are just a sample of possible questions you might ask. Learning the skill of asking the appropriate and necessary questions is an achievement in itself! From the answers you discover that he wants to open this ritual up to anyone who wants to attend. He wants both a time to express his thanks to those who have supported his journey, and a time to have people speak from their heart to him. He is fine with you being creative and surprising him with exactly how the ritual unfolds. He would like a guest book or some memento of the event. Plans for a community potluck meal with him providing the meal basics are already underway.

These few questions give you a great amount of information to compose a ritual intent draft. This will be used to guide you in the ritual development and used in any event invitations or advertising. Here is an example for this intent:

Join with friends and community to witness, congratulate, and support John as we celebrate his transition to work as a trained healer.

Now that you have some limitations in place, it is time to gather a team, if you wish, and brainstorm some creative ways to work within the limitations you have established. It may seem simple. Just gather folks together, tell them what will happen, and let it be done. In reality, constructing the actual ritual, making people feel safe to really open up to each other, and making a meaningful rite of passage for John will involve more choices to make it effective.

This ritual intent was easy, in a sense, because the limitations were imposed by John, the object of the rite of passage. You will find that in developing rituals, limitations can be your friend. Like a blank canvas for an artist faced with unlimited possibilities, an intriguing subject can be difficult to define.

Intent Example: Gratitude Community Ritual

Let's try a broader, less-defined ritual intent scenario. We were charged with developing a ritual to express all we had learned as a festival community over a week of ritual and workshops surrounding the theme of gratitude. We had all the notes from our extensive brainstorming session (see chapter 3) to work from. Gratitude is a large topic with many facets. We had asked many questions and some of the key ideas that jumped out at us were:

- Gratitude is a state of well-being, a state of grace, and a way of life.

- It is optimism that never ends, which brings additional blessings.

- It is appreciating all you have no matter what it is, even your hardships and difficulties.

- A ritual about gratitude might be about making people feel special and might include the careful observation of others, and then a reflection of what is observed.

- If gratitude isn't a core element of your spirituality, how can you express it to each other?

- Words of power: grace, optimism, well-being, positive intentions.

We knew some things we wanted to include in the ritual, which helped in composing the intent. Festivants would be exploring their gratitude in five main areas: their pleasures, heroes, ancestors, challenges, and spirituality. All week, they would add their words of gratitude to cloth banners to represent each area. We wanted to include a path-working and the banners they had contributed to, which would help them connect with all they had learned and experienced about gratitude. Finally, we would connect gratitude to their spirituality so they would carry it home for the year to come.

We started with a few sentences of intention:

We will connect with all the aspects of gratitude for those who have helped and guided us, and bask in thankfulness for our well-being and pleasures. Gratitude energizes our devotion to deity and sustains us, now and in the future.

After reading it several times, and speaking it for a few days, we found it was too specific and did not empower us to really feel and begin living gratitude. It didn't reference how our challenges also need our gratitude.

We took another stab at the intent, using some of our collected words of power:

We have experienced the well-being gratitude offers, a state of grace. Our positive intentions create a new world where we overcome our challenges and sustain our devotion and connection to deity.

After speaking this one for a few days we decided to take a few parts of it, make it more affirmative, and save the connection to spirituality to be revealed in the actual ritual. This is what we finally came up with:

To fully know and embrace the state of grace where gratitude lives. Move past our challenges and enter a new world that our gratitude creates and makes flourish. Bathe in the positive outpouring of well-being and good intention.

(See chapter 2 ritual, "Gratitude.")

We were happy with this final intent. It echoed our words of power, was affirming of our experience exploring gratitude, and set a tone for all the ritual ideas, words, and activities we planned to include.

A well-written ritual intent is a tool to inspire others to join in your presentation. Team members may want to contribute but still be as surprised with the totality of the ritual as the audience is. A rich intent statement leaves room for everyone to imagine what they will experience.

As the specifics of your ritual develop, frequently refer back to the ritual intent. We can get caught up in the excitement of innovative ideas, great character actions or spoken words, or spectacular props, and lose sight of our basic vision for the ritual. You will need to judge the inclusion of each new idea on the basis of whether it moves the message forward or muddies the water! Enthusiasm can lead to additions that may seem to improve the ritual, when they actually distract from the intent.

Keep it simple! A strong, clear message, presented well, will be the most effective way to successfully translate your intent into the ritual experience you envision. No good idea is ever lost. Whether working as a team or alone, take careful and thorough notes on your brainstorming ideas. We regularly refer back to notes or recorded dialogue from past ritual planning for those discarded elements that we knew were great at the time. Each idea may have its own place in a ritual, but not all in the same one!

Description and Title

In addition to the intent, you may need a ritual description, a lengthier paragraph that contains more information about what your participants might expect. Craft the description after the whole outline is roughed out, so you know what to include. The description should contain more practical information about what to bring, where to go, and how to prepare, while still keeping the actual experience planned for the ritual rather vague. It can be aimed more at promoting attendance in event advertising.

Here is the description we developed for the "Gratitude" intent example:

Gather and process from the Heart Chakra to the Sacred Circle. We live in this moment and graciously meet our future with each step. Share your heart and embark on the way of gratitude. Feast to the blessings and delight of the Gods. The rewards of our generosity of spirit return tenfold.

A strong title for your ritual is very important. Like the intent, it should be concise and relevant, declarative and inspiring. The title is where the very first impression is made on your prospective audience. We like to wait until the ritual intent, outline, and description are all complete before considering the title. This way we have the time to allow the right words to bubble up to consciousness. Find a metaphor or symbol that is unique in the ritual and incorporate that in the title. If you name it the obvious "Community Summer Solstice Ritual," you may not inspire much interest. "Live the Longest Light" is more intriguing.

Create an Outline

Now you are ready to fully develop the content. We suggest starting by creating a ritual outline, a framework upon which your content can be anchored. Refer to your notes for ideas that you may want to include, using your ritual intent as a guide. This principle remains the same for whatever group, theme, or intent you are working with.

To make your new ritual outline effective as a tool, keep it present as you work. Take notes on ideas as they arise and sort them into the ritual outline where they might fit. If your team imagination hits a wall, consider a section of the ritual that has been overlooked up to this point: "How can they enter the sacred space in a way that will make this ritual more engaging?" Keep a voice recorder with you so you don't lose any ideas that arise. This is an energizing, exciting, and creative time—don't lose any of it.

Here we have included, as an example, the classic Wiccan ritual outline. It is drawn from small group religious practice and is simply a way of organizing a rite. It is familiar to most folks who attend large group ritual in the Pagan community, and it is where we began.

- Banish: Declare your area a sacred space (and ask disruptive forces to leave).

- Draw: Define the area in which the main protection and effects of your ritual will be contained.

- Bless: By your actions, make the ritual area sacred and symbolically prepared for ritual.

- Call elements/directions: Speak to the elemental forces and invite them to attend and act as guardians for the ritual.

- Invoke deity: Invite the essence of deity to join the ritual.

- Working of intent: An activity that helps people engage with the purpose of the ritual.

- Energy raising: A group experience that heightens the focus of the group.

- Great Rite or feast: A celebration of the ritual purpose fulfilled.

- Release deity: Thanks.

- Release directions: Prepare and release the ritual space.

- Open circle: Bring the ritual to a close.

This *in no way* defines the only way to lay out a ritual, nor are the parts included to be considered essential. For large group ritual, it is often necessary to combine, limit, or restructure these components. Whether you use some, all, or none of these, your participants will need to recognize the subtle signals that ritual has begun, that an extraordinary experience is unfolding around them, and they will need to know when it is over. Account for the primary parts of the outline in some creative way to aid attendees on their journey to the sacred.

We developed the following form for use at the Sacred Harvest Festival. It is loosely based on the outline above. It covers all the basic considerations and ensures that planning has taken place for the major areas of the ritual.

Ritual Flow Questionnaire

1. **Ritual:**

2. **Ritual Intent:** What experience, feeling, insight, or awareness will festivants come away with from the ritual?

3. **Ritual Description:** How do you want it described in the program?

4. **Ritual Numbers:**
   » How many festivants is this ritual designed for?
   » What are the fewest and most participants you need to plan for?
   » Who and how many facilitate the ritual?
   » How many are on your team? Who are they?

5. **Ritual Entrance:**
   » How will festivants be called to the ritual?
   » Where will they gather? An activity at the gather? Song? Chant?
   » Is a ritual explanation or preparatory information needed?
   » Is there a procession to the ritual or a trickle arrival? Activity? Song? Chant? Drums?
   » Entrance at ritual space? Is there an extended gateway or activity at the entrance?
   » Any path-working leading to the entrance?
   » Smudging, asperging, challenge, or receiving of items at the gate?
   » How long will the wait be?
   » Are there any mobility-restricted people who need accommodation?
   » Should they bring chairs? How will they know?
   » When do they enter? Where do they place themselves? How will they know?

6. **Ritual Attunement:**

   » What do festivants form? A circle? A double/triple circle? Groups? An audience?

   » How are they directed to form it?

   » How will you construct your temple or sacred space? How will you make people feel safe and in a contained space?

7. **Implementation of Intent:**

   » What words, gestures, actions, activities, roles, or interactions will manifest the intent of your ritual?

   » How will festivants know what they are to do to accomplish the intent?

   » Will you tell them? Will you show them? Will you need team members to model or use a prop to demonstrate?

8. **Energy Raising:**

   » Is there an energy-raising activity? At what point in the ritual?

   » How is it accomplished? Song? Chant? Movement?

   » What is its purpose? Is it celebratory, for the greater good, to energize festivants?

   » Who directs the energy raised, and how, and to where? How does it end?

   » How do festivants know when to stop?

   » Is there a grounding activity afterward?

9. **Closing the Ritual:**

   » How will people be made aware that the ritual is coming to an end?

   » Will your ritual opening be echoed in your closing?

   » Is there a final crescendo?

   » Do people leave when they feel like it, or are they led away from the ritual area in procession?

10. **Additional Considerations:**

   » Timing of ritual (day, dusk, night); how much wood, supplies, tiki torches, etc., are needed?

   » Feel empowered to modify this form to suit your purposes. Enter, attune, bond, act, empower, ground, thank, and disperse; an outline can be as simple as that.

Ritual: Ritual of the 13 Moons

· · · · · · · · · · · · · · · · ·

Location: Sacred Harvest Festival, 2009
© Judith Olson Linde and Nels Linde

Ritual context

This ritual was produced to support the festival theme "Living the Wheel." It is a celebration of the cycles of the moon and was intended to educate festivants in a hands-on and personal way about the nature of the moons that mark the passage of the year. The challenge was to rotate 12 groups of about a dozen people at a time through a dozen intimate experiences and have it be fast-moving, fun, and educational for families.

Ritual intent

To demonstrate relevant magic corresponding with each full moon of the year using their astrological aspects.

Ritual description

Each Esbat is defined in specific by the whirl of the moon in its cycles. We honor what our moon has to teach us along the path. Gather at 6:45 p.m., join the procession from the Heart Chakra (gathering place) at 7:00; the ritual begins at arrival.

Ritual setup and supplies

Large 4-minute hourglass, bell or singing bowl, individual props (below), center table for hourglass and bell, tables may be needed for some moons. In the circle, each of the 12 moons had a working station set up or space reserved—a twelfth of the circle, like the hours on a clock face. Participants circled up just outside these stations.

Individual props

- Aries: Popcorn, table, tall metal pot with stand, oil, propane torch.

- Taurus: Low planter with one main plant and hundreds of sprouts.

- Cancer: Drilled acorns or beads in a bowl, precut hemp cord.

- Leo: Horned One costume.

- Virgo: Bowl of 14 oranges, knife.

- Libra: Balance scale, 20 thrift store items that all weigh the same (items with some relationship, such as color or shape, but made from varied materials; weight can be added or taken away so the appearance is deceiving).

- Scorpio: Table, Braille box (a narrow box with several holes along the sides just big enough to fit hands through and a top that can be removed), a large textured object (we used a green-man face cast in relief) to identify by touch inside the box.

- Sagittarius: Costume, bow and arrow.

- Capricorn: Cloth squares, scissors, cord, assortment of prosperity herbs.

- Aquarius: Spool of breakable thread.

- Pisces: 6-inch double-sided mirror with handle

- Blue Moon: costume.

- Each moon character had their astrological sign incorporated visibly into their costume.

Team members

13 moon representatives, two incense wafters/greeters, Ritualista, four choir members

Ritual script

The 12 moon people waited a little distance from the circle. At the gate, two incense wafters (there was no time for individual smudging) and the Ritualista greeted participants. They counted participants as they entered and directed the participants to form a circle. After the stragglers were all in, the two greeters and the Ritualista compared participant numbers. The Ritualista went on to open the ritual, while the greeters relayed the participant numbers to the 12 moon people, who divided that number by 12 to know how many to gather into each group later.

Ritual Opening

Festivants entered and formed the circle. With a cue from the Ritualista, the choir moved to the East just inside the circle of people and began singing the chorus of "Behold (There Is Magic)," by Abbi Spinner McBride:

"Behold, there is magic all around us,
Awaken, rejoice, and sing!"

The Ritualista motioned the circle to quiet as the choir sang the verse, which began:

"I am the Air ... "

The Ritualista motioned all to sing the chorus as the choir moved on to the South just inside the circle of people. The Ritualista motioned for quiet again as the choir sang the next verse:

"I am the Fire ... "

The Ritualista motioned all to sing the chorus as the choir moved on to the West just inside the circle of people. The Ritualista motioned for quiet again as the choir sang the next verse:

"I am the Water ... "

The Ritualista motioned all to sing the chorus as the choir moved on to the North just inside the circle of people. The Ritualista motioned for quiet again as the choir sang the next verse:

"I am the Earth ... "

The Ritualista motioned all to sing the chorus as the choir moved to the center. The Ritualista motioned for quiet again as the choir sang the last verse:

"I am the Spirit ... "

The Ritualista motioned all to sing the chorus through once more, and the choir repeated the last chorus line to finalize it. The Ritualista motioned and the song ended.

Character Entrance

The Ritualista greeted the moon characters at the eastern gate with an hourglass, leading them as they walked deosil (clockwise) around the circle, silently counting off one-twelfth of the total people participating. Each moon character joined the circle at a spot close to their station, spaced evenly around the circle. (For example, in a circle of 150 people, if the Aries station is at 1:00, the Aries character steps into the circle there. Taurus counts off 12 people and steps in there, and should be fairly close to their station at 2:00. Gemini counts off 12 people and steps in there, etc. The numbers won't be exact—it's an art, not a science.) All the moon characters joined the circle and motioned everyone to join hands.

The Ritualista:
"Time ... a precious commodity. We spend it, we waste it, we worry it will run out, we ask when ours will come. We mark its passage by many means. The regular cycle of the moon is nature's profound and predictable method, and can guide our daily magic."

The Ritualista set the hourglass on an elevated center altar, and when all the moon stations were ready, rang a bell.

At the bell, each moon released the hand of the person on their left and led their section of people into a smaller circle around their moon station. The moon character ended up facing the inner center altar to be able to see the hourglass. Now 12 circles of people were spaced around the ritual area. At the next bell rung by the Ritualista, who turned the hourglass over, each moon character spoke to their smaller circle in the first person, such as:

"I am the Taurus full moon; here is the opportunity I offer you."

They improvised a few sentences about the moon's essence and then began the working (see below). At the sound of the next bell (warning, 1 minute left), they concluded the working. At the following bell, they said something like:

"Remember this magic when the Taurus (Virgo, Pisces, etc.) moon approaches. Wait here for your next moon cycle."

They then left that group at their station and walked widdershins (counterclockwise) to the adjacent station and said to that waiting group:

"Come with me to experience the next moon cycle," and led the group back to their station. When the bell rang next, they began again.

The Ritualista watched to make sure that all circles were in place and then rang the bell to commence, turning the hourglass over. This process was repeated 11 more times!

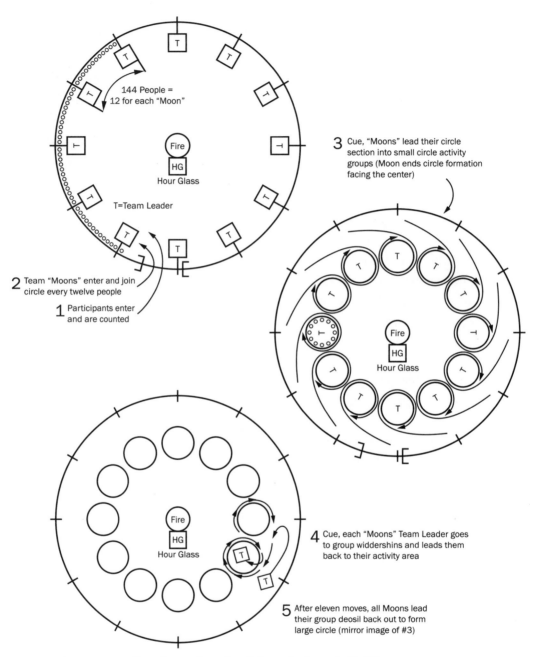

**144 People =
12 for each "Moon"**

Fire

HG

Hour Glass

T=Team Leader

3 Cue, "Moons" lead their circle
section into small circle activity
groups (Moon ends circle formation
facing the center)

2 Team "Moons" enter and join
circle every twelve people

1 Participants enter
and are counted

Fire

HG

Hour Glass

Fire

HG

Hour Glass

4 Cue, each "Moons" Team Leader goes
to group widdershins and leads them
back to their activity area

5 After eleven moves, all Moons lead
their group deosil back out to form
large circle (mirror image of #3)

**Forming and moving 150 people through 12 different
activity groups, and then back into one circle.**

- Participants entered and were counted. Total was divided by 12.

- Moons characters entered and joined with the circle every 12 people.

- At the bell cue, the moons led their section to form a small circle activity group. They ended up facing the center and hourglass. The bell cued to begin moon activity.

- At the next bell cue, each moon went to the adjacent group widdershins and led them back to re-form their activity circle.

- After 11 moves, each activity had been experienced, and the moons led their groups back out to re-form the large circle.

The Moons

At each station, an activity, meditation, interaction, or spell was done that captured the moon essence for application in everyday life.

Aries: *"I am the Aries full moon; here is the opportunity my pull can offer you.* (Note each moon drew from the "essence" provided to speak of their offering.) *My time is to renew your energy, refine your power and focus, and begin that new venture you envision."*

Essence: Energy, power, focus, new ventures. The drive to make something happen.

Activity: An altar held a metal pot containing oil on a tripod. Each participant was given a popcorn kernel. *"The Aries moon is like searing oil, which with our efforts can bring great and powerful personal changes. Close your eyes and imagine a goal that you have never found the focus to attain. Now draw upon your inner energy, and with the aid of the Aries moon as a magnifying glass, see that power flowing into your goal.* (Pause.) *Now place the seed of your goal under the power of the Aries Moon."* Aries turned on the torch and heated the pot and led an energy chant as the popcorn popped.

Ending: *"Remember this magic when the Aries moon approaches."*

Taurus: *"I am the Taurus full moon; here is the opportunity my pull can offer you. My time is to gain abundance in practical ways and remove obstacles to your growth."*

Essence: Money, possessions, luxury, tend your garden, remove obstacles to growth.

Activity: A large planter contained many "weeds." The group surrounded the planter and closed their eyes as a meditation was spoken: *"What obstacles stand in the way of your success and abundance? How can you fertilize your growth? What part of your garden needs tending?"* (Pause.) *"Now think of one word or phrase to empower you, and if you can, speak it as we pluck an obstacle."* Each participant named an obstacle and plucked a weed in turn.

Ending: *"Remember this magic when the Taurus moon approaches."*

Gemini: *"I am the Gemini full moon; here is the opportunity my pull can offer you.* (Made an American Sign Language hand sign.) *My time is for improving communication skills."*

Essence: Short distance travel, business communication, contracts, and transactions. Learning a new language or communication skills.

Activity: Gemini taught a phrase about the Gemini moon in sign language and "thank you." All in turn spoke to their neighbor, and the neighbor acknowledged with "thank you."

Ending: *"Remember this magic when the Gemini moon approaches."*

Cancer: *"I am the Cancer full moon; here is the opportunity my pull can offer you. My time is for hearth, family, home, and regaining psychic receptivity."*

Essence: Family, home, motherhood, pregnancy, finding a new home, scrying, divination, psychic and receptive. Getting cool stuff.

Activity: Each participant assembled a pendulum from a drilled acorn and hemp cord, and tried a simple divination. This item was a takeaway.

Ending: "Remember this magic when the Cancer moon approaches."

Leo: (dressed as the Horned One) *"I am the Leo full moon; here is the opportunity my pull can offer you. My time is to embrace virility and fertility, to muster the confidence and courage of leadership."*

Essence: Male virility and fertility, confidence, courage, strength, and leadership.

Activity: The Horned One verbally and personally challenged each festivant and encouraged them to embrace the qualities of this moon. (This role required someone skilled at speaking from the heart.)

Ending: "Remember this magic when the Leo moon approaches."

Virgo: *"I am the Virgo full moon; here is the opportunity my pull can offer you. My time is to renew your commitment to the vessel that houses you and learn the skills of fitness. The fruits of the harvest provide health, nourishment, and healing for the temple that is your body."*

Essence: Health and fitness, nutrition, healing, improving skills (handcrafts), details, and the harvest.

Activity: There was a bowl of oranges on the altar, a knife, and a cutting board. Virgo passed an orange around the group. *"We have learned to crave the sweet and the greasy, for they offer quick satisfaction. Examine this fruit, see its texture, smell its skin, revel in its promise."* She began to peel and carry the orange around within the circle, showing it. *"With effort we consciously break its seal, the guardian of its gifts, and smell the reward contained."* She separated the orange into segments and handed them out. *"Close your eyes and with all your senses feel the power of the sun contained within, feel the luscious softness, feel the succulent water within to nourish you. Now raise it to your lips, but stop, smell the gift of life you are offered. Imagine the power of the sun, and the land, and the water, rushing in to invigorate you as you place it in your mouth."*

Ending: "*Remember this magic when the Virgo moon approaches.*"

Libra: "*I am the Libra full moon; here is the opportunity my pull can offer you. My time is to find balance and harmony in your relationships and partnerships.*"

Essence: Partnerships, balance, harmony.

Activity: Each festivant selected an item from about 20 on the altar table. "*Take a minute and look around at these objects, and as you see a relationship with another object, talk to its holder and agree to find balance as a pair, or try another if it doesn't feel right.*" After one minute, the pairs stepped to the balance, stated their relationship, and then placed their objects on the balance. Whoa! They balanced! Pairs replaced objects on the altar, and the next pair approached. When all completed the task: "*For when you see and find relationship you are always in balance!*"

Ending: "*Remember this magic when the Libra moon approaches.*"

Scorpio: "*I am the Scorpio full moon; here is the opportunity my pull can offer you. My time is to quest for insight, the inner secrets revealed though transformation.*"

Essence: Insight, occult, psychology, sexuality, transformation, healing the mind, secrets, concentration.

Activity: Festivants surrounded the Braille box and, in turn, briefly reached in to feel the object inside. Different people felt different parts, and working together they made an attempt to identify the object within. (Experiment with 3-second guesses, then 5-second guesses, etc.) Allow more time if the solution hasn't been found when the warning bell rings, but make it difficult enough to fill the 4 minutes. The lid was removed and the secret revealed at the end.

Ending: "*Remember this magic when the Scorpio moon approaches.*"

Sagittarius: (dressed as the goddess Diana, the Archer) *"I am the Sagittarius full moon; here is the opportunity my pull can offer you. My time is to gain refinement of the intellect and hone your path for the long view."*

Essence: Long distance travel, protection, study and learning, writing and publishing, religion and philosophy.

Activity: The goddess Diana offered advice and wisdom to each in turn. She spoke spontaneously of travel and the long journey. *"Aim with accuracy, have the passion to draw the string, the strength to hold steady the bow, and the calm to release it smoothly. Whether in daily life or on your spiritual path, your life must be clearly on the mark. Start relearning all over again."* (This role requires someone skilled at speaking spontaneously.)

Ending: *"Remember this magic when the Sagittarius moon approaches."*

Capricorn: *"I am the Capricorn full moon; here is the opportunity my pull can offer you. My time is to focus your ambition to attain a successful career through organization."*

Essence: Career, success, ambition, determination, organization.

Activity: In a simple spell-working, Capricorn helped festivants make and energize an herbal career-success bundle, and gave directions to keep it empowered.

Ending: *"Remember this magic when the Capricorn moon approaches."*

Aquarius: *"I am the Aquarius full moon; here is the opportunity my pull can offer you. My time is to know freedom, independence, and detachment to form fulfilling bonds."*

Essence: Science and technology, forming friendships, groups, freedom, independence, autonomy, detachment, intuition.

Activity: Aquarius tied thread around each festivant's wrists to bind their hands. Then he offered a meditation that guided festivants to find their personal word that exemplified freedom. The spell was energized by each person, in rapid turns, breaking their bonds as they spoke their word aloud.

Ending: *"Remember this magic when the Aquarius moon approaches."*

Pisces: *"I am the Pisces full moon; here is the opportunity my pull can offer you. My time is to remember compassion and empathy and accept oneself."*

Essence: Creativity, compassion, empathy, self-kindness, meditation, psychic development.

Activity: Pisces had a double-sided mirror concealed. He directed the group to pair up (keeping heights similar by adjusting pairs) and face their partner holding each other's right hands. *"Read the essence of the sacred being within the face of the person across from you."* (Pause for 30 seconds.) *"Now close your eyes for a meditation."* Pisces asked them to dwell upon and summon all the empathy, care, and love that this sacred person deserved. *"Now, keeping your eyes shut, wait for my touch on your hands, and at that moment, open your eyes and project that love out to them."* Pisces moved around the circle and held the double-sided mirror between the festivants' faces so they saw their own reflection when they opened their eyes, and then touched the joined hands pair by pair.

Ending: *"Remember this magic when the Pisces moon approaches."*

The Ritualista gave the final bell cue ending the complete series of 12 moons, and each group was led back to re-form the circle. The Ritualista said, while walking the circle:

"But this is the ritual of the 13 moons, and how can that be? Every few years, once in a Blue Moon, a sign will have a second moon within it. The Blue Moon appears to amplify the—"

The Ritualista was interrupted by the entrance of the Blue Moon character, who walked the circle, saying,

"I am the 13th moon. When I appear, be ready for the magic of the long time, of your life. For magic done within my influence can aid you in the major changes you seek!"

The Blue Moon bowed and joined the circle at the East.

The Ritualista tipped the hourglass sideways, saying, *"Our time is well passed!"* and rang the bell to cue the choir, starting the song "The Wheel Turns," by Eala Clarke, with verse additions by Ivo Domínguez, Jr.

As the song was sung, the Blue Moon joined the Ritualista, and they moved to face each direction in turn: East, South, West, North, and into the center as the song ended.

The ritual team shouted together, *"Hail and farewell!"*

The Moons walked out through the ritual gate, leading a procession out of the circle and ending the ritual.

Photo by Jenna Touchette

Photo by Jenna Touchette

Aries Moon and Libra Moon characters (left to right).

SIX

....

The Ritual Begins

Laid before me, the Tree of Life, in all its glory. I enter and find a mythical place of
Strength, the Tower, the Hanged One, the Empress. Each has a story to tell, a scent or
taste to offer, and the path to the Crown is uniquely mine alone. The Fool serenely
welcomes me, and I am offered food and drink as I try to digest what just
happened. I wander back to my tent feeling spiritually elevated and satiated.

TAROT PATH-WORKING RITUAL

Often rituals are scheduled to allow a period of time for participants to gather, to acclimatize
to other participants and the ritual purpose. This can happen within or near the ritual space,
or it can happen at a remote place in preparation for processing to the ritual site. The first
thing to imagine is what participants encounter when they arrive at the ritual site or gathering spot and how they are prepared.

Earlier we described the team role of the greeter. This person is charged with ensuring that each participant is welcomed, introduced to at least one other person, and given
any personal instruction or printed handout produced for the ritual. This is where the
ritual begins, because a welcomed participant is already entering a sacred state of mind.
Although the audience will have gotten information about your event through advertising or an invitation, this is your last opportunity to prepare participants for the ceremony.

One option is to hand out a written ritual program. It may have the ritual title, intent, description, and even an outline (order of service). It may include the lyrics for any songs to be sung in the ritual. Be sure to include contact information for the ritual team or sponsor, and note how and when feedback can be offered after the ritual. Once you offer a written program, keep in mind that unless everyone has a pocket, one of their hands will not be free to use during the ritual.

The greeter also performs another function, that of making the initial connection with the ritual team. They can respond to any immediate questions, and they become a familiar point of personal contact after the ritual.

We often use this time of arrival and gathering to teach songs or chants to be used in the procession or the main portion of the ritual. You can also begin establishing the ritual purpose at the gathering place. Use appropriate spoken words, activities, sensory experience, or theater. You can choose to consider the ritual as actually beginning here, as people gather in anticipation, and apply everything you have learned about setting the ritual stage as they arrive.

Gathering at the ritual site presents some problems, but with forethought they can be overcome. A common problem is that people naturally converse and remain in their own world when left in a crowd waiting for an event to start. They can splinter into small social groups and may need to be drawn back to their purpose in attending. Providing a focus for their attention will naturally solve that problem. Invite community announcements. Begin a song or chant, or drumming and dancing. Startle the crowd with action or humor. A jester or any distinct character will draw attention and stop conversation. When the time has come to begin, attention can then be readily transferred to the next step in the ritual. Avoid disrupting whatever mood you have begun building by saying, "Okay, the ritual is going to start now, please pay attention!" Why not be creative here, and through a sensory experience, a visual or auditory cue, demonstrate that the ritual is about to begin?

People can be brought into the ritual from their point of arrival in several different ways. How they are brought to the ritual will also depend on their number, the site, whether you are indoors or out, and how big a team you have. When considering the method you will use, look to your ritual intent for guidance. Your choice should reflect an option that moves your ritual purpose forward!

Processions

A procession moves your participants from the gathering spot to the sacred ritual space or ritual gateway. It is a symbolic journey from the normal world we experience, the mundane, to the sacred. You may have attended a traditional funeral where a hearse and procession of cars arrive at the gravesite. People exit the cars and assess their surroundings, and walk in silence to the ceremony. The solemnity of the event and social customs have dictated the nature of this procession, which prepares us for grief, remembrance, and burial. Silence allows us to reflect on the person lost to us and our own mortality, and to attune ourselves to the occasion.

In community ritual, the procession should be a time to prepare for the entry into sacred space. It can be silent, or it can include drums or other music, chant or song, or theater. It can be led by members of the ritual team, costumed and speaking in character. A procession can happen spontaneously and with little organizational form. It can be a time of bonding with the community of participants, or an individual walk focusing on one's own inner world.

What feeling will best aid your participants to prepare for the ritual? It could range from buoyant frivolity to quiet anticipation, from fear and dread to joy and pleasure. Imagine your large group led by a couple of silly jesters or a fairy. Could they do the bunny hop or form a conga line? Would someone dressed as the Reaper and carrying a scythe create a somber tone? If you have a symbolic prop to use in your ritual, why not carry it at the head of your procession? Don't underestimate the power of an easy but focused chant to create a feeling of shared experience.

It is always best to have at least one member of your ritual team in a procession. Everyone is usually excited to get started and an appropriate pace needs to be established. Kids will want to run ahead, the elderly may need more time. Set a pace that keeps your participants together! This is a bonding activity for participants, and moving together as a community supports that feeling.

If you want to sing or chant, keep it simple! It may seem a small matter to walk and vocalize, but it isn't easy if the words or tune are unfamiliar. We can get easily winded when walking! A procession is marginal exertion, but add the strain on breathing that a song or chant represents and your participants can lose their ability to energetically contribute. The more complex, energetic, or important singing is to a procession, the more members of your team need to participate. It is better to have a procession in silence than to plan for one with many facets and components that falls apart on the way because it cannot be sustained. We don't want our ritual to feel like a failure or too much effort right from the start!

• • • • • • • • • • •

Example

In our largest ritual (see chapter 13), we used a method that alternated drumbeats with short phrases. This call-and-response was very effective in setting a pace and creating a warm invitation to join the procession and chant, energizing and embedding the theme into the participants and procession.

Sing tonight [boom—boom] Plant a seed [boom—boom]
Dream tonight [boom—boom] Come tonight [boom—boom]

(A lead caller shouts the upcoming words during the double drumbeat so the procession can easily learn and join in as an echo.)

Sometimes participants want to bring items to a ritual. It could be drums, rattles, or shakers. Maybe they have a blanket or chair to sit on, or a wrap if it turns cold when outside. Plan for how you will handle this in a procession, or even provide a cart or wagon to be part of the procession. We often have processions that lead to a path-working gate and then the path leads to the main ritual site. We love a raucous procession with drums and rattles. What if these items inhibit participants in the path-working? We solved the problem by processing past a blanket at the edge of the ritual site and dropping off our instruments there, modeling this action for the participants. We then finished the walk to the path-working gate in silence, reinforcing the ritual mindset taking root.

At night, or if it supports your ritual purpose, people may be asked to carry a candle, flashlight, glow stick, incense, or another item for use in ritual. Candles are beautiful for a procession, but flame and melted wax can be a fire hazard or prohibited indoors. Be aware how each of these items affects a procession. Ask yourself if the "effect" on the procession really supports the ritual purpose or inhibits it. Plan for items carried to be held for the duration of a ritual, placed in a clearly designated location, or disposed of when arriving at the ritual site.

Drums and other percussion instruments can add rhythm to a procession that gets everyone moving together. They can also become a chaotic force that drowns out a group or solo voice. Percussion tends to dominate tempo. If your ritual team cannot lead the percussion in a procession, choose a few strong percussionists you can trust. Keep the tempo moderate to slow, and simple. Someone will need to control the procession pacing, keep everyone together, and may need to adjust on the fly so the procession arrives intact and prepared.

Processions are most used out of doors but can also work great indoors. You can have a gathering spot just outside a door or in a building entryway and then process down a hall into a room. If there is only a doorway between two rooms, you can process the outer circumference of a gathering space before entering the room of the ritual site. Another option is to enter a doorway and process the outer circumference of the ritual room itself upon entrance. However you choose to include a procession, know the reason you are including one. Is it supporting your ritual vision somehow?

Whenever we plan for participants to move in ritual or a procession, we need to consider how those with limited mobility can be accommodated. These are not just people considered handicapped, but anyone for whom mobility presents a challenge. The elderly may not be as steady on their feet or able to navigate obstacles. Families with young children may have strollers or need to hold hands. Participants with limited endurance may simply not be able to walk more than a few yards. Often all it takes is advance thought to accommodate mobility issues. A few minutes removing or marking obstacles outdoors may be all that is needed. Providing a team member to offer aid at a bridge, narrow passage, or obstacle can solve the problem of universal access. When these options won't work, we usually provide transport to the ritual site before the procession. Most people with disabilities are happy to know they have been thoughtfully included even if their ritual experience is different in a small way. If the totality of your ritual is challenging and requires adept mobility, reconsider how you promote, advertise, or assess your audience. You may have varied from what your community needs by not planning for a diversity of mobility needs.

Path-Workings

Path-working is a term sometimes used to describe a visualized internal journey. We have expanded its meaning to encompass an actual physical journey as part of ritual. A ritual path-working can take many forms. It can be a method for organizing a complete ritual experience, flowing from beginning to end moving through several locations. A path-working can be an extended entry into a ritual site or a portion of a ritual, occurring any-time during it.

Path-workings are effective when participants need to receive an individual experience within a large group. This can be accomplished by setting up one or more experiences along the way to the location of the main part of the ritual. Here it becomes an experiential procession of sorts. If you are outside, position members of your team in secluded areas along the path to offer an emotional or sensory experience. A path-working is possible indoors and even within a single large room. Create stations using concealing cloth or props to create the effect you want. Path-working used to bring participants to the ritual site will allow them to attune to the ritual mindset. If you can keep them in that state until the entire group is as-sembled, you may be able to abbreviate the process of establishing sacred space.

A series of encounters can set up an expectation and prepare participants individu-ally for resolution once all have arrived at the main ritual site. They may hear whispered questions, they may see a prop or scene that reappears later in the ritual, or experience a smell, taste, or touch. You might have them "force" their way through obstacles in the path or receive something relevant on the journey. This can be done indoors using a hallway or passage to make it seem a journey. Use path-working when you want a part of your ritual to be enhanced by a solitary experience.

. . . .

EXAMPLE

When we incorporate a costumed figure that represents deity or who plays a major symbolic role in ritual, we sometimes provide a decorated cot for them to "lie in state" as participants pass by in a path-working. This gives an opportunity for them to see and connect (or interact) with them in advance of their appearance in the later, gathered group portion of a ritual.

In very large group rituals, a path-working can be used to divide participants into smaller groups where they may experience a portion of the ritual more intimately than as a whole but not individually. A path-working within a largely attended group ritual can easily create a bottleneck. After rehearsing and thinking through the experience, we can often identify problems in advance and counter them. You should plan to provide guides to aid in a smooth movement along the path. Never assume how people will act or pace themselves in a path-working. There are some who will race through and some who will crawl in their thoroughness to experience the path completely. Plan to accommodate both and keep everyone moving without harming the ritual mindset and purpose.

We like to have our whole team also experience the parts of a ritual that are individual experiences. If you line up your ritual team in the order in which they are encountered by participants, each member of the team can then experience the ritual by leaving their station to join the main group immediately after all the participants have passed them. If we have a sound group, choir, or musicians, whenever possible we ask them to serve double duty and act as invisible guides in key parts of the ritual.

Whenever you use a path-working, remember it is a part of the ritual. It needs particular attention to every detail, because it has many opportunities to lose its relevance. Consider how each aspect of the path contributes to the ritual, just as you would with any other technique.

Gateways

In ritual, a gateway can be either a physical structure or prop that acts as a doorway, or an unseen barrier established by the actions of the ritual team and then opened by the team's actions or words. A gateway of some type is desirable in most rituals. We want participants to clearly feel, "Here you are outside the ritual; now you have entered."

If your participants are gathered at your ritual site, you can still establish a gate to move the participants from a mundane crowd into a ritual space. When faced with a room full of people milling about, draw them through a gateway at one edge of the room to redefine them into participants now entering a sacred place for ritual.

Your gate can be as simple as two people, torches, flower pots, or any other props that define the two sides of a door. We have also had gates so elaborate that the entry gate became the heart of the ritual!

A gate can serve many and multiple functions:

- To establish the entry to ritual space

- To transition from mundane interaction occurring outside the ritual space

- To challenge or to provoke thoughts from entrants verbally or physically; they must do or say or hear something in order to pass through

- To smudge, bless, or anoint participants

- To slow down or regulate the entrance rate of participants

- To provide participants with any objects or props they may need within the ritual

- To actually begin the experience of the intent of the ritual: a sensually elaborate statement of what is being entered

Some gateways are visual works of symbolic art. You could create one that people will somehow add to as they enter or leave something upon as they exit. Gateways can move participants through darkness or from darkness into light. A gate can provide physical contact, visual illusion, a gauntlet of sound or voices, or a potpourri of odors or tastes. Whatever your choice, it should be tailored to fit and reinforce the ritual intent, and flow with whatever is to follow, not be a gimmick or an isolated experience. The gateway will be as important to the purpose of the ritual as the effort you put into designing it and integrating it into the ritual plan.

· · · · · · · · · · · ·
EXAMPLE
A powerful and simple gateway that just requires the availability of six or more people (and a regulator who stands at the entry and spaces people a few steps apart) is a whispering "gauntlet." If your team or choir does not have other duties during entry, they can do double duty and help with this. Space team pairs a few steps apart from each other along

the path, facing inward with enough room for a person to pass between them. Provide short phrases for each pair to whisper in each participant's ears as they are briefly paused. Use words that support your intention and/or provoke thought such as: "Prepare for the great mystery," "You enter the abyss." Because the whispers are simultaneous, participants may miss the full phrases, but be assured the words enter the subconscious! The gauntlet can be adapted and used with percussion, sound, or many other sensory offerings.

One of our ritual glitches came within a wonderfully planned ritual when we had recruited a last-minute volunteer to smudge, bless, and cleanse participants at our entry gate. We did not know that the procession would gather nearly 200 people, nor what a vague term "smudge" was! As our team members were all acting within their characters and roles, it was 15 minutes before we realized the length of the entry line backup and the slowness of entry. Our smudger was doing a very thorough job, as she had been taught for personal ritual. She was wafting smoke up and down both sides and over the hands and feet of every participant. We hastily adjusted once we realized the difficulty. Even a brief rehearsal would have caught this misunderstanding before it had affected the ritual.

Your ritual participant numbers, type of procession or path-working, and entry through a gate into sacred space all need to be coordinated to flow smoothly. Especially in rituals with more than 50 people, a concise gateway method is advised. You can build the ritual intent at a gathering place, create an energizing and supportive procession, and have an amazing entry method or visually stunning gate, only to have the momentum crumble apart because of a 40-minute line to enter the ritual space.

When a gateway or entry may cause a long wait time, you can provide a community activity for those in line. A powerful chant or song, or sustained drumming or music, will help keep participants focused. Socially we are conditioned to have little patience for waiting. You may be able to use that impatience to further the intent. What could you do to encourage introspection among those in line? People who are physically uncomfortable or new to community ritual are the most vulnerable to losing focus while waiting for entry. If you lose the attention of your ritual audience right from the start with a boring wait time, you may never get them back.

Ritual: Tarot Path-Working Ritual

·················

Location: Sacred Harvest Festival, 2008
© Nels Linde and Judith Olson Linde

Ritual context

This ritual was one of the largest and most theatrical we ever facilitated. All the tarot trumps were represented in full costume, presenting their own personal experience to festivants who encountered them. More than 200 people passed through the path-working, some coming back a second time since each trip was unique!

Ritual intent

Participants will experience the trumps of the tarot personified and at their essence. Their random choice will determine the path they follow through the Qabbalistic Tree of Life.

Ritual description

Tarot trump personas will conduct a brief walking meditation for those who draw that path. Participants will work their way up the Tree of Life through these meditative experiences as the draw of cards directs them.

Ritual setup and supplies

The Qabbalistic Tree of Life was laid out on the ground with wide florist ribbon. From Kether to Malkuth it measured nearly 100 feet long. Tipareth was the middle point, Kether nearest the ritual circle, Malkuth farthest away. The Temple of Malkuth was set up as the entry point. Festivants were smudged on entering the temple.

Devil trump, Fool trump, and High Priestess
persona (left to right, top to bottom).

Each Sephira (with the exception of Kether, which had a more elaborate setup) had a tiki torch, a blanket or rug for waiting, and a large pouch containing Hebrew letter cards, which determined randomly the path each person would take. There was a 10 x 17-inch tarot trump placard placed at the beginning of each path. These depicted the trump card and its corresponding Hebrew letter. Because the 14th, 19th, and 27th paths were accessible from either end, they had two placards, one at each end. (The B.O.T.A. website has Paul Foster Case's trump images available for purchase and download in black and white.[17] Print on legal size paper, color appropriately, mount on foam core, and you have your placards.)

The journey was one-way only—that is, from Malkuth to Kether. The paths each person took were determined by drawing a Hebrew letter card from the pouch at each Sephira. We downloaded the Hebrew alphabet from the Internet, made the letters about ¾-inch-high and bold, printed multiples onto card stock, and cut them into 1-inch square cards. We put the letters into each pouch to send participants on a journey in the direction of Kether (be sure to have plenty of extras of each letter, as you may have to refill if you get a large turnout). So, for instance, the pouch at Malkuth had tau, shin, and qoph as options. Yesod offered resh, tsaddi, and samech. Hod offered peh, ayin, and mem. Netzach offered a trip across peh as well, but also nun and caph. Tipareth was the starting point for lamed, zayin, gimel, heh, or yod. Refer to the arrows on the diagram for the rest.

Team members

Ritualista, at least 23 trump personas (two at Lovers), two greeters, exit guardian, wrangler. For this ritual, the more help, the better.

This ritual cannot be done without a dedicated crew of people willing to "own" their role. They should immerse themselves in the card they will act out, learning as much as possible about its meaning, correspondences, colors, and Qabbalistic associations. They are encouraged to creatively express their card in costume, and asked to somehow incorporate into it the Hebrew letter associated with their card. Each trump has a recommended taste and scent for their meditation and will need to devise a method of carrying these so they are easily accessible.

---

17   Builders of the Adytum, http://store.bota.org.

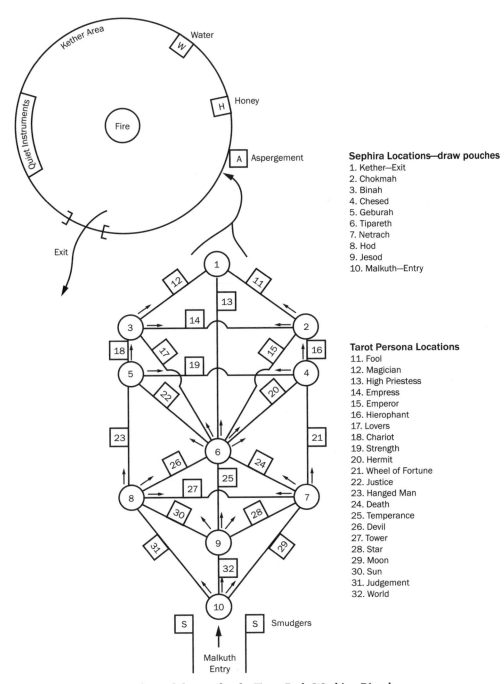

Sephira Locations—draw pouches
1. Kether—Exit
2. Chokmah
3. Binah
4. Chesed
5. Geburah
6. Tipareth
7. Netrach
8. Hod
9. Jesod
10. Malkuth—Entry

Tarot Persona Locations
11. Fool
12. Magician
13. High Priestess
14. Empress
15. Emperor
16. Hierophant
17. Lovers
18. Chariot
19. Strength
20. Hermit
21. Wheel of Fortune
22. Justice
23. Hanged Man
24. Death
25. Temperance
26. Devil
27. Tower
28. Star
29. Moon
30. Sun
31. Judgement
32. World

The path layout for the Tarot Path-Working Ritual.

Trumps will meet each festivant (or groups of 2 or 3 as necessary) at the starting trump placard. Conduct this meditation by *slowly* walking them up the path a way, saying the first line, then stopping and asking participants to close their eyes, and then delivering the rest of the meditation. The trumps then offer a sensory experience and poetic words, finishing with *"The path of [trump name] is now yours,"* and walk or wave them forward. Festivants then have the last half of the path to meditate on what they have experienced as they slowly move to the next Sephira. Since the **14th, 19th,** and **27th** paths have two entry points, the Empress, Strength, and the Tower will be taking participants from either end. Once the participant reaches the next Sephira, they can wait there until they are ready to move onward.

Ritual script

A solemn drum procession announced the ritual's opening, but festivants could wander down and experience the path-working from that time onward until its close. Once in the entrance temple (Malkuth), festivants were individually offered a draw from the pouch, which set them on their path. (Tell festivants to keep their Hebrew letter cards as a record of their journey. If they replace them into the wrong pouches it will become very confusing very quickly.) Judgement, the World, and the Moon were waiting a few steps up their ribbon-marked path. All the other trumps were at their reception point Sephira. The tarot trump personas each conducted a brief walking meditation for those who drew that path, and the festivants worked their way up the Tree of Life through these meditative experiences. The participants drew a letter from each Sephira pouch and followed instructions on to the next path. They waited until the trump of the path drawn was finished speaking to the current participant and was available, and then continued onward. As each festivant had to wait until greeted to move on, the trumps returned to their starting Sephira after each festivant was waved forward. (By random draw, some paths will have more activity and backups may occur.)

The path ended at Kether, where the Ritualista guided festivants to a large resting area around the fire. Here they were greeted with a water aspergement, snacks, and water to drink, as well as soft instruments (flute, didgeridoo, rattles) and chanting to create ambiance. The festivants stayed as long as they wished and left via a ribbon-marked exit at the South, which led around the East edge back to the road so as to not disturb path-walkers on leaving.

Below is what each trump character offered as participants approached them. The brief meditations and sensual offerings used by the trump characters were based on visualization exercises in the book *The Shining Paths* by Dolores Ashcroft-Nowicki.[18] The poetic words spoken at the end were taken from *The Book of Thoth* by Aleister Crowley.[19]

FOOL: *"The space between the pillars is pure light. Naked, and unencumbered, you embrace the new journey still ahead. You stand on the precipice, all of manifestation spread before you. As you look down to your own body, you find yourself clothed in the rags of a wanderer, holding a staff and a yellow rose. With a bark, your black dog leaps from the edge, and you follow, slowly spinning to your destiny."*

Taste: Fennel seed. *"You will set your hand to the plow of experience, and sow the seeds of knowledge."*

Scent: Peppermint or neroli. *"Your memories are the fruit of your past and your future. How will you preserve them?"*

The Fool (Book of Thoth): *"Know Naught! All ways are lawful to innocence. Pure folly is the Key to Initiation. Silence breaks into Rapture. Be neither man nor woman, but both in one. Be silent, Babe in the Egg of Blue, that thou mayest grow to bear the Lance and Grail! Wander alone, and sing! In the King's palace his daughter awaits thee."*

MAGUS: *"Bubbles slowly rise from the primordial ooze, through the past, present, and bursting at the surface, forming the future. A hand reaches down and plucks one up, then another hand, and as the bubbles rotate slowly, being juggled in the air, they take on form and light and color, until all the shapes that dictate form dance before you. A brightly costumed juggler appears, claiming these hands, as the objects of our world vibrate to life. He says, 'As above, so below.'"*

Taste: Dill. *"As the shapes fall to earth around you, the juggler turns and walks through the doorway of a simple cottage."*

---

18   Dolores Ashcroft-Nowicki, *The Shining Paths: An Experiential Journey through the Tree of Life* (The Aquarian Press, 1983; 2nd ed., Loughborough, UK: Thoth Publications, 1997). Adapted with permission.

19   Aleister Crowley, *The Book of Thoth* © Ordo Templi Orientis. All rights reserved. Used with permission.

Scent: White sandalwood, lemongrass, or benzoin. *"Turning back he asks, what spirits will share your house?"*

The Magus (Book of Thoth): *"The True Self is the meaning of the True Will: Know thyself through Thy Way! Calculate well the Formula of Thy Way! Create freely; absorb joyously; divide intently; consolidate completely. Work Thou, Omnipotent, Omniscient, Omnipresent, in and for Eternity."*

HIGH PRIESTESS: *"Ahead the star Sothis. A camel leads you on the way of the mystic in the desert night. An infinitely deep chasm blocks your way, with only a rickety plank to cross it. A jackal appears and starts across. You follow, and it creaks and splinters. As you step across, it splits and falls with no sound. The Jackal now dissolves and you walk a paved path up a hill. Two glowing pillars appear extending to infinity in front of a veil of deep blue mist. As you approach soft wings encase you and the mother's voice sounds, 'Who follows the star, with no hope, are those who journey to me.'"*

Taste: Lemon. *"As you are so I was. As I am so you will be."*

Scent: Jasmine. *"Who so crosses the abyss can stand before me and say, 'I Am.'"*

The High Priestess (Book of Thoth): *"Purity is to live only to the Highest; and the Highest is ALL: be thou as Artemis to Pan! Read thou in* The Book of the Law, *and break through the veil of the Virgin."*

EMPRESS: *"You are in a dark, tight passage. You know there is light and struggle to reach it. You feel the need to push and finally break free. You are held in the mossy arms of the green earth, in a courtyard old as ages. Framed by a vine-covered archway stands a woman of great beauty. She is the Mother, with all that that entails. She tells you the story of the creation, and of your creation, in a language lost to time, yet you hear and understand."*

Taste: Vanilla. *"She cups your face and plants a kiss on your forehead."*

Scent: Rose. *"Who enters the door, who leaves? Who keeps you from the out-stretched nurturing hand?"*

The Empress (Book of Thoth): *"This is the Harmony of the Universe, that Love unites the Will to create with the Understanding of that Creation: understand thou thine own Will! Love and let love. Rejoice in every shape of love, and get thy rapture and thy nourishment thereof."*

EMPEROR: *"Following the brightest star, you walk a moonlit forest trail. As the full moon rises you feel yourself lifted skyward. You fly past the moon and each planet in turn, until the glowing temple of the zodiac forms about you. Below you is a great castle, its round table visible to you as you peer through the window. The light focuses on the ritual chalice there, as it glows brighter and brighter."*

Taste: Ginger. *"Just as it seems too bright to hold your gaze, you see within it the face of the supreme."*

Scent: Bay leaf or petitgrain. *"Do you see deity in your own vessel?"*

The Emperor (Book of Thoth): *"Use all thine energy to rule thy thought: burn up thy thought as the Phoenix."*

HIEROPHANT: *"Above the glowing hearth fire, a tapestry of the winged bull hangs. As you look closer, the scene develops perspective, and then becomes real. You stand atop the dais, dressed in white, ready to perform a royal wedding. As the winged bull leads the couple up the steps to you, you hear the ring of the smith's hammer, drawing iron into nails at the anvil."*

Taste: Thyme. *"Once offered the chalice of tears by pure white hands you now are blissfully wedded with the higher self."*

Scent: Cardamom or rosewood. *"What can wed you to your higher consciousness? What fear holds you back?"*

The Hierophant (Book of Thoth): *"Offer thyself Virgin to the Knowledge and Conversation of thine Holy Guardian Angel! All else is a snare. Be thou athlete with the eight limbs of Yoga: for without these thou are not disciplined for any fight."*

LOVERS: *"You walk along a seashore, warm with summer breezes. You see, rising from the water, a sword, brilliant in the sun. As you approach, you see yourself reflected on its mirrored surface. The image is you but not quite; it is a [insert opposite here, male or female] version of you. The sword dissolves as your twin steps forward, embracing you, and you continue your walk together, knowing love, knowing there is no separation."*

Taste: Lavender or peppermint. *"What is the sword that parts you?"*

Scent: Lavender, geranium, or peppermint. *"What girdle binds you together?"*

The Lovers (Book of Thoth): *"The Oracle of the Gods is the Child-Voice of Love in thine own soul! Hear thou it! Heed not the Siren-Voice of Sense, or the Phantom-Voice of reason: rest in Simplicity, and listen to the Silence."*

CHARIOT: *"The horses carry you forward over the hill. Ahead on the vast plain you see a walled city. As your chariot draws near you see many people brimming the battlements cheering and waving. You see also that the walls of the city are crumbling, the homes and buildings are derelict, the people are not well fed. You summon your power, you call for aid, and commence the rebuilding."*

Taste: Coriander or carrot. *"How can a kingdom rule itself?"*

Scent: Chamomile. *"Which of your boundaries needs rebuilding?"*

The Chariot (Book of Thoth): *"The Issue of the Vulture, Two-in-One, conveyed; this is the Chariot of Power."*

STRENGTH: *"Before you crouches an old one, above a figure in a black cloak. As they raise fists to punish again, you see your dark twin in their eyes. The crouched elder becomes you as a child, running toward you with a brightly wrapped gift. The child turns into a sweet lion, and you pet its mane. It twists and snarls to bite you and as you grasp its jaws, it melts into a gold cup filled with liquid. The first drink is bitter and foul, the second sweeter."*

Taste: Rosemary. *"The third sip is sweet honey."*

Scent: Juniper berry or neroli. *"What experience must you tame?"*

Strength (Book of Thoth): *"Mitigate Energy with Love; but let Love devour all things."*

HERMIT: *"Bearing a lantern, you tread the castle path across the drawbridge and enter the courtyard. You shuffle into the darkened chapel where screened alcoves hold other seekers. As you hold your vigil in prayer, you examine your hands—each line and crack, a story or lesson learned."*

Taste: Caraway. *"At dawn you awaken naked, and as you leave to greet the dawn you find a new monk's robe about you."*

Scent: Wintergreen or sage. *"What helping hand do you seek to fertilize your growth?"*

The Hermit (Book of Thoth): *"Wander alone; bearing the Light and thy Staff. And be the Light so bright that no man seeth thee. Be not moved by aught without or within: Keep Silence in all ways."*

WHEEL OF FORTUNE: *"You walk the winding path toward the mountain, join-ing the stream of pilgrims of all tribes and classes ever upward on the quest. At each crossroads hawkers wave and offer directions, distraction, and shortcuts, some obvi-ously false. You console the lost ones and find your sack of gold ever growing, as you move upward following the soaring eagles."*

Taste: Nutmeg or clove. *"Finally, you see the mountain top, and it is covered with weary travelers, palms faced toward you."*

Scent: Cedar. *"Do they wave in accomplishment or seek to ward you away?"*

Fortune (Wheel of Fortune) (Book of Thoth): *"Follow thy Fortune, careless where it leads thee. The axle moveth not: attain thou that."*

JUSTICE: *"You enter the eight-sided temple of the sun. You see the four altars of the elements, and smell the scent of herbs beneath your feet. At the white marble altar stands the young goddess Maat, who demands truth with her eyes. The thrones of the 42 Karmic Assessors line the hall, waiting to question you. Maat stands aside, and light fills the altar to radiance."*

Taste: Spearmint. *"Your eyes adjust to see the golden scales thereupon."*

Scent: Myrtle or palmarosa. *"What is the lesson to learn in this life?"*

Justice (Book of Thoth): *"Balance against each thought its exact Opposite. For the Marriage of these is the Annihilation of Illusion."*

HANGED ONE: *"In a gigantic workshop, a pottery, he gently picks you up and as you spin on the wheel, clay forms around you. Done now, you are hung upside down to dry. From upside down, you see things differently, more clearly, without distor-tions. You are placed in the kiln to burn away the dross. Small cracks make their way through the shell, and you know what and where these flaws are. You are set on a table and with sharp taps from his hammer, the pottery shell falls away."*

Taste: Caraway. *"Have you forgotten your real self was inside?"*

Scent: Wintergreen or sage. *"What deep knowledge will bubble up into the light?"*

The Hanged Man (Book of Thoth): *"Let not the waters whereon thou journeyest wet thee. And being come to shore, plant thou the Vine and rejoice without shame."*

DEATH: *"Through the crowd you push your way to the river. A boat awaits with priests ready to prepare you for the journey. As the boat pushes off, you are laid upon a litter and a heavy silver mask is put over your face. The boat bumps against the shore and your litter is carried up to the stone monument, and then down into the bowels of the pyramid. Timeless stillness enfolds you. (Pause.) Like a hawk you hover, looking down at your still form. In a spiral you descend to rejoin your body."*

Taste: Vinegar. *"Do you live this life fully?"*

Scent: Cypress. *"Do you walk in two worlds?"*

Death (Book of Thoth): *"The Universe is Change; every Change is the effect of an Act of Love; all Acts of Love contain Pure Joy. Die Daily! Death is the apex of one curve of the snake Life: behold all opposites as necessary complements, and rejoice."*

TEMPERANCE: *"Staff in hand, you hike at dusk across a wide desert. You approach the largest oak imaginable, the heart of a most sacred place. As hoofbeats pound in your ears, you see centaurs approaching from behind. You try to hide and fall into a dark pit. As your eyes adjust you see snakes all around you. One glowing, golden snake approaches and bites you painfully on the leg. You are filled with memory and knowledge of the ages. You watch as the snake entwines upon your staff and becomes solid with it. Glowing now, it lights a tunnel back to the desert surface."*

Taste: Bergamot. *"The staff turns to a fine bow in your hands, and you light an arrow skyward. It leaves a rainbow trail as it arches to the horizon."*

Scent: Hyssop or angelica. *"Why do you wait? You are the foundation."*

Temperance (Book of Thoth): *"Pour thine all freely from the Vase in thy right hand, and lose no drop. Hath not thy left hand a vase? Transmute all wholly into the Image of thy Will, bringing each to its token of Perfection. Dissolve the Pearl in the Wine-cup; drink, and make manifest the Virtue of that Pearl."*

DEVIL: *"You walk a corridor of mirrors reflecting your image, and as you move, your image distorts and becomes twisted in illusion. Hysterically laughing, a goat rampages past, horns and tail breaking mirrors, your falseness falling like shards of turmoil. The corridor becomes cave-like, walls filled with drawings of new gods drawn over the layers of old."*

Taste: Sage. *"The goat rushes back past, out now into the plain. A scapegoat carrying the sins of your tribe with it."*

Scent: Patchouli. *"To which illusions are you enslaved?"*

The Devil (Book of Thoth): *"With thy right Eye create all for thyself, and with the left accept all that be created otherwise."*

TOWER: *"On the gory field of battle, swords arc, clanging, and you run uphill to the mouth of a cave. You find a large, golden, glowing egg inside, and as you gaze at it, you see visions: villagers gossiping and insulting one another, and then retiring to their isolated hovels standing in ruin. The egg begins forming the cracks of hatching. Memories flood you of times of strong desire, creative leaps you have made, and of your own naked image."*

Taste: Black pepper. *"A sharp red tongue and then a jagged mouth breaks through the egg, and with a crash it shatters and the Phoenix breaks free and lifts to the heavens."*

Scent: Pine or sassafras. *"Who does your voice aid? What sword does it wield?"*

The Tower (Book of Thoth): *"Break down the forces of thine Individual Self, that the Truth may spring free from the ruins!"*

STAR: *"By starlight you walk the misty path between twin rivers, lush and verdant at dusk. Above the creatures of the night glide past. Below all is ethereal and beautifully calm. Enjoy the path of perfect, completed nature. Ahead the evening star is bright as a beacon."*

Taste: Lime. *"Gazing in the rivers the vital silvery fish swim here and there at random."*

Scent: Camphor or eucalyptus. *"How do you reach within and gain the prize?"*

The Star (Book of Thoth): *"Use all thine energy to rule thy thought: burn up thy thought as the Phoenix."*

MOON: *"The mist clears between twin crystal pillars. On either side stand a wolf and a dog, and the sound of a thousand beating wings fills you. You circle a small fern-lined pond filled with giant goldfish. A large weather-stained stone phallus marks the path to the temple of white stone. Two leopards flank the steps, and lounging there is the hoofed, horned piper, rubbing fine oil on his brown skin. From the open doorway above, the draped figure of the Goddess of Love appears beckoning. As the breeze wafts animal musk and exotic perfume to you, they retire to the inner temple, smiling."*

Taste: Marjoram or honey. *"As you turn to walk away, you see the phallus has now turned to a bright marble statue of lovers entwined and is decorated with fresh flowers."*

Scent: Sandalwood. *"Do you weep for those who would not listen?"*

The Moon (Book of Thoth): *"Let the Illusion of the World pass over thee, unheeded, as thou goest from the Midnight to the Morning."*

SUN: *"Soaring over forests and meadows of rich vegetation and fields of glorious bright flowers, you glide above the white marble city with its temples and schools and observatories and land at the steps of the center of learning. You ascend between lions of stone to greet sages and teachers. They teach that to forgive is to remember and to begin anew."*

Taste: Tangerine. *"How does the wick burn so bright in the candle, and only strengthen with the pain of fire?"*

Scent: Frankincense or cinnamon. *"How do you light the darkness?"*

The Sun (Book of Thoth): *"Give forth thy light to all without doubt; the clouds and shadows are no matter for thee. Make Speech and Silence, Energy and Stillness, twin forms of thy play."*

JUDGEMENT: *"Follow the salamander to the spirit of primal fire. Stepping onto the bed of glowing coals you feel your essence, your body, burn away, as you transform through the fire. The eyes of the gorgon and your own past incarnations burn into you as you rise from the flames like the Phoenix. Reborn by the smith's forge, you seek to quench your new form."*

Taste: Basil. *"Between lies the middle path."*

Scent: Pennyroyal or anise. *"Cleansed, where do the guiding divine hands at each side lead?"*

Judgment (Book of Thoth): *"Be every Act an Act of Love and Worship! Be every Act the Fiat of God! Be every Act a Source of radiant Glory."*

WORLD: *"Walk the path of descent. Be stripped of all trappings, assumptions, self-image, personas, and ornaments. Descend into the underworld, past the phantoms of the dead, and monstrous beings. Cross the narrow bridge over the river Styx, past the Watcher of the threshold. You are the guest of the night of time."*

Taste: Pomegranate. *"Now impaled on a cross of equal arms, you spin slowly in space, and find truth."*

Scent: Myrtle or vetiver. *"What will you miss about leaving your physical body?"*

The World (Book of Thoth): *"Treat time and all conditions of Event as Servants of thy Will, appointed to present the Universe to Thee in the form of thy Plan. And blessing and worship to the prophet of the lovely Star."*

SEVEN

·········

The Sacred Space

I come with the expectation of a typical chest-beating Men's Rite, but find myself
challenged by several, including a man with a child. The smell of copal is thick as I enter,
named as a God of Summer, and honor my ancestors. Water splashes my feet, and the
men sing and drum, and begin to awaken him, shrouded on a throne. It is just a man,
but no, as he rises it is Enki, the Father, drawn to this rite. He hears my voice and
offers wisdom, and I honor him with my dance. My ancestors, the Gods,
they are all here in this sacred place. I know it deep within.

RITUAL TO ENKI, THE FATHER

It is important that some act prepares the ritual space for ceremony and helps create a feeling of safety. To be vulnerable to a new and intimate experience requires that a level of trust
be established. Even in a ritual produced as a theatrical event, the "audience" may need a
specific time and experience to become unified and prepared. We call this establishing a sacred space, and there are many ways and levels of depth you can use to accomplish this. The
greater the trust and intimacy you see your ritual intention as requiring, the more of these
techniques may be needed to establish your sacred ritual space.

Some spiritual systems do not establish a sacred space. Their ritual experience is founded on a belief that the world in its entirety is sacred, so why is there a need to take ceremonial action to "make" it safe and sacred? If your audience represents a defined group that has this expectation, it is best to respect that in how you define sacred space. If you have a mix of people, choose a method that is efficient and symbolic to accommodate those who expect some act to make the space sacred, and yet does not offend those who don't need this process.

The Entry Challenge

Here the participant is confronted with a test of some type that must be passed before entry to ritual is allowed. This can be a question to be answered, an emotional response like fear to overcome, or an actual physical test. We consider this a method to begin creating sacred space for ritual because a challenge acts as a filter for the intention of your participants. It is designed to make people feel safe for the intimacy of ritual. The challenge makes people declare they are attending with a certain nature. They might be asked:

- Do you enter this ritual with an open mind?

- Do you enter this ritual with an open heart?

- Do you enter this ritual with malice for none?

- Do you enter this ritual with willingness to speak your truth?

The challenge question might also affirm their intention: "Do you open yourself to change?" Once each participant has given the affirmation, everyone in the ritual knows that, at least by their words, they have this common reassurance.

The challenge may be physical. A temporary blindfold might be required to demonstrate that you "blindly trust those who join with you in this ritual." Create a narrow opening and require entrants to "force" their way through. Two or more people can be shrouded or tented, and act as physical guardians.

EXAMPLE

For a Samhain ritual, we once created a 20-foot tented passageway hung by rope from the trees. Participants had to push their way through, past smells, whispers, touch, and people who stood close together outside the passageway.

A knife, sword, or staff can be brandished to confront the participant. This can be to demand the entrant's name, as was done for hundreds of years, from behind a cracked open door or in darkness: "Who goes there?" This hearkens back to another time when any spiritual experience outside the predominant religious tradition was a real risk taken by ritual participants. Passing a physical challenge with a weapon, no matter how symbolic, makes the presumption they will speak truthfully and enter the ritual with the proper authority or attitude.

We have also used physical illusions to challenge. An infinity box (see chapter 12) is a prop used in low light conditions to simulate a bottomless crevasse. An angled mirror reflects tiny LED lights on the underside of a piece of plate glass, creating multiple reflections, and the illusion of an infinite distance. The box was topped with 1-inch-thick tempered glass, thick enough to hold 500 pounds. In a darkened gateway, ritual participants were guided to step onto the glass with the challenge, *"It takes trust and courage to cross the abyss. Now take that first step into your happiness."*

Even knowing it could not possibly be "real," people were extremely reluctant to step onto a space that appeared to go 30 feet deep in the ground. To overcome the fear of falling into a deep well was the challenge participants had to cross.

Whenever you include a challenge of any type, you need a team member to supervise it. You really want all prospective participants to meet the challenge, but what do you do if someone fails? If the challenge is verbal, a team member can be in place to discretely whisper the answer if needed. With a physical challenge, an alternate route into ritual or an offer of physical help should be available. In many Wiccan traditions, if one fails the challenge or does not have the group password required, the gate guardian might ask those already in the sacred space, "Can anyone vouch for this person?" Then anyone already past the gate challenge can help the person be admitted by vouching for them.

In Wicca, a common entry challenge is "How do you enter this circle?" For many the classic challenge answer of "In perfect love and perfect trust" is either irrelevant or impossible to expect from participants in a large group ritual. If you decide to use an entry challenge, it should be designed to match the intimacy of your ritual, your community's expectations, and the nature of the ritual purpose. Never allow a challenge to alienate your audience; it is just one tool in creating sacred space!

Make Holy

To experience ritual as a sacred act, we need to feel holy. Most of us have grown up with an underlying feeling that somehow we are just not worthy to come together in grace. The acts of cleansing, clearing, and blessing ourselves and our ritual declare we are both worthy and ready to together embrace the sacred. These activities of purification come in many forms, can blend together, and occur at any time during a ritual. Commonly they occur early on, at or near the ritual entry point as part of our inward movement to experience ritual.

Cleansing can be represented by physical activities such as sweeping, washing, or dusting. The "gunk"—unwanted thoughts, feelings, and concerns from our daily life—may be brought into the ritual. Some people can release these energies with just a thought or a phrase. Others will need a structured activity.

Cleansing can also be a step in defining the boundaries of our sacred space. A classic cleansing activity is sweeping the boundary of the ritual space outward. This can be done with a broom or pantomimed as an action. It can be done silently or with words that declare what is being "banished" or swept from the ritual space. Expressing the intensity of your intention is what will make it effective for your community to feel safe for intimacy.

Other activities can be used as well. A person or group can blow their breath outward from the center, like blowing off the dust. *Asperging* is the act of sprinkling a congregation with water. This is usually done by dipping a hand or small leafy branch in water and shaking a sprinkle above or upon the feet, hands, or head. Asperging can also be considered an act of blessing, anointment, or defining a ritual area if it is framed in a different context.

Example

During a men's ritual celebrating Enki, the Sumerian Father God, the boundary was formed by carrying a gourd of water and a large, leafy branch around the circle, dipping into the water, and asperging the participants' feet. To support the intimate sharing and devotional nature of this ritual, this symbolic boundary was reinforced by repeating the asperging blessing several times during the course of the ritual.

Sound can be used to cleanse a ritual area. Strong focused words declaring your intention are very effective. For whatever other cleansing method, carefully choose any words you add. Breath can produce a whole range of sound. Instruments that produce lengthy sustain or resonance, such as bells, chimes, gongs, and singing bowls, work well, as do flutes, didgeridoos, and drums.

The act of blessing is the infusion of something with holiness, spiritual redemption, divine will, or approval. It can take place at any time from when participants gather until they exit a ritual. Blessing will often take place near a gateway and early in a ceremony to help create a sacred container. Blessing near a ritual's end will signify the ritual is coming to a close and help people leave with a sense of the sacred.

Tradition can define specific forms and times for blessing. In any rite of passage, they are traditionally included for the people at the focus of the rite—for instance, the bride and groom in a wedding. In a devotional, ritual blessings are bestowed with the force of the deity being honored in the ritual. The act of devotion defines the participant as being worthy of redemption or approval by the deity. The nature or historical context of worship will frame what kind of blessing is most appropriate in a devotional.

Blessings can be as simple as sincere words directed at another. In many religions, they are performed by a priest or priestess who says the prescribed words with intention and may make specific hand signs or motions. They may face or touch each individual directly, or bless all the participants at once.

Blessings can include an anointment of oil or water or even earth. Smudging the body with smoke from incense, sage, or sweet grass is a form of blessing. Any substance representing the alchemical elements (Air, Fire, Water, or Earth) can be used, or any organic substance that supports your intent. Imagine stepping barefoot in rich, black earth as a blessing for a springtime ritual. We have even been blessed with Nutella.

Whenever you touch a participant with an oil or compound, you should have prepared them for the experience earlier. Many people are allergic to substances. Unless you have disclosed this blessing ahead of time you will need to ask each person for permission. We sometimes offer the advance instruction to motion "no" (a hand held up) if you wish to be exempt from an anointment or blessing. This can avoid confusion and disruptive discussion during the ritual.

Blessing becomes sacred by the intention behind it. In community ritual, blessings are most effective as an intimate and personal act. They are the perfect time to establish the authenticity and sincerity of your ritual team. A blessing offered casually or without intention certainly doesn't reflect divine will and may not even feel like an act of approval. For people who have lived on the edges of community, without a feeling of belonging, the simple act of blessing can provide a powerful impact to your ritual participants.

Blessing serves several functions. It creates a sacred atmosphere and acknowledges the hallowed nature of each person. Blessing helps people discard feelings or thoughts that may keep them from opening to the intimacy of your ritual. Sharing this moment of personal holiness generates a bond between the person blessing and the person being blessed.

Create a Safe Place

A circle is a very versatile shape for any gathering of equals. A circle of people creates a natural boundary in its circumference and affords a space where everyone can see and hear everyone else. A circle is resistant to the establishment of a separation between performer and audience, something that may or may not be an advantage to your ritual purpose. It is easy to assume ritual takes place in the shape of a circle, and that participants are in a single row at the boundary. If your ritual takes place indoors, people will most likely assemble at the perimeter of the room, so your "circle" may be square or rectangular. You can offer formal rows of tables and chairs for people to sit in or gather them into a casual crowd. Whatever shape your intention brings participants together in, creating a safe place will define a boundary for the ritual container.

You can create a boundary either in advance or during the ritual. A boundary prevents the unwanted from entering and keeps the shared intimacy within. It can be either a very visible and real thing or a jointly held definition, or both. The need for a boundary to create ritual space will depend on your community and your ritual. For some people, establishing a boundary is critical, and for others it is a purely symbolic act that is unnecessary.

A substance like salt, flour, or cornmeal can be poured around the border of the ritual area. Rope, crepe paper, and even string lights create a continuous and flexible boundary. Many of these can be used indoors or outside. In a room, the walls themselves can form the boundary. Outdoors, simple garden lime (an inexpensive white powder made for lawns and gardens) is safe and easy to use. Whenever possible, choose something that will symbolically support your ritual purpose. Often a public ritual will draw observers, and it can become confusing to determine when an observer becomes a participant (if you choose to allow this). Using a physical boundary to define the space solves the problem. You are either in and participating, or outside and observing.

A person dramatically walking the edges of your ritual space will help establish a boundary. If they carry a tool that points—a knife, sword, staff, cane, broom, a laser light pointer— these can reinforce what walking feet create.

Words used with power and authenticity will establish a boundary. They must be said with loud force and authority, and a visual reference adds to their effectiveness: *"I see a wall of glowing light rise up from the floor, surrounding us, to shelter and protect us!"*

The engagement of your participants in the process will reinforce whatever action you take. Try this silent and effective method which can be used with nothing but hand movements:

· · · · · · · · · · · ·

EXAMPLE

Once all participants are assembled, the leader raises his hands up to his chest and down to a palm-forward position, dramatically modeling a slow, deep breath and releasing it. (Participants mimic this action.) Then with slow and exaggerated exactness the leader presses his left hand to his heart, bowing his head forward. With careful deliberation, he presses that hand to the heart of the person to the left of him. Finally, he reaches down and clasps the person's right hand. This action is silently passed around the circle until everyone is holding hands.

It helps to have other team members to the left of the leader to help model this action. It is up to you to assess the comfort zone of your participants. If hand-to-heart contact is too intimate, touch their shoulder instead.

Whatever you do to engage your ritual community in the establishment of sacred space, a minimum of words and a demonstration of the seriousness by which you do it is usually more effective than a lengthy, wordy, and elaborate method done casually or with insincerity! When participants experience a serious attitude in creating the boundary of a sacred space, they will feel the safety needed to open themselves to the intimacy of your ritual.

Even in a group of 200 people you still need a safe place for attendees to open themselves and experience the intent of your ritual. How you establish this should be a response to several factors. What is the ritual experience of your participants, and their level of knowledge and trust with each other? What is the depth of personal vulnerability demanded by your ritual intent? How many people are involved? How much time do you have or choose to allow to establish a safe place? What physical conditions are you working with? The answers to all these parameters will help define your best choices.

Guardians

You may have a ritual team member who has offered to reinforce the boundary as a guardian or tiler. These two roles are similar, but not the same. A guardian remains outside the ritual space, and he or she should be aware of that limitation. A tiler acts as designated guardian and also the handler for disruptions or upsetting circumstances within the ritual space. That role needs to be defined in advance. A tiler needs experience and skills dealing with people in distress within the ritual experience; a guardian does not.

People chosen for these roles can be physically impressive, but more importantly they should be calm, reasonable, and firm. A confrontational response by a guardian will only inflame any situation, and projecting calm resolve is the primary characteristic to assess in assigning this role. If a ritual is being disrupted in any way that is threatening, the team leader should halt the ritual immediately. The most that is expected of a guardian is to stand between any disruptive forces and attempt to diffuse the situation as the ritual participants disperse by direction of the team leader.

Determine in advance what distance observers must keep and have the guardian intercept them before they disrupt the focus of participants. If there are limitations on when late arrivals can become participants, the guardian can either inform them of this or welcome them into the rite.

In many spiritual traditions there are otherworldly forces which may be called upon to provide a guardian role for containment and safety when a ritual takes place. The cardinal directions (North, East, South, and West) or their alchemical elemental natures (Earth, Air, Fire, Water) can be acknowledged as spiritual guardians of the sacred space and honored or invited. Guardians can be of any number and may be mythic creatures, deities, or personages from history. The important aspect of inviting spiritual guardians is that your audience recognizes and accepts them as being up to the task. Your preparation, props, or words of incantation should clearly transmit who they are and what is asked of them. If you do call to spiritual guardians to help you create your ritual space, be sure to include a time near the end of your ritual to thank and release them from their duties.

Attunement

Attunement is the process of bringing a group into a harmonious or responsive relationship. It is valuable in ritual because it helps everyone bond together and get emotionally, spiritually, and mentally on the same page. When we are only observers in a social group, we easily slip into our own world, separated from those around us. At some level the purpose of your ritual asks people to risk sharing themselves. A feeling of bonding with each other will facilitate that sharing. Attunement is the preparation for intimacy.

Attunement may feel like a pause in the ritual action. It is an invitation to be fully present and aware. Many of the actions we have already talked about—blessing, sweeping, anointing, and so on—can also act as a ritual attunement. A special moment of attunement is appropriate for those who are the focus of a rite of passage. During a marriage ceremony, for example, it is the time set aside for the couple to feel their new relationship as a couple but within the context of the ritual.

Attunement can be accomplished by using a whole range of actions, from subtle and quiet to rowdy and boisterous. Any action that helps bring people right into the here and now of their experience will be effective. A group can be brought into harmony with the phrase, "Let's all take a deep breath, and as we slowly release it, let go of any emotions we are holding on to, and feel this moment." Incorporate a physical touch: reaching hand to hand, or to shoulder, or waist, or even surrounding and encountering an icon or symbolic prop. Any of these, when done reasonably simultaneously, will result in group attunement.

Sound can accomplish attunement within a group. A singing bowl, a didgeridoo, or a bell provides resonant tones to help people break their train of thought. Sound can also be reinforced with words: "As this sound passes through you, know that it resonates in each and every person here today." A group song or chant can provide an attunement, but it should be something very easy, or taught in advance of the ritual, so everyone can join in. The whole idea is to present a readily shared experience, rather than one in which people revert to observing.

The directive phrase to "ground and center" can be enough in some communities to attune everyone by connecting themselves to the stability of the earth and their core selves.

· · · · · · · · · · · ·

EXAMPLE

Imagine your ritual team spreading their feet slightly and rocking back and forth until they find stability. Then they spread their arms and close their eyes. As they draw in a deep, slow breath, their hands swing up toward their chest, and then back out, slowly exhaling.

Through the use of dramatic modeling, even an audience unfamiliar with the terms or process can come into attunement, can ground and center themselves, with no words explicitly spoken.

· · · · · · · · · · · ·

EXERCISE

Make a list of ways you can incorporate a method of group alignment or attunement that you can use. Mark any ones that best contribute to the ritual intent you are working with. How can they be specifically adapted to work even better with your ritual theme? Add this to your ritual notebook.

Become Sacred

Part of the journey to take sacred back is to claim your own ability to share your authentic self in ritual. Many of us have learned to keep safe by staying isolated within ourselves, keeping our feelings and fears from showing, and by trying to appear perfect. To share our vulnerability is risky, but it is the only sure way to reveal our true selves. Once we have taken this step as ritual leaders, we can make that sharing the norm. How deep into our human nature do we expect ritual to take the community? The authenticity we share as a team will define the level of empowerment others feel to take the risk of embracing our ritual purpose.

In this chapter, we have discussed all the actions we might take to establish a safe and sacred space for ritual to take place in. We have related the importance of a serious dedication to our ritual purpose in every action. Dedication is not enough. Once a ritual is underway, every interaction is also an opportunity to build a space where perfection is not the expectation. What you provide is a place of safety for each person. For an experienced ritual team, any limiting factors to our connection as humans are already shed by this point.

Establishing authenticity always involves risk taking. We take the risk that someone will see who we truly are, not accept us, and then reject us. We remove any personal barriers that allow us to hide from each other. If we do this successfully, the distance that resides between even strangers can fall away and the intimacy of being human together can blossom.

Here are some ideas to help you encourage releasing obstacles to intimacy. The window to the soul is said to be in our eyes. An action that asks people to gaze into each other's eyes is a good place to start. This can be designed so your ritual team leads this process. Participants can be randomly matched with one another or paired up by an integrated ritual process you have designed. Brief instructions can help get started: "As you pass by, make eye contact with each person. In that brief moment you hold each other's gaze, affirm and acknowledge their sacred nature." For this process to work participants need to gaze significantly past that comfortable time of one or two seconds.

A personal interaction can be passed around your ritual and include a touch, phrase, or an answer to a question. These have to be structured carefully to be received well, and can even involve role playing: "Turn to the person on your left and as you meet their gaze, welcome them to the world as you would welcome your own newborn." Introducing these types of challenges for participants to meet is very risky, but when successful the human connections made are tremendous.

Presenting oneself as completely vulnerable as an individual can draw out authenticity in others. This can come in the form of a heartfelt story from an individual or a sincere dialogue between two or more individuals. When we contribute in a leadership role, we will often have occasion to stumble, forget our words, or make a very public blunder. If we can handle these mishaps acknowledging our imperfection, without emotional turmoil, and offering ourselves acceptance, we firmly connect with all participants. Our primal response when faced with observing a real experience of pain or joy is to open ourselves, and that opening can become infectious in the ritual setting.

The most vulnerable we can be before others is to be fully nude. Nudity is certainly not appropriate in many settings, but being confronted by it can serve to "shock" ritual participants into responding with their true feelings. It is really hard to disbelieve, be angry at, or reject offerings or gifts from a nude person. They are so vulnerable we accept them as authentic almost automatically.

We have not even gotten to the "meat" of the actions that will move our community toward our ritual purpose. What we have done by this point is created a sacred space, a safe container for sharing intimately at whatever level our purpose requires. Many of the ideas, techniques, and concepts we have discussed will be repeated as we move on to developing the heart of the ritual. For many people, feeling safe in public ritual is an experience that will have profound effects.

Ritual: Ritual to Enki, the Father

....

Location: Pagan Spirit Gathering Men's Rite, 2008
© Nels Linde

Ritual context

This was offered as the men's ritual at the Pagan Spirit Gathering in 2008. It was both an invocation and celebration of the Sumerian god Enki. This was also a ritual to acknowledge the men going through and having completed an adult rite of passage. The ritual included about 60 males, from babies to kids, teens, and adults. It was the first men's rite at this event that allowed a biological female who self-identified as male to attend.

Ritual intent

To celebrate and reclaim the archetype of Father with the fellowship of other males. This ritual is open to all who self-identify as male. Some children and teens may attend. Participants are encouraged to bring drums and rattles.

Ritual description

A devotional experience for self-identified males with Enki, the Father. Bring drums, rattles, and shakers!

Ritual setup and supplies

A small fire was in the center of a ritual grove. An altar was at the north for honoring mentors. This was a small table with a basket of candles and a lighter, and a slab of wet clay smeared flat to accept small vertical devotional candles. Next to the altar was a large gourd filled with water and a fresh leafy oak branch for asperging feet. Near the fire slumbered Enki, semi-nude and fully painted, crowned with flowers and leaves, sitting upon a decorated throne. Enki was embodied by Breighton, an experienced priest who had worked with Enki for several intense weeks and invoked Enki for a lengthy period in the ritual.

Ritual props

Costume and paint for Enki. A decorated chair/throne. Two tubes of metal screen wrapped together in paper and bound to resemble a scroll. Inside the tubes were 75 bisque raku clay disks with an embossed male figure, pierced so they could be strung on a cord as a necklace. This scroll represented the "ME," the Sumerian wisdom of the gods and guide to life that the goddess Inanna steals in myth. Tongs to remove the scroll from the fire later were next to the throne. A bowl of animal crackers was near the gate. An open bottle of wine was available for libation. Near the ancestor altar were 75 god name tags, 75 candles, and enough clay to make an altar base layer to insert candles. A lighter, smudge supplies, an oak branch, and water in a gourd.

Breighton as Enki.

Team members

Entry guardian, three challengers, smudger, Namer, Enki, Ritualista.

Ritual script

As the males approached the outer path gate, all the ritual team sang in welcome, using a variant of "Come Brothers Come," by Peter Soderberg (Sparky T. Rabbit) with the phrase "Horned God" replaced by "Enki." Participants joined in singing at the gate, and the ritual team dropped out of the singing as they took on their path roles.

Gate Setup and Process:

The guardian at the gate acted as a regulator, allowing one festivant to enter at a time. He had a sign on his chest to prepare the entrants: "All that enter become Gods, but even Gods may have weaknesses" and "We must honor our ancestors and mentors." Three challengers along the path to the ritual area confronted each participant:

The first asked: *"How do you enter this circle?"* (Participant answered.)

Next, a man with a child said, *"Declare what brings you pride!"* (Participant answered.)

The third asked: *"Who do you honor?"* The participant answered, then the third challenger replied: *"Honor them within,"* and directed them onward to the ritual area.

At the ritual area entrance awaited a smudger and a Namer. The smudger cleansed each entrant with copal burning on charcoal in a small cauldron. Participants then passed to the Namer. He had a tall basket of 75 adhesive name tags that declared each participant a god and included a symbolic petition to Enki, based on a human weakness related to the god source. For example:

God of Summer Wind: Too impatient to listen
God of Lightning: Quick to anger
God of the Canals: Desire to control

The Namer let each man draw one blindly, and to each the Namer said, *"Thou art God,"* and applied the name tag, then waved them in.

As they passed him to enter the circle, the Namer said, *"Enki slumbers."*

The Ritualista greeted each male as they entered and directed them to light a candle for a mentor or ancestor at the North altar, saying, *"Honor those who came before."*

As participants filled up the ritual area, the entry song faded and a new song was started by the ritual team, accompanied by rattles: "We Are Spirit," author unknown, with descant. A basket of rattles was available for use.

When all had entered, the song ended and the Ritualista said, *"Enki, Father of all, awaits our voice. Each here carries strength and seeks the healing wisdom the Father offers. Let us wake him!"*

The team started a song of awakening, "We Are Your People," by Beverly Frederick, with drumming and rattling.

The Ritualista and smudger walked the circle with burning copal and asperged participants' feet with the leafy branch dipped in water. The Ritualista sprinkled Enki with water to awaken him as the song came to a crescendo and ended.

Enki awakened from slumber, surprised and glad his sons had sought him. He sat up and said, *"Who seeks the wisdom of the Father?"*

The Ritualista came forward first, modeling the proposed action, and offered his tag to Enki, saying, *"It is I, God of Summer Wind. My breeze warms us all, yet I sometimes am too impatient to listen. Please, help me, Enki!"*

Enki took the Ritualista's name tag and stuck it on the scroll of the ME, saying, *"The Father listens without the limit of time. Let me take your burden and add its resolution to the wisdom of the ME, our guide to a happy life. Be free of your burden!"*

Two more from the ritual team went next; one read the written tag weakness, the other obviously ad libbed to show the participants could speak about their own weaknesses if they preferred. Ad libs were empowered by participants as they modeled this process.

Enki said, *"Who else seeks wisdom?"* and the process was repeated until all participants had been allowed an opportunity to speak to Enki.

In some instances, Enki added personal private advice to aid the petitioner. Drums, shakers, and clapping were started by the team to accompanying a brief personal dance by one petitioner. The dancer made his mark in the sand in front of Enki in completion, and the team fell silent. Periodically when there was a lull, or when Enki needed to reinforce his invocation, the Ritualista cleansed Enki with copal and wafted it around the circle, or asperged the participants' feet with water using the branch.

When the process was complete, Enki said, *"The Gods present are free of all these burdens, but who will now wrestle with them? We need new creatures lest these burdens return upon us. I, Enki the Father, will create men that they may build the world. Formed with the guidance of the ME, they are birthed with all they need to find happiness. Aid me in this task!"*

The song of release was started by the team: "We Are Opening Up," by Gladys Gray. The team started to clap, and later to whoop and howl, as the Ritualista took the tongs, picked up the scroll of the ME, now covered in the weakness tags, and held it over the fire. When all the paper was burned off, the metal screens surrounding the tubes were opened and the clay figure tokens were revealed and put in a basket. The energy reached a crescendo and broke.

Photo by Nels and Judy Linde

**The Enki bead after burning off its
wrapping as the ME in the ritual fire.**

Enki walked the circle, displaying the charred clay token figures, and said, *"Behold, the humans will do the work of the world, and when they seek the wisdom of the Father, let them remember this symbol, and the wisdom of the ME as their guide."* Enki placed the basket of tokens at the North altar of mentors and ancestors.

The Ritualista poured a libation at each quarter and at the center as he walked the circle. As he was moving, the Ritualista said:

"Let these new creatures find the wisdom of the Father to know the Earth, our home for all creatures; Air, the words of power; Fire, fertility in all things; Water, the seed of life; and in the Spirit, their hearts, and to remember those who came before. Let the men of the world reflect the wisdom of the Father in all things."

Enki said:
"These humans have been born with the ME, knowledge to build a happy home and make the land fruitful. Take this symbol that by your hand the trees be large trees. May your bulls be large bulls, and have the cry of wild bulls. May the great ME of the gods be perfected for you. May your silver be gold. May the land, and everything you have, increase and your people multiply!" Enki then handed a figure token to each participant, as the participants added clapping and rattling.

Enki asked: *"Who here dedicates themselves this gathering to seek the wisdom?"* Dedicants from the men's rite of passage candidates came forward for a personal blessing. Enki sprinkled them with water and said spontaneous words of blessing.

The ritual team started the song of celebration: "Rise with the Fire," by Starhawk. Everyone drummed and danced to a final energy-raising crescendo. The Ritualista and Enki moved to the gate so at the crescendo all was ready to end. The Ritualista said, *"Go forth and praise the Father, and when doubt and weakness come, ask: "What would the Father do?"*

As all exited the circle, Enki handed each participant an animal cracker and blessed each with a kiss. The Ritualista gave each participant a piece of string on which to hang the token amulet as a necklace.

EIGHT

....

Engage the Subconscious

It is a luscious path, filled with color, and sound, and words to delight the senses.
Each stop engages my chakras, setting them to vibrate and glow. I enter the sacred
space to joyous singing, and I am brought before the radiant Goddess with bounty
about her, and she offers me my shining crown. In the darkness I join a hundred
others, basking in their collective glory, heads all aglow. I listen, sing, and soak it all in.

JOURNEY INTO THE LIGHT RITUAL

From Starhawk about ritual: "A ritual that works moves us emotionally. It speaks to our Younger Self through the language of the senses, using color, smells, tastes, actions, rhythm, music, poetry, and dance to make us all participant heroes of our own stories."[20]

Before we begin to elaborate on the practical aspects of building effective ritual, we have one more important element of ritual to consider and decide how to include. How will you take your ritual intent, the story you wish to tell, and engage your audience in a way that they become personally involved and invested in the ritual? Reaching directly into your participants' subconscious through symbols and sensory experience is the quickest and surest method to engage your audience.

---

20   Starhawk, "Creating Community Ritual."

Most of these engagement techniques involve stimulating the senses. The rest of the methods involve directly touching the emotional foundations within our audience. How the personal engagement you incorporate into a ritual ties into your intent will define how your audience will personalize the ritual and be affected. Without this intimate and individual connection, all your efforts will likely be seen as just an entertaining pageant.

Symbols and Symbolism

We are surrounded by symbols, from the familiar octagon stop sign to the peace sign "V" from the 1960s. They are a visual shortcut to a concept or emotion. They can also reflect the complex or archetypal roots of human experience. Symbols enrich and define our experience in ritual. Whenever you are tempted to use words of explanation in ritual, first explore visual images that can convey your intent. Even those that are uncommon, or from ancient or foreign cultures, will resonate with your audience. There are symbols that will elicit a primal response from humans, much as a hummingbird will be drawn to anything red as a source of sweet food.

In ritual the perception and impact of every action and word are heightened in importance, taking on symbolic meaning whether you intend them to or not. The secret to creating effective ritual is to recognize this and make choices about what you present rather than leaving it to chance.

Think about the state or condition that you want your participants to attain. What images are relevant to the intention or the process of getting there? Here it is helpful to make a brainstorm list of every bit of symbolism you can come up with. Some will seem weaker or stronger, but most symbolism gains its impact in relation to its context. A long list of potential symbols appropriate for your ritual will give you more ideas to consider. If you get stuck looking for the right symbolism for your ritual, use library and Internet resources to search for ideas that will work. We sometimes consult "spell" books as they often contain lists of symbolic references for many concepts and situations.[21]

---

21   One example is Patricia Telesco, *Spinning Spells, Weaving Wonders* (Berkeley: Crossing Press, 1996).

EXERCISE

Take any common ritual theme and create as large a list of symbols as you can that might help to realize the intention. For this example, use "transformation." We'll start you out: fire, a butterfly, an ice cube, and a diamond. Build on this list in your ritual notebook.

There needs to be an understandable relationship between the symbology you use and the response you are reaching for. Care needs to be taken so as the ritual unfolds the connection becomes obvious. You do not want to have to tell your audience, "The seed represents our new beginning"; you want them to absolutely know that with all their senses, intellect, and heart.

Don't overthink symbols and substitute an abstraction for something that you can simply provide. You don't need a symbol for fire if you can provide a campfire, candle, or torch. A pan of black dirt is "the Earth." Making a sacrifice can be offering a lock of hair, which *is* a real sacrifice.

Symbols have such a deep impact on our subconscious that unless you pay close attention, the experience is internally digested and you are affected with hardly a notice. As a ritualista you need to be fully aware of what you include and why. Only then can you integrate and refine your use of symbols to move your participants where your ritual intent directs you.

Vision

It is essential in creating ritual to develop your ability to visualize. You must be able to see the ritual unfold as you imagine a participant would experience it. This aspect will often dominate, defining the theme and intent. The visual experience can be tightly controlled. All of your participants will receive a nearly identical visual experience.

Imagine your basic ritual plan through the participants' eyes. With each portion, use your mental "rewind" button and try imagining different visual techniques and images. Is costuming important? What does the movement within the ritual look like? Can simple tasks be enriched by how they appeal to the eye? If you are creating an attunement activity to bring participants closer together, for example, is there a visual method you could include to support that goal? With experience, this storyboard run-through and sensory enrichment process becomes second nature.

Visual impact can deeply engage the emotions and the spirit. Many factors will influence the visual aspect of your ritual. Just as in home decorating, color sets the mood and promotes a particular emotional response. Take any emotion, such as grief, joy, worry, or love. Now brainstorm a collage of five images that evoke that feeling for you. Visual representations in the ritual context can magnify their power. Incorporating them into a ritual gateway, masks, costuming, or any ritual props increases the personal engagement experienced by participants. Incorporating visual symbolism into a central shrine is a great way to bring focus to it.

Costumes can be essential to create ritual characters that are instantly recognized. They can be important if there is a theme your team is working with, or even if they need to be readily identified.

Do not ignore the importance of ambient lighting when planning a ritual. It is a factor that is easy to take for granted. We have offered rituals outdoors in conditions from full sun to the dark of night. People squint and burn when they stand for any length of time in full sun. Our well-planned makeup and visual effects will seem garish and our props awash in hot glue when seen in bright light. Ritual thrives in an atmosphere of visual mystery. Dark of night can be fantastic, but only if participants have enough visual cues to know what they are experiencing. A large central fire and a torch-lit perimeter can work, but much visual detail will be lost. If electricity is available, string and rope lights can provide a good quality light. Mount them above head level on ropes or wires, and keep them safely out of the way. Mirrors can offer double duty as both a prop and to amplify and direct soft lighting after dark. Twilight or deep shade has the advantage of soft light and yet ample visibility. Timing a ritual just before darkness is tricky. We usually visit the site ahead of time with a sunrise and sunset table and watch the light as it fades to schedule the ritual optimally.

Indoors, you can have more control over lighting, but you will likely have to provide it. If the existing lighting is too harsh or not suitable, plan to add what your ritual needs. It may take extra effort to secure and install the right lighting, but it will make a world of difference in how the experience is seen. Note how much emphasis is put on lighting in a theatrical production the next time you attend a play. It is usually one area where expense and planning are not spared! We occasionally offer ritual at a local church meeting room.

They have several lighting options, from perimeter down lights to selective and dimmable ceiling lights. This is optimal for a walk-in space. When planning for an indoor ritual, be sure to check with the site owner about fire codes. Most commercial spaces restrict the use of open flame (such as candles).

We tend to take the visual for granted. Sometimes the smallest details will be those that stand out and define the ritual. Take whatever time you need to thoroughly imagine each visual detail and plan for the quality of illumination. Your audience will notice the difference through their experience.

Sound

The sense of hearing is easy to engage in ritual. We are continually bombarded by noise, sometimes without even realizing it. This can be intense and startling, the subtle hum of the natural world, or the din of the city. All of life's most important moments are associated with sound. What is the pitch of grief, of death or tragedy? What music evokes elation or ecstasy for you? Even the tiny chirp of a cricket can stimulate our memory to times of solitude or contemplation.

Sound, more than any other sense, can also be a disruption to personal engagement in ritual. Traffic noises, idle conversation, or a child in distress can distract from spiritual purpose. The use of your voice, whether speaking in authority or explanation, can be just as distracting. "Together, we cast this circle, hand to hand, heart to heart," combined with appropriate gestures, engages your participants. "And now it's time to cast our circle, so all join hands, forming a circle" says the same thing but is more a voice of direction and does little to captivate. With the exception of the theatrical voice, engagement in ritual should be enticed with sound, not commanded or instructed.

Which sounds build toward an energetic release and which ground us in safety? We all have felt the powerful urge to move upon hearing a gospel song. Now combine sound with the movement that complements gospel: hand-clapping. This can rhythmically charge a song or chant, or be a percussive element all in itself. A finger snap is a simple act and subtle sound, yet the magic of one person starting a basic beat with it and a hundred joining in can become both a large sound and a bonding experience.

The shattering crash of metal, the resonance of a gong, the gentle patter of a rain stick—these all have the power to support a story, shock the psyche, or gentle the soul. These small additions can make the difference between accomplishing a transformative impact and only being entertaining. Enrich the experience of your ritual by adding appropriate background sounds: a singing bowl, a whisper, a rattle, the sounds of water, a bullroarer,[22] or even a simple stick clacking.

Add to the ritual sound the power of phrased words and the human voice. Most traditional religious experience has associated sounds. We both fondly remember the call and response of the Latin Catholic Mass. Vocal toning, using voice to express specific sounds, can shift the mental, emotional, and spiritual perspective of your participants. Rich harmonies are easy to create when the constraint of words is removed from our vocalizations. With both song and chant, we add the direct message and lyric phrasing to communicate and reinforce our intent. The musical quality of song and the rhythmic power of chant have energized whole spiritual movements. Songs are a standard technique for providing unifying and bonding personal experience in ritual. They are so useful we may be tempted to add a song whenever the ritual needs something. As with any technique, overuse can diminish its effect.

You can use music, sung or instrumental, to frame ritual actions into a desired emotional context. There is a whole industry of writing scores for movies based on this principle. Who hasn't felt "foreboding," or "victory," or "sorrow" from a well-composed soundtrack? Emotional response in your audience can then be used to support your ritual intent.

But what about the sound of silence? Silence is always framed by some type of sound at its beginning and end. The absence of sound has an undeniable impact. A pause commands attention. An action performed in silence augments its importance. A quiet moment can provide time for an action or experience to be absorbed and internalized. Use silence sparingly and with discretion. Imagine the sound of your ritual taking place. What does a participant hear at each portion of your ritual? Make choices to orchestrate the audible experience to increase the impact of each part of your ritual.

---

22 A weighted aerofoil of wood attached to a long cord, swung in a large circle to make a characteristic roaring vibrato sound.

Percussion and Rhythm

Percussion is a rhythmically defined form of music. It can involve and affect people in many ways. Increased tempo will energize movement, adding tension that builds to a crescendo. Mimicking natural sounds adds depth and induces connection with the environment. Steady, throbbing rhythms are used to induce trance-like states.

The use of percussion and rhythm is invaluable in aiding the flow, pacing, and energy level of a community ritual. We immediately think of drums, but there is a wide and diverse vocabulary for both percussion and rhythm. Percussion can be everything from a hand clap, finger snap, mouth slap, or foot stomp, to a rattle, bell, gong, or drum. Rhythm is simply a pattern of percussion and we can use our breath, guttural sounds, or the music of metallophones. We can beat upon logs, or even use staving, in the manner of Scandinavian ancestors.[23] Percussion can also be your biggest nightmare. Once unleashed it can take over your ritual and simply encourage individual egos waiting for applause.

Percussion Uses in Ritual

- Gathering point: Draw people together, begin engagement, and set the ritual ambiance.

- Procession: Move participants together to the ritual site and create a feeling of unity and excitement.

- Entry: Provide ambiance and cover the sounds of any verbal challenge if needed. Percussionists in two lines can provide the gate into the ritual area.

- Banish: Use percussion sounds as a tool to cleanse the ritual area.

- Circle casting and elemental directions: Use sound to call attention to and focus on actions.

- Energy raising: Build energy with rhythm.

- Decompress: Add percussion after ritual to transition out of sacred space and mindset.

---

23 Staving: The rhythmic tapping of a wooden staff against a wood floor or the earth.

Types of Percussion and Rhythm Tools

- Shakers: Hollow with beads or other objects on the outside. They are loud, great for emphasis and keeping a beat, but hard to control.

- Rattles: Hollow with grains inside or items that all clang together. Best for fine control and individual emphasis, use in the lead spirit-worker role.

- Bells/wood blocks: Loud and sharp sounds, best for keeping the tempo of large groups in sync.

- Middle Eastern drums: Best for intricate solo accents and quiet rhythms.

- Hoop drums: Best for slow, meditative, or heartbeat rhythms, or in the lead spirit worker role.

- African drums: Best for loud, large groups, energy raising, and processions.

Considerations for Using Percussion and Rhythm in Ritual

- Volume: Use an appropriate percussion tool for each situation.

- Engagement: Keep rhythms simple if you want others to join in.

- Avoid distraction: Don't overwhelm key verbal or action portions of the ritual.

- Pay attention: Percussionists must know and follow start and stop cues from team leaders.

- Build energy: Support percussion with movement, facial expressions, volume, and tempo increase to help build the energy.

Plan in advance how you will integrate any percussion you include. Request percussionists to talk to the officiants before beginning or at the ritual gathering location. A blanket inclusion empowering anyone to add percussion can lead to auditory chaos and disruption! Instruct percussionists to be especially sensitive and appropriate to the flow and energy of the ritual. They need to always watch for signals from the leaders who guide the ritual. Remember, with rhythm less is often more. To manage a percussive energy raising, have a signal for acceleration and volume increase, and then have a clear signal to stop. Percussionists should focus on the ritual facilitator, not each other!

Words

Words are in some ways the least effective tool in our toolbox, yet they will always be important in ritual. For our words to be effective they need to flow naturally from us, and also contain exactly what our script and intention moved us to create. There really is no substitute for memorization of words essential to our role in ritual. We each individually will have a limited capacity for memorization, so it is important to limit the words in our roles to the essential. The K.I.S.S. (keep it simple, stupid) principle applies throughout ritual planning but especially in composing any scripted words.

When you write a word script, design it so the key words are easy to remember in relationship with each other, and then accept that the sentence structure can vary upon delivery. You are memorizing the essence and content, not the exact words. For example, your notes might say, "Welcome to a celebration of the effort Fred brought to his studies," which can be spoken in many ways. It could be spontaneously spoken, something like: "Today we come to this sacred space to share in a celebration of the six years of dedicated focus Fred has brought to his studies to reach his goal." This way you memorize the content and don't have to obsess over getting the exact words correct. This relieves your anxiety and makes it more likely you can speak with authentic confidence, which is more important.

The use of rhyme to help the speaker remember lines and engage the audience arises in the origins of both ritual and theater. Rhyme is a technique that has been used in many of the epic poems and myths of the world. It reaches deep into our psyche and by itself creates a ritual mindset, just as our childhood rhymes did. Rhyme grabs our attention as we listen for how the thought will complete itself. Like percussion, a rhyming rhythm can be a trance-inducing factor in ritual. Composing in rhyme takes more time and effort, but the result for your ritual is well worth it. Your ability to use rhyme will grow with practice. Once you work with rhyme in ritual you will find it makes memorization much easier.

We used rhyming language exclusively in a series of folk magic–based rituals. We created a "standard" ritual opening that was completely spoken in rhyme. By using it for each of four rituals (with some small variations) we were able to limit memorization and also connect the ritual series together thematically. For this work you will find a good rhyming dictionary and thesaurus invaluable.

There are alternatives to memorization, but they have real limitations. Carrying a written script during ritual is a temptation but a very problematic answer. You have a piece of paper to drop, lose, or become illegible. One hand is always occupied. Your attention and focus are taken away from the presentation by every few seconds having to glance at your script. This disconnect inevitably diminishes the authenticity of your words. Usually the lighting is too dim to read by anyway. Many ritualistas need reading glasses, and where do you carry those? In specific situations you can mitigate some of these factors by having scripted words written on a prop. Now you don't have to hold a script or use your hands, but you can't avoid the other hazards of being dependent on a written script. In a complex ritual, you might have a simplified outline printed and in a pocket. When the focus of the ritual is on another team member you can then catch a quick glance to refresh your memory. Even writing cues or notes on your hand or arm is preferable to carrying a script.

The ritualista should be familiar with the tools of the poetic trade: literary devices.[24] Many of these devices help you create not only evocative language but also a script that is easier to memorize. Commonly used are:

- Metaphor: A comparison that doesn't use "like" or "as"

- Allusion: An indirect reference to something without mentioning it explicitly

- Pacing and meter: How you pause and the speed of your words

- Consonance: Repetition of consonant patterns, typically at the end of words

- Assonance: Repetition in vowel sounds to create internal rhyming in phrases

- Alliteration: Repeating the first letter sound in multiple words in a row

---

24   "Literary Devices," www.literary-devices.com.

Another way to limit memorization is through the use of a narrator or reader. We used this technique once when we were confronted with a ritual script that was way too wordy and memorization-dependent, with little time to prepare or rehearse. What we did was simplify the script where we could, and the ritual roles became acting parts. Wherever dialogue was needed, a person at the edge of the space read the scripted lines in a loud, expressive voice. The actors only had to make motions that indicated they were taking the speaking role.

You will find the scripting of effective words and memorization is one of the most time-consuming parts of producing a community ritual. When immersed in this task it is a great incentive to again ask, "Is there a way to communicate what I am trying to say here without the use of words?" This is the time to look deeper into your ritual toolbox for answers! Maybe a song, chant, or action conveys just the right words.

Once your ritual begins, the use of spoken words should be limited to those scripted and essential to the ritual. Each time we use words to talk about something outside of or in explanation of the ritual experience, we draw people out of ritual consciousness. Never start a sentence with "And now we will…" As soon as you say that phrase, the likelihood of a shared experience has diminished considerably.

Voice: Songs and Chants

We have all felt the hair rise on the back of our neck during an empowered and enthusiastically offered song. Whether with unified voices or rich harmonies, human voices joined together have inspired and energized communities since the first fire.

Several of our most memorable rituals have developed completely around an inspiring song or chant. In each case, what made it possible was that the song itself told a story or declared a theme within its essence. With a powerful artistic creation to work from, the ritual intent expressed what the song evoked within us. Don't be afraid to write your own songs! They can be very simple and you can focus the lyrics exactly on your intention. Judy wrote this song for the "Gratitude" ritual using an easy-to-learn melody:

Walk in the way of gratitude, walk in the way of gratitude,
Walk in the way of gratitude, walk in the way of gratitude.
All around me, open my eyes, see
Blessings aplenty, give it freely.

Lyrics can connect directly with your ritual intent. We collect songs and chants covering a wide range of topics because we never know when one will be needed. If you can't find or compose what you need, ritual songs can be an adaptation of a popular tune. Simplify your words and apply them to existing lyrics. It is a team's dream situation to have a choir available to support a ritual. Working with a group willing to rehearse, you can use music that is complex or lengthy. You will find people able to harmonize on the spot in ritual. It is always a wonderful surprise to hear a simple song explode into multiple tonal parts.

If you are depending on your ritual participants to carry a song, especially for building a crescendo, plan on a simple tune and lyrics, and try to introduce it prior to the ritual. As people gather or during a procession are great times to get exposure for the song. If you have a website or your group has an electronic newsletter, secure or make a digital recording of your ritual song and post a link to it in advance. Get your community humming your ritual tune before they even gather!

If you want to include songs, you need at least one strong vocal leader. They need to have a loud, pleasant voice, and be able to project the tune and lyrics clearly and without too much stylization so your participants are able to join in. They also need a sense of rhythm. Keeping a consistent pacing will help everyone follow along. Many songs need to start on a specific note to be in the vocal range of a majority. If you do not have perfect pitch for beginning a song, purchase a small pitch pipe to use. Consider taking a couple of voice lessons to improve your skills and assess your voice if song is something you wish to add to most rituals.

Chanting is an ancient method to energetically empower your ritual wishes. Chants can be very easy to compose; just a few key words are enough. One of the anonymous classics from Pagan practice is still one of the best: "Earth my body, Water my blood, Air my breath, and Fire my spirit."[25] An easy tune, hand motions, and many descants (supplemental chant parts) have since been added, but the power is in the brief descriptive words and strong metaphors. Sometimes just describing what you are doing in ritual can become a chant.

---

25 "Earth My Body," www.flutopedia.com/song_earth_my_body.htm.

You have included a working for participants to ask their ancestors for help in guiding their way forward into the future. Here is a chant to energize that portion:

"Ancestor wisdom, whitened bones.
Dark before me, light the way home."

Try chants out in advance of the ritual. Sometimes what seems perfect for one person in the shower is droning or boring when a hundred people repeat it for ten minutes! Chants will naturally speed up to form an energetic peak. Make sure that as it accelerates, yours doesn't turn into a tongue twister.

In both song and chants the use of the round is powerful. We have designed whole rituals around a well-worded three-part song. When spoken with two or more starting points, even a simple chant becomes a magical entrainment with the energy of combined voices.

You can use a meditation tool, the OM, as a very effective energizing tool. Use a series of three pitches getting ever higher. Start comfortably low, and let it resonate until it dies away. Raise a few notes and OM again. Then finish with a comfortably higher pitch. Add some harmonies. Start with your hands relaxed at chest level and lift your arms with each pitch until fully extended above your head. The energy felt by your community will be palpable!

Growing up, we all learned to recreate sounds with our voices. An auditory interpretation of the sound of footsteps, machines, electronics, even automated processes can be integrated, just as old radio shows were enriched in this way. The human voice can mimic many natural sounds. We have all barked, howled, buzzed, and recreated sounds for fun. To draw these simultaneously from your participants requires advance planning and modeling to succeed. A group improvisation of spontaneously created sounds can offer a unique chorus of powerful natural sounds.

The Intimate Senses: Taste, Smell, and Touch

The senses of taste and smell are invaluable tools for the ritualista. While ever so subtle compared with sound and visual effects, they reach deep into the human psyche. They can evoke memories of the past, of childhood, of trauma, and of joy. They can generate an intense physical or mental response in individuals. In the Jewish Passover seder, for instance, the bitter mixture of horseradish, the maror, symbolizes the bitterness of slavery endured in Egypt. The taste is meant to transport people back to the slavery of their ancestors, with the ritual purpose of remembering the importance of subsequent freedom.

There are seven basic tastes: bitter, salty, sour, astringent, sweet, pungent, and *umami* (savory). Our taste buds can detect extremely small amounts of these and the subtle mixtures are endless. There are also tastes that stimulate our heat or cold sensors, such as cayenne or spearmint. For group distribution, stick to single substances that evoke the feeling you seek. Certain acids can be used to enhance sour tastes. Each acid imparts a slightly different tartness. Acetic acid gives vinegar its taste. Citric acid is found in citrus fruits and gives them their sour taste. Unripe persimmon causes a very unpleasant astringent sensation on any part of the mouth it touches. Honey is often used to represent the sweetness of life.

Taste is a difficult sense to safely offer participants. First, participants must be warned of the substance used to prevent allergic or sensitivity reactions. Then they must get the substance to their mouths without creating a health hazard. It is not safe for a large group to dip their fingers in a substance and transfer it to their own mouths; the vessel will be quickly contaminated. In some cases a disposable tool, a tongue depressor or cotton swab, may be a practical method. Best is to have a method that can dispense a small amount by dripping, dropping, or shaking on a participant's own finger. Then the distribution vessel (typically an eye dropper or powder shaker) can remain sanitary and people can choose not to taste.

Consider the use of both fondly attractive smells and nasty ones. A whiff of Play-Doh brings most people immediately back to their childhood. The scent of a corpse flower will fill one with a sense of the dead and decaying. An easy way to present odor is to use a wicking material saturated with essential oil. Hung on a path it will vaporize into the air. Hunting supply stores sell products specifically designed to efficiently distribute scent.

Heating, in a candle or in a potpourri warmer, is also a very effective delivery method. We often use the sense of smell to support and increase the effectiveness of other sensory encounters: visual, sound, or action.

Smell requires close or actual physical contact to be effective, and so is not appropriate in all situations. In this age of allergies and sensitivities, participant awareness of the content of products they will be exposed to, and provision for alternatives, must be provided for.

Touch can be used as an intimate or nurturing action. Slow and gentle touch, on appropriate body areas, will be perceived as comforting. Touch can be used in blessing individuals, in creating bonds, and in theatrical expression. It can be subtle, firm, gentle, and, using very structured techniques, dramatically evocative. In many blessings the third eye (forehead) is marked or anointed. Touch does not have to mean body contact. A whisper carries the touch of another's breath. Passing through a veil involves feeling the fabric. Touch can occur when squeezing by or passing through an obstacle. Being aware of how the sense of touch is engaged adds another layer of understanding to your ritual skills.

Touch, like any sensory method, should not be assumed to be a casual act. As a ritualista you must be sensitive to the fact that, for some, touch is a risky intrusion into personal space.

Movement and Dance

People love to move. Movement and dance are actively energizing. The trick to using them in ritual is to get participants started, help them overcome their inhibitions, and then know how and when to end! Once your audience gets moving they may not want to stop.

The "all dance" method refers to what we have seen in many ritual outlines: "At this time, all ritual participants dance." With a community experienced in ritual, making this outline note become a reality can be very easy. With an older, more sedate, or inexperienced group, this directive will fall flat. Typically, to start an "all dance" energy raising, a cue is given to a group of percussionists, musicians, singers, or hand clappers. You need something to set a beat to move to. Ritual shills or team members start by modeling the activity. With eye contact and inviting gestures, team members entice those who are eager to participate to the center, hopping, skipping, or dancing—just get them moving! As soon as they have one participant dancing, the team member focuses on the next. Usually the participant, now left alone, will get the idea and bring another person in. The process continues until everyone who is inclined to is moving.

A problem you may encounter with this method is that people have relative mobility, and often are less than flexible about their comfort zones. Some move frantically fast, others are more limited, and some may not want to move at all. You may be expecting people to grab one another and attempt to make the hesitant participants move. If your community is comfortable with that, and people know it's coming, it can work. What is worse than a lack of activity is when people leave feeling they were bullied and "forced to participate." If dancing as a means of raising energy is a new method for your people, and particularly if there is insensitivity to personal boundaries, it can be a disaster! An "all dance" event is potential anarchy, so prepare to be flexible in how it will play out. Plan to have a cue or action by your ritual team to coordinate bringing the dance to a crescendo and a conclusion.

A more controllable movement approach is to have your ritual team gather people in pairs, foursomes, or small groups. Within these groupings simple steps or movements can be taught, adapting to the sensibilities, limitations, and tempo of the individuals in each group. You have a much greater chance of getting a large percentage of participants involved in this way. There are dance patterns and movements a little research will find that are specifically designed to engage groups and draw them in.[26] Movement doesn't have to be wild galloping! A simple "grandmother step" (right foot forward, now together, left foot forward, now together, either done sideways or forward) can be done in tiny increments, with grace and intention and including those from young children to ancient ones!

The spiral dance is a good technique to add movement as an energizing event. The spiral dance has some very positive features: participants all hold hands, they are guided to pass by each other face to face and can engage each other with their eyes as they pass, and they all end up in the center to reach a crescendo!

---

26   Dances of Universal Peace, www.dancesofuniversalpeace.org.

How to Lead a Spiral Dance

Slowly! That is the first thing to know about leading a spiral dance. Always bear in mind that your pace at the beginning of the dance will impact the whiplash factor at the end of the dance, so no matter how slowly you think you are going, you are probably still going too fast. But let's go back to the beginning.

Generally, you're going to want your spiral dance to happen during the energy-raising part of a large group ritual. Either you're going to be inside a very spacious area, or you will be outside. Whichever the case may be, this cannot be done without someone getting hurt unless you take precautions ahead of time. There should be no obstructions, no altars, no trees, or anything else that people can trip over. Make sure that you scrutinize the surface that people will be dancing on. If indoors, are there rugs? Anything loose? A change in levels? If outside, holes or divots in the ground? Rocks or branches? How many people, and how much space do you have? If you have enough clear space so that the people in the circle can stand right next to each other and hold hands, and there is no obstruction within the circle, you're probably fine. If you have a fire in the center of your circle, you are going to have to be aware of how close you are bringing people to that fire. Another problem is you might not have enough people to fill your space. Don't let them be spread out; have people hold hands until the circle is closed. That should do it.

If you are the person leading, find some way to take your bearings or pick a visual point of reference that's outside the circle, so you know when you've gone around once. The people across from you before you start will be moving and you will not be able to see what's on the other side of anyone across from you, so your visual point of reference should be something that is a little taller than a person.

When you are ready, drop the hand of the person to your left and start to move to the left, slowly, passing just in front of that person. Those in the circle follow as they are guided by their joined hands. Keep moving one full time around the circle; continue about halfway past the point where you started, slowly; and then turn toward the person on your right. One way to make sure that each person makes that turn easily is to take a moment to make eye contact with that person as you turn to face them. Now as you continue (SLOWLY) past each person, make that eye contact. This is the magic of the spiral dance! Continue on until you have passed the last person in that line of people. Remember, that last person will be the person whose hand you let go of when you started (unless they're switching places to mess with you).

Now you have to put your faith in the dance or in physics or in magic, or you just have to let go of control, because you have to continue this slow one-step-at-a-time dance, facing out, for one more circle. At this point you have a choice to make. You can turn again and face the person to your right, and make that eye contact again with each person as you move past them. This will reverse your spiral, bringing you and the line of people you lead back facing inward along the perimeter of the circle.

The other choice you have with a spiral dance can be used to gather everyone close together around a center point. Once you see everyone has been turned facing out, you turn inward facing the center, with your back to the person on your right. Now you are going to continue spiraling toward the center of the circle, making your circle smaller each time. Keep it slow, and concentrate, because at this point everyone is going over the same territory that you have covered, so you want them to have plenty of opportunity to catch up. Keep winding slowly toward the center until you all become a tightly wound, huddled mass. Don't forget, if there is a fire in the center, you need to stop moving once you reach a safe buffer area around the fire. You will not know when all of the people have finished their inward spiral. You will have to depend on your senses to tell you. If you are singing or chanting or in any other way raising energy, here is your point of climax. Revel in this moment—it is truly splendid.

Challenging the Intellect

Our thinking, analyzing selves can be tricked into engaging our subconscious in ritual. We have used activities that challenge people intellectually to bring forward an intuitive result. When problem solving, puzzle assembling, unscrambling, or decoding ritual actions occupies our conscious mind, our subconscious is free to explore any theme presented by the ritual intent. This is not necessarily the best or easiest tool for your ritual toolbox, but when you need something unique to pull out of your hat, it can present a very profound experience.

You can use riddles or questions whispered to participants to help them think about subjects relative to your ritual intent. They can be used to provoke thought, or the answers (or clues to the answers) can be presented later within the ritual. You can develop a team-building activity by dividing participants and offering a problem or riddle to solve in order to progress on in the path or ritual. Incorporating these mental exercises into engagement with a prop, or revealing later how the answers add to a larger context, ties them to the overall ritual. As with a challenge, compose your questions so the exact or "right" answer is not primary. What is important is the process.

· · · · · · · · · · ·

EXAMPLE

In a tarot-themed ritual, we had a 4 x 6-foot puzzle commercially made of an artistic rendering of the Fool card.[27] In the ritual we divided participants into eight groups and gave each person a puzzle piece, each with a color-coded back. We had them write their name on the back of their piece for later retrieval. Each of the eight groups in turn, as other ritual activity continued, was given a chance to assemble their puzzle portion (without ever seeing the full image). Once all eight groups had assembled their portion ,the whole image was displayed. At festival's end, we flipped the puzzle over and participants were invited to find and take home their piece as a gift. Participants have showed us their piece years later, connecting them to the ritual and the process.

People love to do craft projects in ritual. The hands-on work of creating or decorating a prop engages the mind. The desire to excel keeps them focused on the task and distracted from whatever symbolic content they may be creating. The later realization of what they have made will increase its impact. In the ritual "They Will Remain" (see chapter 9), we had participants block-print leaves and flowers with simple potato stamps and paint onto two clear, masked acrylic sheets. Later in the ritual the masking was removed to reveal male and female deity figures which were then assembled into an exit gate. The realization of what the participants had unconsciously created reinforced the symbolism of the ritual.

---

27   We used the Seeker card from Joanna Powell Colbert's *Gaian Tarot*, www.gaiantarot.com.

Fool card puzzle and participants retrieve
their puzzle piece as a gift at festival end (left to right).

When offering a craft project, care must be taken to determine what happens to any leftover materials. How are they removed from the ritual space or kept out of the way until the ritual is finished? If the project makes a mess or gets onto participants, you must provide a cleanup station. If they take something with them, it is good to have them mark it or add their name. Items can get lost, and they will want to be able to identify their own creation. Sometimes a project will support a transformation theme, and if you plan on burning it, make sure the materials are organic and safe to burn. This type of activity needs to be designed to encourage full participation. People can be inhibited when feeling their "talent" is on display; many won't participate if it feels competitive.

Consider each activity in your ritual outline as an opportunity for a sensory engagement by your audience. Design your use of the senses to enrich and develop your ritual intent. Our unconscious mind and spiritual state of being are most integrally connected to the raw data we get from our senses. Let the sensory experiences you include tell the story. A well-crafted ritual uses the senses to allow the story to be perceived by the unconscious self.

Ritual: Journey into the Light

....

Location: Sacred Harvest Festival, 2012
© Nels Linde

Ritual context

This ritual was offered as the main last-night ritual at Sacred Harvest Festival 2012. It started at dusk and had about 180 people participate.

Ritual intent

To experience our chakras opening to the sacred and to bask in the light of community and infinite love!

Ritual description

A path-working opening our chakras, and gaining a sense of the divine within each of us. We empower our community for the next year's journey, embracing and filled with the light of the crown chakra. This ritual will involve a path-working with a 20-minute wait time to enter; please bring a chair if needed. Bring rhythm instruments for the ritual procession and ending, and bring your voice! Join in the procession from the Heart Chakra gathering place at 8:00 p.m.

Ritual setup and supplies

See the ritual script and path-working details descriptions below.

Ritual team members

Crone: Dressed as a wise woman, she acted as the path regulator.
Woodwose: A "man of the woods," bare-chested, ragged, and fierce.
Maiden: A beautiful young woman in fine dress.
Deity: A serene Mother figure in fine dress, with her hair braided into a crown.
Two bass drummers (became wranglers after the path emptied).
Singers (at least four)
Six Sirens dressed as dancers in leotards and bright tops. They put on mirrored gloves and brought the gate veils to the circle, to be used as sheer flags, as the path emptied.

Six chakra activity path-workers (in order):

1. Costumed as the Bull, at the red veil, root chakra gate. He played a hoop drum.

2. Costumed as the Fish, at the orange veil, sacral chakra gate. He played a didgeridoo.

3. Costumed as the Ram, at the yellow veil, solar plexus chakra gate. He played a bell chime.

4. Costumed as the Dove, at the green veil, heart chakra gate. He played a rattle.

5. Costumed as the Lion, at the blue veil, throat chakra gate. She played a chirping bird call.

6. Costumed as the Owl, at the indigo veil, third eye chakra gate. He offered an anointment with water.

Ritual script

A procession was led by the ritual singers from the gather location. It swung by the ritual circle for instrument or chair drop-off on the way to the path entrance. The Deity figure was observed in passing, saluting the directions and making the ritual space sacred. The procession moved on to the woods path entrance. Waiting there were all the chakra gate ritual team members (six Sirens, six chakra activity path-workers), the Maiden and the Woodwose (both cloaked), and the Crone. A double-wide two-person path was set up along the woods path, passing through veils set 12 short paces apart.

On arrival at the gate to the path-working, the procession song ended, and the Crone said: *"Begin deep breathing before you enter, in and out through the nose only, making a small hiss at the back of the throat as we breathe in and out."* The Crone also had this written on a card to pass back down the arrival line for latecomers. The festivants formed a double line, and the singers began "Prepare Yourself" by Abbi Spinner McBride (16 bass drumbeats per verse).

The Crone was the path regulator, allowing two festivants to pass with each verse of "Prepare Yourself." The ritual team entered first in order of their encounter along the path: chakra gate pairs, then the Woodwose and Maiden, then the singers.

Two bass drummers were on each path end, in sight of each other, and kept a synchronized slow walking beat in time with the song. One added a bell chime cue every 32 beats (or two song rounds). Pairs walking the path took 12 steps/beats to move to a chakra pair and pass through the veil, 4 beats to center and prepare, 12 beats for the activity, and then 4 beats to absorb the veil activity and move onward.

Path-working details description

Five pairs of path-workers were spread along veiled chakra gates, each 12 steps apart. These gates represented the first five chakras from root to throat. One half of each team pair was costumed or marked in some way as the appropriate associated animal, and offered a sound activity directed at each pair of participants as they approached the veiled gate. As participants passed through the veil they made the verbal Bija ("seed") sound said to activate the particular energy of that chakra. They were aided by a Siren team member who helped guide the participant pair through the veil, offered them a scent, and then whispered words sending the participant pair onward to the next chakra gate.

Red veil gate: A hoop drum was played, directed toward each participant's root chakra in turn. They were passed though the veil to the Siren while making the Bija sound *"Laaaumm."* The Siren offered an optional scent, cedar, and touched the participant pair to send them to the next veil, saying, *"Breathe deep and connect with the fiery center of the Earth. Pull that energy up until it glows at the base of your spine and feel that red glow expand."*

Orange veil gate: A didgeridoo was played, directed toward each participant's sacral chakra in turn. They were passed though the veil to the Siren while making the Bija sound *"Vaaaunnngg."* The Siren offered an optional scent, orris root, and touched the participant pair to send them to the next veil, saying, *"Breathe deep and connect with the viscous mantle of the Earth. Feel that orange energy rise into your womb or prostate and feel that orange glow brighten."*

Yellow veil gate: A bell chime was played, directed toward each participant's solar plexus chakra in turn. They were passed though the veil to the Siren while making the Bija sound *"Rummmm."* The Siren offered an optional scent, dragon's blood, and touched the participant pair to send them to the next veil, saying, *"Center and draw from the ground below you. Feel the yellow fertility of the soil become your core. Let that boundless yellow swell."*

Green veil gate: A rattle was played, directed toward each participant's heart chakra in turn. They were passed though the veil to the Siren while making the Bija sound *"Hummmm."* The Siren offered an optional scent, copal, and touched the participant pair to send them to the next veil, saying, *"Breathe deep and pull up the green living energy of the Earth. Fill your heart with the pulsing green glow that is life."*

Blue veil gate: Near the woods' edge at the blue veil gate, a chirping bird call was played, directed toward each participant's throat chakra in turn. They were passed though the veil to the Siren while making the Bija sound *"Yummmm."* The Siren offered an optional scent, frankincense, and touched the participant pair to send them to the next veil, saying, *"Draw the blue energy of healing sound from below. Feel the throat expand in empowered blue glow as you join the mantra "Yummm."*

Indigo veil gate: Festivants now exited the path and approached the "true mirror" at the ritual circle edge. This was a prop that mirrored in reverse, so participant pairs saw themselves exactly as others view them. At this indigo veil gate, a third-eye anointment with water took place. Pairs were passed though the veil to the Siren while making the Bija sound *"Shaauummmm."* The Siren offered an optional scent, mugwort, and moved the pair to the "true mirror," saying, *"Rise and fill the third eye with the deep indigo of divine vision. Swell the soul until it moves past the night sky to join with the light."* Participants gazed into the "true mirror" and saw themselves reversed, as others see them.

Participants then passed by a gauntlet of singers, all singing the first verse of "Held in the Heart," by Abbi Spinner McBride.

One singer took each of the entering pairs by the hand and led them to the Deity figure, who was near the center, sitting facing the fire. The singer then returned for another pair.

The Deity sat in a sacred shrine surrounded by candles and incense. A lotus blossom was on her head, and she held a large bowl of grapes. The Deity met the eyes of each participant as each was given a violet glow-stick crown. With a radiant smile, the Deity said, *"Grow toward enlightenment."* A bar chime was rung by the Deity as each participant touched their crown. The Deity made the Bija sound *"Aaoouummm,"* and offered the scent of lotus as she motioned for them to join the others.

Participants formed a tight, multilayered circle bounded by torches, leaving a small center area open. They were sitting on blankets and singing together. The Crone's entry into the path signaled it was empty, and the ritual team followed through to the circle behind her, in pair order. The team pairs removed and brought all the path gate veils, which were now carried as flags.

As the last festivants passed into the circle, the second verse of the song was sung by the singers. The Crone and chakra activity people (bringing their instruments) now passed through the chakra veils into the circle. The path-working portion was complete. All participants were seated and singing together in the approaching twilight, wearing their glow-stick crowns.

Symbolic drama: The torches were now extinguished by the team so only the small central fire was lit. The Maiden appeared from the woods, exuding love and joy. Holding a lit candle, she slowly walked around the inner, open circle area. A coarse Woodwose, man of the woods, broke through the circle holding a spear. In silence he stalked the Maiden in a crude dance and then was drawn in, fascinated by the flame. He got closer and closer, then threw his spear to the ground and knelt before her. She spread her arms and kissed him on the forehead, freezing him in place.

The Crone entered the ritual circle and raised the bowl of grapes for all to see. The drum, didgeridoo, chime, rattle, and bird chirp sounds all returned together as she said:

"Raise your voices in the holy sound, to bless our bounty as the crown of infinite love becomes open."

The Deity started the sound *"Maaaaaaaaaaaaaaaaa"* and all joined in. After 20 seconds, the Crone said, *"So mote it be."*

The Deity rose and gave a lit candle to the Woodwose. She then took the bowl of grapes from the Crone. The Sirens entered, wearing their mirrored gloves. They gathered in a tight group behind the Maiden and the Woodwose, facing the participants. Four of the Sirens reached around the Maiden and Woodwose, moving their mirrored hands behind the two candles to shine the light and reflections back to the circle of festivants. The song "We Are Opening Up" by Gladys Gray was begun by the singers.

As this "illuminating" group slowly moved deosil, facing the crowned participants, the two remaining Sirens carried a large veil that spanned over the wide circle of people. It was slowly drawn deosil across the heads of the festivants, as the illumination group passed. The Deity followed behind and placed a grape in each festivant's mouth. The perimeter torches were relit after this group passed by all the circle participants.

While the song, illumination, veil, and Deity worked their way around, the fire in the center was being stoked. Once the action and removal were complete, the song accelerated until it ended with repeating *"We are opening, we are opening."* An energy-raising dance began, led by the Sirens carrying the colorful chakra flags and circling. When the crescendo peaked and crashed, all team members modeled touching the earth as a grounding.

The ritual team gathered in the inner circle. They faced the East, South, West, and North in turn and uttered *"Maaa,"* bowing in unison to each direction. The Deity nodded in agreement and walked out of the ritual circle through the gate. The other principal characters followed. The singers started the second verse of the song for a procession back to the gathering spot.

NINE

·········

Awe and Wonder

I wind through a torchlit path and encounter two serene figures lying with eyes closed, a man and woman, painted and gaily dressed, covered in flowers. Who are they? Why are they here? I enter the circle and quickly find myself decorating panels with paint using potato print blocks. The task is a collective joy, and I help a child add their part. It is strangely mysterious and yet fun. I am led to experiences, and voices speak of the frailty of all the grove surrounding me. Together we all call to the Gods of wild nature, and they come, bearing gifts! As our voices raise in song into the night, our work is revealed. Though the Gods are leaving us, and our time here is done, we truly know They Will Remain!

THEY WILL REMAIN RITUAL

"The most beautiful thing we can experience is the mysterious. It is the source of all true art and all science. He to whom this emotion is a stranger, who can no longer pause to wonder and stand rapt in awe, is as good as dead: his eyes are closed."

ALBERT EINSTEIN

Awe is that sense of magic we experience from encounters with the mysterious. Using all our ritual tools, we want participants to leave having had that feeling of wonder. It can come in many forms: expanding our knowledge of the natural world, the sacred nature of ourselves, our community, or our relationship with things beyond ourselves. The heart of community ritual is found in creating a place to experience these emotions that increase our well-being. In this chapter, we explore some techniques to take the ritual journey directly to wonderment.

Guided Meditation

The aim of a guided meditation is to fully allow each person to make their own unique mental journey. When done well, participants encounter a profound multisensory vision.

It is difficult to incorporate an intense guided meditation like this into large group ritual. The technique requires an inner quiet and comfort for each participant, and they all must be willing to embrace the process in order for it to work. A completely developed guided meditation that can be the primary focus of a ritual is best done with groups of less than fifty. Work indoors where comfort, the climate, lighting, and intrusions can be tightly controlled.

More often, an abbreviated meditation and a compressed induction process are used to briefly create this kind of personal experience as part of a larger ritual outline. For large groups the purpose might be to encounter one place, concept, symbol, or deity, and use each participant's response to frame and enhance the balance of their experience. Participants might visit the Underworld, the Tree of Life, or encounter, say, a goddess of the hearth like the Greek Hestia. Then later in the ritual they might interact with a symbol or prop representing the Underworld, or the Tree of Life, or a costumed character representing Hestia.

Multiple voices simultaneously guiding induction, with participants divided into smaller groups, is one technique you might use to be effective with a larger group. Have your participants slowly walk in a circle, on a labyrinth or down a path, with the meditation delivered in segments as they move past. The *judicious* additions of ambient sounds and smells can provide more layers of sensory involvement. With a community ritual, we also need to be able to structure meditation so that whatever we individually experience, the journey will support the intent.

Before you write, consider the purpose of your meditation and define the result you are looking for. It helps to visualize the meditation repeatedly in detail, from beginning to end, making note of any significant symbols or events you want to include. Think carefully about what visual, sensory, and symbolic touchstones your words will provide and how they tie together with the ritual purpose. The entire journey will eventually develop to the point where you can begin writing. A guided meditation should be thoroughly composed. Even experienced leaders do not attempt to improvise when the details of the voyage can be so important.

Guided meditations usually follow a recognizable structure. You will prepare participants to be receptive to the alpha state[28] by getting comfortable and relaxing. Begin with gentle directives: "Close your eyes, and take a deep cleansing breath." A technique commonly used to begin is to ask the listener to visualize entering a cave, building, or opening under a tree. As they walk down a staircase, steep path, or ladder, reinforce and deepen their relaxation with each step.

As the meditation begins, describe in very general terms what the participant encounters. You want to encourage use of the senses to engage participants' imaginations so they are immersed in the experience, while letting them fill in the details. If you describe encountering a doorway, ask participants to note what it looks like, what may be written on it, or what it sounds like when they open it, and what they notice about the room. A meditation can also be a story, one with characters and a simple plot. Continue to reinforce relaxation occasionally and remind everyone they are safe and secure as you progress.

Participants should be restored to normal waking consciousness gently and gradually. Guide the listener back to the starting place of the meditation. Have them return to the doorway or stairs (whatever they encountered at the beginning), counting them back to a wakeful state as they move toward the entrance. Carefully help them reclaim their awareness and enter back into the world around them. Keep some salt handy—if anyone has difficulty returning, help them place a small amount on their tongue while sitting on the ground.

Some simple tips to help you get started and avoid common mistakes:

- Make sure everyone can hear you.

- If you are reading it, be conscious of your paper rustling. Any ambient noises can be very distracting.

---

28 Being relaxed with the mind emptied and open to experience the moment.

- Be aware that people will race past your voice if you take a long time to describe the next step. For example, if you say "the water ahead," they may have already turned the lake you want them to see into a river.

- Speak in brief phrases with a relaxing cadence, ending phrases with a lowered pitch.

- Give general descriptions and then allow or ask them to fill in the symbolic details: "What sounds do you hear?" "Do you see anything near the large tree in your view?"

- Keep the whole meditation in the same "person." Use either "you" or "we" consistently.

- Avoid references to time. Each will be sensing time at their own speed and will be jarred when you say time-defining words like "now," "immediately," or "suddenly."

- Phrases that are unconditional and undemanding work best: "Allow yourself to ...," "Pause here until you have heard what may be offered," "Something may be drawing your attention."

- Before returning, add an instruction to remember what they have experienced. This can be really helpful for some participants.

- Allow enough time for everyone to be comfortably returned, and check in with each individual before moving on with your ritual.

The ability to write and deliver a guided meditation is a skill that you need to practice to develop. Start out by recording yourself for critical listening. There are many resources available to develop the skill of leading a guided meditation. If you wish to include this in your toolbox, practice on small groups of friends and get their criticism after each session. You may think what you offer flows seamlessly, but they will let you know where you lost them at every turn!

Invocation and Evocation

Your community may be blessed with people who can welcome a sacred presence or deity itself to enter or speak through them to a community. This is a skill that you don't just choose to develop for the occasion of a community ritual. Both invocation and evocation take time, talent, and work to develop fully. We will call people who have this ability "spirit workers."

Invocation is the calling of a spiritual essence into oneself. For invocation to take place, each spirit worker and each specific deity will have requirements. These might include personal purification, prayers, supplication, or offerings to the deity, and specific words or an incantation to initiate the possession. When an invocation is taking place, the spirit worker opens herself or himself to be literally taken over or "ridden" by the god form and may interact as a deity with your ritual participants.

> Nels: *In the "Ritual to Enki, the Father" (see chapter 7), I was helped by a spirit worker, Breighton, who had already worked with Enki in the past. He was willing to attempt a sustained invocation during the ritual in order to speak personally to most participants as Enki. In preparation he offered devotion and prayers for several weeks to enhance his relationship. During the course of the ritual, whenever his god connection started to wane, I would pause the interaction, offer Enki's favorite scent (copal incense), and asperge the feet of all the men around the circle with water sprinkled from a leafy branch. This allowed Breighton to maintain his invocation for nearly an hour.*

Evocation is to "call forth," the summoning of the spiritual essence of a god form. The deity's words or actions are expressed through the spirit worker, who remains fully aware of themselves. The term "aspecting" is also used to describe the manifestation of a particular characteristic or god form in this manner. People disagree about what actually happens during aspecting. Some see this as having the deity enter into them. It may be tapping into their own divine relationship. It is usually observed as a heightened trance state.

Asked to design the annual ritual opening of the drum area at Pagan Spirit Gathering, we chose a deity pair we were familiar with and had worked with in the past, Inanna and Dumuzi. At about the middle of the ritual, we were called to enter as god and goddess. We had planned an interaction where Dumuzi unsuccessfully courted Inanna with strawberries in the South, and then whipped cream was added in the West. In the North came bread, and finally, in the East, honey was added. The honey finally won Inanna's heart and they kissed. They then proceeded to give honeyed bread and strawberries and cream to the several hundred energy-raising, dancing participants. Evocation worked here in part because of our past relationship with the deities, the time in private to evoke their essences before entering, and a basic script to follow without words. Even though we have little real acting ability, the evocation of these familiar deities was perceived as powerful and authentic.

When invocation and evocation are successful, the authenticity of the experience is immediately felt by participants. These two methods are differentiated because they provide distinctly different experiences. Because deity is allowed to take possession of a spirit worker in invocation, we have to let go of any scripting for the ritual. An invoked deity will do, speak, and act as it pleases, and the connection can be lost at any time. That possible interruption needs to be incorporated into the planning.

During invocation, a deity might speak either to participants individually or to the group as a whole. The deity might act out a story or express emotions relating to your ritual purpose. Some specific devotional rituals are solely designed to provide a community with deity interaction.

During evocation, the spirit worker will have awareness and more control over what happens. The actual "summoning" uses words that are designed to resonate with the human subconscious, and speak specifically to the deity who is being called forth. Once the evocation is successful, the spirit worker can offer the essence of what the deity intends to communicate.

Bacchus, Dionysus, or Pan might be chosen for a celebration. Diana and Inanna have "warrior" and strength associations. Pele is the fire goddess of volcanoes of the Hawaiian islands and would work to support transformation themes. A devotional ritual can accommodate more education for your participants about the deity's nature before aspecting takes place. Deities who are commonly known and resonate with the ritual purpose are most often the best choice.

You should only attempt either of these methods with the help of a skilled spirit worker. These techniques are only appropriate within a sacred context, where spiritual possession will be accepted. Both of these interactions are more likely to be welcomed in a community where they have been experienced before.

Interactive Iconography

Ritual uses the language of symbols, metaphor, and allegory. Say your ritual theme has transformation as its goal. Plant a seed, crack an egg, pour water, pop a balloon—all these actions demonstrate change. You can show your participants what transformation looks like, or you can make it possible for them to use their hands and do it themselves. Doing trumps observing every time. When each person is given the opportunity to effect that change, on a subliminal level they know for a fact they have that power. When we experience this in ritual, it integrates the memory of transformation and our capacity to create change.

Your ritual intent can be symbolically translated by using one well-designed prop as a focal point. How could this be added to, written upon, or somehow touched by everyone? Whether a shrine, special gateway, or the main prop focal point, you can provide writing or drawing tools, strips of cloth, ribbons, string, stick matches, feathers, or almost any item to decorate it. For devotional rituals you might include an opportunity for each participant to add a written prayer or symbolic addition as a demonstration of connection to the deity. Allowing participants to add their own pieces to a ritual element gives them a sense of ownership of the ritual intent. Touching something forges an energetic connection to it. This connection endures long after that direct touch is severed.

. . . .

Example

In the ritual "They Will Remain," we used two life-sized pieces of clear acrylic framed in wood with stake legs supporting them to make two low tables. Participants used carved potato printing blocks and paint to stamp on the sheets. (We also had a bucket of water and towel if they made a mess of their hands.) We had precut the adhesive film that Plexiglas comes with into male and female outlines and removed that portion of the film. The potato block designs had specific patterns on them (flowers for Flora, seed and leaf images for Jack in the Green). Later in the ritual we removed the film outside the figure outlines, revealing the male and female images fully painted. They were then mounted vertically on poles to form a gateway to exit the ritual. This echoed the two earthy deity figures who were invoked and called into the circle, and then exited the ritual.

Gifts

A great way to embed the intent of your ritual into your participants' consciousness is to have them be given, make, or in some way personalize an individual token. If this is something they then take home, it will become a direct reminder of the experience. We are handed items daily that have no meaning, which we toss as soon as we see a trash can. How do we make this item memorable? If we incorporate a symbolic focal point into the ritual, the gift can be a lasting representation of this larger image. If you create a tree to represent your community as a focal point, you might use a small disk of wood with a tree image burned into it as a gift. Many ritual intents include a reference to beginning a new path based on the ritual experience. Cement this intent within participants by giving them a seed. Use an acorn, sunflower seed, pomegranate, popcorn, or any garden seed as a gift to remember their new start. Add writing, carving, a container (such as a bag), or color marking to make it more personal and connected with the ritual moment.

....

Example

You may have created a prop to interact with, add to, or decorate. Design it so later in the ritual a piece of it can be disconnected and given to each participant as a gift. You might use a plant or tree prop (replicated, handcrafted, created in ritual, or artificial) to interact with. Later, remove the leaves and present them as a gift of remembrance or symbolic reference to participants.

A gift is something given. Seems simple enough, but to be effective, how it is given is critical. It could be something each person receives upon entering the ritual space. This works well if participants don't need their hands free. Will they be clapping? Joining hands? In that case, a gift that is worn, like a bead strung on a cord, works better. A gift necklace is in contact with the person and their awareness through the balance of the ritual. We have offered clay bead necklaces for many years, which are made in advance using press molds (see chapter 12). The first ritual then includes the giving of this gift to every participant, to be worn throughout the coming week. We have found people wearing and treasuring this gift years later, as a reminder of that week's experience.

Rather than simply putting your gifts on a table at the entrance or exit of your ritual, have a person actually bestow them. The giver can imbue them with relevance through their manner. If they are handed out like a high school worksheet, they will be received with that much significance! A common stone can be a gift, and the right presenter with dramatic technique can make it seem like the most important, magical stone ever received. Personal interaction such as intentional eye contact, a special touch, an anointment, and even a kiss can become the "wrapping" that binds the ritual purpose to each participant's awareness.

If the gifts you provide are all unique, a random draw by participants works to make them feel the one they receive is meant for them. If you use this method, make them draw without seeing the individual items, from a bag or a raised basket or bowl. If you allow participants a visual choice, invariably some will want to take a minute to dig through every gift and find their preference, slowing the process.

Having participants pass or give gifts to each other can be powerfully bonding. This is a technique suitable to support a fellowship ritual. Modeling by ritual team members is a good way to use this technique. There is a risk in that process: the community-building aspect of participant giving can easily be diluted by a casual or insincere approach. Often in producing community ritual, the role of passing something out is assigned moments before the ritual. Communicating the importance of the manner in which every role is expressed is necessary, and particularly in giving of gifts.

Written affirmations can be a gift your people give to another participant. Writing materials for a large group take a lot of management and planning to successfully work without bogging down a ritual. To streamline the process, offer another activity at the same time, maybe a song or chant. We all think our handwriting is perfectly legible, but it often isn't to others—something to consider if this is to serve as a gift.

Before closing the ritual, somehow connect the token to the emotions that the ritual has generated. Once linked to the subconscious, every encounter with this symbol will help them re-experience it. We do this by "energizing" the gift to anchor these feelings to take home and use in individual transformation. Have participants pass their gift through a small flame, dance with it, anoint it with holy water, or toss it in the air! This group act, charging a gift with intention, can easily become the ecstatic portion of your ritual.

In "Ritual to Enki, the Father," a pierced clay disk with a male figure embossed on the surface was incorporated into the two scrolls forming the "ME" (laws of the gods of Sumer) prop. Seventy-five disks were laid on edge and then surrounded with metal screen and paper to create the scroll-tube look. During the energy-raising portion of the ritual, the ME was added to the fire, and after completion, the discs were unwrapped and given with a cord by Enki to each participant as the ritual ended. This connection of the group energy, deity, and the gift cemented its importance to the ritual experience.

Charging, or energizing, can be a mystical, metaphysical act, harnessing and focusing the will upon a ritual symbol. This is great if you work with a community that has a common experience and belief in that power to energize by will alone. Energizing is also a simple and verifiable experience. Take a room of quiet people and get them all clapping, and the energy of the room is completely different. It has changed from passive to active.

A brief period where ritual participants hold, look at, or engage a ritual symbol or gift is appropriate to establish your focus. For them to really take it all home, most people need something a little more active! Write a chant or find a suitable song to help integrate the gift with your intention. The more creative you are at integrating and making connected and relevant this energizing of the gift with your ritual intent, the more successful and memorable it will be.

Altars and Shrines

In a religious context, an altar is any structure upon which offerings, devotion, or sacrifices are made. Permanent altars are usually found at shrines, temples, churches, and other places of worship. In community ritual, altars can have a very practical purpose: a place to keep whatever physical tools, props, or devices you will need to have access to. There is no requirement for a ritual to have an altar. Many rituals have other focal points, and the tools that team members need can be carried in pockets, bags, or baskets.

Ganesha shrine.

When you do include one or more altars or shrines, you must recognize them as a focal point for participants. If you acknowledge the four cardinal directions as forces to aid or protect you, an altar, shrine, banner, person, or some physical object is useful to mark them. Each direction has hundreds of natural and symbolic correspondences that can be incorporated. Because of their religious origins, the altar itself and the area around it are seen as endowed with greater holiness. It is a mistake to place an altar without care or attention to detail. For whatever the purpose, it becomes a focal point, and if it appears unimportant to you, that casual concern will get transferred to an assessment of the balance of your ceremony.

Altars do not have to be elaborate to be beautiful additions and support your ritual theme. A handsome cloth can cover a rusty TV tray table or an overturned storage tote and provide just what you need with thoughtful and well-placed decoration. In a ritual working with the nature of the year's 13 moons, we divided the large group into 13 smaller groups to have a personal experience with each moon. Most moons had their own interactive altar, and on the main central table all that was present was a large-scale hourglass prop, used to both regulate smaller groups moving from station to station and to symbolize the passage of time.

However you include an altar, treat it as a sacred focal point. A powerful altar is a representation, a microcosm, of your ritual intent. Every item present should be carefully chosen and placed so when the participant looks at the altar, they can understand the reason behind it.

Thor shrine.

A shrine demonstrates devotion to a deity, ancestor, hero, or similar figure of awe and respect. Since it is specifically designed to honor, it is usually larger and more involved than an altar. A shrine should be well thought out to include every aspect and sensory addition that the focus of the shrine would want. Shrines furnish a place or method for visitors to express their devotion. Classic offerings you might provide are lit candles or incense, food, water, wine, flowers, coins, a bell to ring, or a guest book for any personal mark or writing. You could have participants each create a small prayer or message to add. This can be written on paper, cloth, or bark or offered for burning to a fire or candle.

Shrines serve as a tangible form to express what might be happening inside us. A community can, through this act of creation, move past strong emotion, especially to help heal the pain of loss or tragedy. Shrines help us remember, reflect, grieve, and honor the losses that individually overwhelm us in the moment. Making and adding to a shrine can itself be a ritual. Shrine building lends itself to the spontaneous creativity of many hands. Often all that is needed is a pile of supplies, a basic support structure, and permission to play, and an incredible sacred space will appear!

Keep in mind that both altars and shrines are tools. They're meant to help you, not become an obligation or burden to your team or the ritual. In most community rituals, they are set up before and taken down after the ceremony. In those cases where you have a secure outside or reserved inside location, structuring in participant access to a shrine or altar can be a great way to create engagement before you even gather, and long after the ritual ends. You might design an element of a shrine to be preserved and portable and arrange further public display and interaction with it. The pentacle constructed of brooms during the Veterans' Pentacle Rights Ritual (described in chapter 4) was displayed as an interactive shrine in several locations over the next year. Visitors added their own ribbons as offerings and prayers.

Ritual Props and Decorations

The ritual experience is magic. When community ritual helps people view and experience themselves and others in a different way, it opens a doorway for participants to transform themselves. This can be in deeply profound and personally immediate ways, or in perceiving themselves as truly spiritual beings, alive within a spiritual world.

Cernunnos shrine.

A ritual prop (from the theatrical term "property") is an object used by ritualistas to further the intent or experience of a ritual. Your props should also be part of your site decoration, but not all decorations are props. The difference between a decoration and a prop is use. If the item is not touched or symbolically interacted with by a ritual performer or participant, it is a ritual decoration. Ritual decorations will support your ritual through one of our perceptual senses. A shrine that is only a visible support for ritual is a decoration; when participants make an offering or somehow energize, engage, or contribute to it, it becomes a prop.

Props and decorations are not essential, but they can be really useful. Unlike a repeated theatrical performance, community rituals are usually a one-time event, and often props are destroyed or have only this one use. Why then would we go to the effort and expense to add these to a community ritual? The answer is within the nature of the ritual experience.

Many of us have been raised with skepticism. We have been disillusioned by our experiences and may come to a group ritual with the attitude of "I'll believe it when I see it" rather than from the mystical place of "When I believe it, I will see it." That is to be expected. Props and decorations bring to ritual a sensory experience that can reinforce our unspoken beliefs, so we begin to see it with our own new eyes.

Ritual props can help us suspend disbelief, shedding the common perceptions, laws of nature, and foundational truths we live by. We can then be open to magical and mystical perception of our world and ourselves. The power of symbology to engage the subconscious can be integrated into most props and decorations. One of the best gateways we have seen in an outdoor ritual was also one of the simplest. It was a 7-foot-tall vulva-shaped doorway made of bent saplings tied together at the top. Hanging from it was a child's globe of the earth, like a clitoris. It was used for a ritual to connect with the essence of Gaea, and made a perfect symbolic entryway for this ritual, literally and symbolically entering the womb of Mother Earth.

How you integrate props and decorations into your community ritual is often limited by time, energy, funding, and personal commitment. Since we rarely have unlimited amounts of any of these, we need to prioritize which areas of our ritual will benefit most from the support props offer. Look again to your ritual intent: what did you come up with?

For a celebratory intent, you may want decorations that are visually exciting. Design a gateway adorned with flowers or bright colors, a seasonally decorated altar, or a boundary laid in pebbles, sunflower seeds, or cornmeal. Oversized, exaggerated ritual tools or costumes make a statement seen by all. Display a robust feast to create a feeling of bounty or celebration.

For a rite of passage, focus prop design on the transformation. Use a physically or visually challenging entry. Set up a pictorial history altar documenting the passage. Design a prop that changes shape or viewpoint during the ritual, something that transforms itself to echo the particular nature of the rite being celebrated. The symbolism of the seed or an egg can be easily adapted into functional props in a rite of passage.

For guided meditation rituals, auditory props can be really effective. Create a mini-waterfall, add nature sound effects (crickets, frogs, birds, rustling, or wind noises), provide a relaxing atmosphere, or offer comforting smells. A labyrinth pattern of movement laid on the ground either as a pure walking experience or with altars or other personal props along the route is effective in these types of rituals. One of the best gateways we have used is the gong gate.[29] This is a pair of decorated 2-inch PVC supports slid over fence posts. Hung from these is a series of lengths of metal pipe cut to sound a pentatonic scale. Participants walk through the gate as these gongs are played with soft mallets, surrounding them with sound.

Rituals that deal with highly emotional or confrontational internal themes can incorporate the visually ominous, calling up cultural archetypes and stereotypical images to stimulate emotions. Imagine what death, sorrow, fear, pure joy, or elation might look or sound or feel like. Classic images of death are skulls, bones, and decomposition. Imagine an improvised tent that isolates participants for a moment in complete blackness. What is it like to emerge from the darkness of the womb to the light of day? How can you symbolically recreate that transition?

---

29   Designed by Hank Knaepple, for Harmony Tribe, Inc.

The gong gate.

For a sense of mystery, we have used characters dressed in black leotards with outlines of white bones traced upon them. We decorated their faces and gave them black gloves with small round mirrors hot-glued to the palms. These characters surrounded the ritual area, dancing up to participants and offering their reflection. Well-designed props need no explanation. Their symbolism should be obvious or their mystery part of the intended design.

Illusion

Nels: *As a prop-building enthusiast, my greatest joy is designing props that create a magical space for personal growth or transformation. I have come up with amazing props to "launch" people into a state where the intent of the ritual can take place. There are illusions from the stage, the circus, and even chemistry class to draw from.*

Classic magic-show illusions can be adapted to the ritual stage. Imagine receiving a gift in ritual that magically appeared from behind your ear. Sleight of hand is difficult for an amateur to master, and these skills need to be convincing if you attempt to use them! Mirrored illusions, magical appearances, and mid-air suspension of items require planning and the audience's directional viewpoint. The physical transformation of one prop into another makes a powerful statement of change. Flash paper that seemingly burns from nowhere and disappears may be an old trick, but it still works. We used a "true mirror" in ritual to allow participants to see how they really look to others. It is a device with multiple mirrors that shows you your image exactly as others view you, rather than a reversed reflection.

The elemental forces of nature, displayed in an innovative way, can help generate within the participant that suspension of disbelief which is essential to wonderment. Many of your most effective prop designs can be inspired by the amazing properties of the physical world. Remember that foaming volcano you built in elementary school? How about two cans and a waxed string stretched between them as a telephone? The arc of static electricity moving between two poles. The echo of voices in a large canyon. Magnetism can make items move or form shapes without any apparent cause. Even the simple explosion of popcorn can be fascinating! Chemical additions to flames can magically add unique colors. The myriad forms of combustion and fire trickery, when in an outside space and safely presented, touch some of our deepest fascinations.

It is critical to design prop interactions to flow smoothly and quickly with large groups of participants. You may need multiple paths so several people can have an individual experience at the same time. Thorough testing and rehearsal are needed to ensure that all props work and are safe, the timing is well understood, and the actions will not slow the whole ritual down.

As with every part of ritual, effectively executed is best. Fantastic props or illusions that don't quite make it have the opposite effect on the mind. It is easy to get distracted and over-emphasize props in your efforts; they are just so much fun! Keep their use in perspective with the overall flow of your ritual. One really well-designed prop is more memorable than five that drain your effort and don't quite fit the ritual or move participants to better experiencing your intent. Sometimes your prop ideas are all so exciting, you are tempted to include them all. Resist, and save some to adapt for your next ritual!

Ritual: They Will Remain

· · · · · · · · · · · · · · · · ·

Location: Sacred Harvest Festival, 2006
© Judith Olson Linde and Nels Linde

Ritual context

This ritual uses a standard opening which we have often used for a series of rituals with a unifying theme. The standard ritual opening supports the overall theme but is repeated in each of an arc of rituals. This has the effect of creating a unifying element between the rituals and evoking the feelings experienced in the previous one. It also has the advantage of allowing us to put increased effort into refining one good opening, and then having it ready for the next ritual in advance. It allows participants to focus on the rite knowing already how the space is made sacred. The entire series of rituals was written in rhyme. This ritual is a great example of participants creating an iconic prop, connecting it with live deity figures, and seeing the prop transformed during the ritual.

Ritual intent

Reawaken our awareness of the forces of the natural world. Where do we fit, what do we face? Male and female, an inspiration, gift, and magical resource. Join in, lend a hand, build a shared vision.

Ritual description

Maybe not within our lifetimes, but quite possibly in those of our children, the "beauty of the green earth" may have been paved over completely, the "white moon amongst the stars" might be just another venue for advertisement, the "mystery of the waters" might be how we can find any clean enough to drink, and the "secret desire within the heart" may be to get back to the way it was. In my despair I try to keep perspective, I try to remember that the forces of nature are beyond our control, that only life can generate more of itself, and that without constant tending, the trappings of civilization would be swallowed up by Gaia's regenerative force. This ritual is about being touched by the archetypes of that force, and a reminder that "When we are gone, they will remain."

Ritual setup and supplies

Two 2 x 6-foot panels of acrylic, with the clear protective sheet cut out to form a resist mask of silhouetted figures with arms raised (masculine on one panel, feminine on the other). Each panel has a wooden 2 x 2-inch grooved edge as a stiffener. They have two pipe flanges on each edge for later vertical mounting. Each panel is supported on the north side of the ritual circle with 1 x 4 x 24-inch notched stake supports, three on each side. Panels are parallel and about five feet apart. The panels are designed to be removed and then inserted and held vertically in metal rod stakes forming an exit gateway. Several bottles of craft paint: pastel pinks, blues, and white for Flora; greens and browns for Jack Green. Several stamps cut from potatoes: for the Jack designs; acorn, leaf, lizard, handprints; for the Flora designs; spiral, dragonfly, butterfly, flower bud. Metal pie pans for paints. Four elemental altars on the circle, with supplies for the altar experiences: North, a small stone; East, a bowl of fairy dust glitter; South, a tiki torch; West, a bowl of water, a sponge, and a stone with a hole through it. Each altar team set a division, a small separation, in front of their altar to allow a bit of privacy for each festivant's passing. Cots for the deities to lie in state. Acorns and flower petals.

Diagram key

- [R] = Regulator/Greeter (1)
- [G] = Guardians (2)
- [E] = Elemental experiences (4)
- [W] = Whisperers (4)
- [P] = Printing helpers (8)
- [B] = Wash bucket
- [M] = Mounting rebar poles for exit gateway (4)

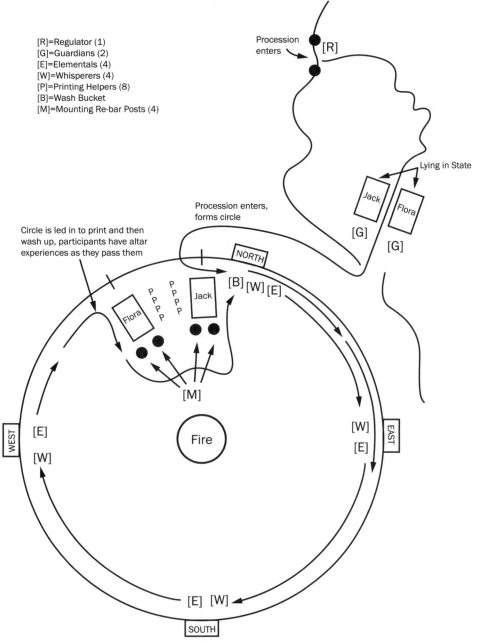

[R]=Regulator (1)
[G]=Guardians (2)
[E]=Elementals (4)
[W]=Whisperers (4)
[P]=Printing Helpers (8)
[B]=Wash Bucket
[M]=Mounting Re-bar Posts (4)

Procession enters

[R]

Lying in State

Jack

Flora

[G]

[G]

Procession enters,
forms circle

Circle is led in to print and then
wash up, participants have altar
experiences as they pass them

NORTH

[B] [W] [E]

Jack

P P
P P
P P
P P

Flora

[M]

WEST

[E]

[W]

Fire

[W]

[E]

EAST

[E] [W]

SOUTH

Layout of the They Will Remain Ritual.

Team members

Regulator/Greeter; Flower Face; Jack Green; four elementals with potato fork (N), broom (E), scythe (W), and staff (S); two guardians; Ritualista 1 and Ritualista 2; eight block-printing helpers; hand washer; choir. (Four altar experience helpers were recruited in ritual.)

Ritual script

The festivants processed to a woods path where each was greeted by the Regulator and warned: *"Touch not what you see on the journey."* Festivants walked the wooded path that led to the East ritual area gate.

Flower Face and Jack Green were the god and goddess of the wood. They were in costume, painted, and covered in flower petals and acorns, and were lying in state on cots along the path. Guardians were in place protecting them.

Standard folk ritual opening

The festivants entered through the gate and formed a circle. Four elemental team members wandered around outside the circle as if no one was there. They carried a potato fork (N), broom (E), scythe (W), and staff (S). Entering the circle, they took their respective places in front of altars, facing into the circle. Ritualista 1 entered the circle with a rhyming chant:

> *"In a clearing on a moonlit [cloudy, twilight] night, illuminated by firelight,*
> *Assembled here we circle round, to see what blessings can be found*
> *In the company of other folk, and what magic we may invoke."*

Ritualista 1 paused at each direction and signaled with a tambourine, saying a simple rhyming call:

(East) *"Where the moon rises and dawn breaks the day, on scented breeze newness wafting our way."*

(South) *"To the South lie the sands of fire, choices made, the loin's desire."*

(West) *"In the West the misty shore, rainbow's end, the ocean's roar."*

(North) *"To the North the mountains of stone, caves of my ancestors, antler, bone."*

As Ritualista 1 mentioned each direction, each elemental team member turned to their altar, lit their candle, blew a kiss to their direction, and then turned back toward the inside of the circle. Rotating slowly in the center with her arms out, the Ritualista continued:

"The Lord and the Lady are present here too, and spirit, as always, within each of you."

Ritualista 1 walked the circle, saying:
"What they call progress in our day is watching nature slip away.
As every hour more acres fall to industry and shopping mall.
Whooping crane flies the open field, a vision of wonder to me revealed.
Her habitat shrinks every day. How long can it go on this way?
All life is programmed to succeed, from man to whale to tiny weed.
And if unbalanced would indeed replace all other life on earth,
Man's vanity is Gaia's curse."

Ritualista 2 continued:
"Yes, but Gaia lives, and rules this land with balance, wisdom, and steady hand.
The blight for us seems evermore; for her it's just an open sore.
Her fecund power fills the night with verdant bounty and savage might.
When we have need she shares with us. Now, take her seed and plant it thus."

Ritualista 2 demonstrated printing the panels with the potato stamps and paint, and then, beginning just left of North, the participants were led into the circle to paint/print the panels. Quiet percussion accompanied this work.

Prop activity detail

The two panels were arranged in parallel between the gate and the central fire. Between the panels were eight assistants, paired up back to back, four to each panel. They each held a pie pan with a different color paint and a potato stamp. The line of participants, drawn from the circle at the North, moved south toward the central fire outside the Flower Face panel, and then back north along the outside of the Jack Green panel. Participants added one or more prints for each panel. If a participant was too enthusiastic or meticulous, they were told, *"Less is more."*

The festivants then all proceeded around the circle deosil (clockwise) and at each altar had an encounter. After completing their printing, the participants continued in a line to the experience at the Earth altar. The Earth team member took each person one by one and whispered an elemental wisdom riddle:

Earth: *"Some things you cannot change, you can only feel."*

The Earth helper (spontaneously recruited from the circle) held the participant's foot and dropped a small stone on it. The participant was sent deosil to the next altar, and the Earth team member took the next in line from the completed printing circuit.

Air: *"Some are here for a moment and then gone."* The Air helper put fairy dust glitter on the participant's hand and blew it away (not toward their eyes).

Fire: *"Some are bright and affect us forever."* The Fire helper took the participant's hand and waved it through the tiki torch flame (high enough to be warm but not burn).

Water: *"Some move through us without us knowing."* The Water helper poured water from a wet sponge through the hole in the stone onto the participant's hand.

The festivants rotated around the circle until they passed the four altars, then continued around again, following the line of festivants until all had completed the four altar and printing experiences as they passed them, and were back in their original positions around the circle.

Ritualista 2: *"We invoke and call Flora and Jack in the Green to come to us from their wooded home."*

Ritualista 2 led all in chant as Flora appeared out of the forest and entered the circle: *"Flora, green lady, gold berry, petal maid, rise again ... come to us."*

At the end of the chant, Ritualista 1 said: *"She blossoms from primordial mud. First seed, then root, then stem and bud."*

He then began the chant to Jack Green: *"Woods wise, green man, horned one, Jack, rise again ... come to us."*

Jack Green appeared from the forest and entered the circle. The chant ended and Ritualista 1 said: *"Honey of love, from the dark he is born, to rise with the sap and sleep with the corn."*

Flora and Jack Green went round the circle with baskets and handed out flower petals and acorns, respectively, to add to each person's "folk magic" pouch (received as a gift in an earlier ritual). While this was happening, the ritual guardians raised and moved the panels to their vertical exit gate positions, insert the mounting rods through the panel brackets and into the earth. The print helpers removed the panel-printing support stakes and all printing and washing supplies.

These activities were accompanied by the song "When We Are Gone," by Anne Hill and Starhawk. When the gifts were all given, the song ended, and Flora and Jack Green together removed the masks from the panels to reveal the male and female silhouettes, and then stood facing each other. For the ritual exit, they created an archway by touching hands as children do in the game "London Bridge Is Falling Down."

Ritualista 1: *"We've gathered in the moonlight, in our home under the trees.*
We cast our sacred circle and shared the mysteries.
Remember the healing of the fire, the trust of tribe and kin.
Remember the touch of nature's core, the power you have within."

Ritualista 1 took up a combined basket of acorns and flowers and walked once around the circle, tossing a few at each altar as the candles were extinguished by the elemental team members and they blew a kiss to each direction. She ended at the North and exited through the gateway created by Flora and Jack Green, followed by the elemental team members, who aided in the festivants' departure from the circle.

TEN

·········

Raising Energy

It is the last night of a week of intense community ritual at a festival. Following a winding 20-foot snake puppet, the procession has led us along the Serpent Path on the Tree of Life. As we passed by, tarot trump characters spoke in mystic tongues. Our path ended at Kether, marked in the twilight by a central blazing fire. The Fool has led 250 excited, dancing souls here, singing, "We are your people, join us!" I wait in the South, dressed in my flame costume, my sword growing heavy as I mentally run through my lines of farewell as the King of Wands. The crescendo must be over, I think, as the energy begins to wane. No, they are still moving, still dancing, and now a lone singer overlays, "Follow, follow your heart! Deep in your heart, you know the way home." The group chorus and drumming picks it up, and the volume and energy soar yet again. My heart is pounding with adrenaline and tears of joy come as this sacred moment stretches on. My people need this. I can wait.

PATH OF THE SERPENT RITUAL

You have brought your community into sacred space, opened their minds and hearts, given them a sensory experience to move them toward embracing your ritual intent. Now what? Similar to bonding your ritual community together with an attunement, at this stage of the ritual you will want to provide a time, structure, and action to unify around fulfilling your ritual purpose.

You can again pull out your ritual toolbox and use the senses to center around an activity to summarize and bring focus to that purpose. This is the critical time where you either move your community to embrace your intent or let them leave feeling mildly entertained. Use your written intent as your guide. Read it out loud. Have you educated, celebrated, created fellowship, marked a transition, offered an act of devotion? Before you move to clearly empower and accomplish your purpose, verify you are still on track!

As ritualistas, somewhere between the first time we discuss a ritual theme or intention and our planning stages, we have an inspiration that we just know will be effective and that we settle on as the "hook." This is the action, focus, experience, or environment we are creating that we see as capturing the essence of the intention. During the ritual, the details of our gathering activity, procession, entry, and making a safe and sacred ritual space directly prepare us for the hook experience. Often the hook involves a sensory engagement of the subconscious integrated with one of the experiences of awe and wonder from chapter 10. We are vague here defining a hook because the solutions to ritual are limitless; as soon as we make rules to define what we can do, an idea appears that breaks them all!

Empowering and Energizing

In ritual, people move from a sense of wonder to the optimism that together they can make something happen, either for each person, for their community, or for their environment. In whatever manner you have brought your community to this point, you need to design something to create a feeling of empowerment. Empowerment is a tool to help your community internalize the intention of your ritual. We cannot integrate what we experience within ritual unless we have permission to make it our own, to take possession of the sacred and shared purpose we now have, to *take the sacred back*.

The attractive force of community ritual is found in action, the hook that embodies the intention and the purpose. This is the empowerment that is at the heart of your ritual. Any activity that participants take control of, such as a themed song led by strong voices, will accomplish this. The lyrics may inspire people to add in harmonies or transform it into a multi-part round. Once you get participants invested in it, they will feel and build upon the sense of empowerment. If you are in a place where it is possible to have a large bonfire, building it, lighting it, adding tokens or prayers to it, and dancing around it are all empowering activities.

Look at all the symbolism you are using and find an activity that participants can take ownership of with their energy. You need this to be integrally linked to your purpose. In celebratory rituals, it is an appropriate moment for a symbolic act related to the nature of the experience, celebration, or rite of passage.

Many activities can promote a feeling of empowerment. Creating a situation where participants must rely on their communication to accomplish a goal in ritual is empowering. Any trust-building action that demonstrates group reliance on each other or calls on them to act in strength and unity works. So will achieving what seems impossible until the group focuses mind and muscles upon it, such as moving or building with boulders, logs, or earth.

Some of our best ritual hooks have combined and integrated a prop that participants have contributed to and a song, chant, and dance to empower them. In the Theseus myth–based ritual (see chapter 3), after the battle between Theseus and the Minotaur moved out of sight, an empowering song of release was started. As the energized song reached its peak, the head and mane of the Minotaur were brought back and mounted on a pole next to the central fire. The mane was covered with the shadow traits participants had added earlier, and as it was added to the fire, the song (and now dance) reached a crescendo with participants moving toward the fire. This was a perfect empowerment for participants to release unwanted shadows from their psyche.

In another ritual, a group chant was used to call Flora and Jack in the Green to enter the sacred space from their wooded home. When they appeared each in turn, the empowerment felt was palpable. One of our most effective empowerments was also the most whimsical and fun. At the conclusion of the Stone Soup ritual (see chapter 12), participants were given popcorn kernels with the question: *"What seeds can you plant to ensure our community grows?"* They added these to a 4-foot beeswax poppet drilled with hundreds of holes to receive their "seeds." After being smothered in Crisco, this poppet (supported by a sheetmetal circle) was laid over a large hot fire with these words: *"With the sweetness of magic, with fire transformed, join power and hands! Make our image reborn!"* As the empowering song and dance surrounded the fire, a fountain of popcorn came shooting out of the fire.

Creating Ecstasy

The excitement of celebration expressed as a unified group is an uncommon occurrence. Imagine if you could help facilitate a ceremony where a large group of people could directly feel what the ecstasy of an "ever-expanding universe" was like? Now translate that feeling into a shared sense of increased well-being. The group experience of things much larger than ourselves, an intimate shared feeling of empowerment, creates a sense of elation and excitement—of ecstasy. The need to experience ecstasy has been diverted in modern society to expression through taking drugs, video gaming, gambling, sex, and most any thrill-seeking, adrenaline-producing activity. Community ritual can provide a safe and empowering place to reclaim this basic human drive as a positive force.

An ecstatic experience is not necessary for a successful ritual. You can plan for an ecstatic energy raising and never quite get there. You can plan for an empowerment activity that shifts into the ecstatic without intending to do so. In either case you need to be prepared to recognize when ecstasy has arrived, and be able to bring it to a climax and back to earth.

The ecstatic experience provides an altered state of consciousness. Participants feel a diminished sense of self and an increased unity with the group mind and, extended further, a part of the cosmos. The creation of ecstasy in ritual is almost like mass hypnosis. Once a few individuals cross over to the ecstatic state of mind, it becomes infectious and spreads rapidly through your ritual participants. Modeling by your team can be very effective for this, in effect giving permission to those who may be too inhibited to go there on their own. Your team, however, also needs to maintain a connection to their role as ritual leaders.

The natural curve in which this rising feeling of ecstasy takes place is sometimes called "energy raising." It builds through a group process, reaches a crescendo, and helps people internalize the experience as it dissipates. We sometimes call this the "all dance" portion of a ritual, because movement is such an effective tool for experiencing it. Any of the ritual tools you are gathering can be creatively applied to accomplish this. The goal is to find and integrate the one energy-raising activity most effective for your particular ritual. A powerful group experience can fall completely flat if it doesn't clearly bind the feeling of euphoria and connection to the group and the ritual intention. The words of a song or chant, the tempo of music, percussion, or dance, the visual or sensory experience presented as you guide this ecstatic moment, will all define how the ritual is remembered.

An ecstatic experience can be included in many types of rituals as an energy-raising technique to help empower your ritual purpose. This is often the most difficult point in a ritual. If the ritual has led participants to a feeling of safety and emotional readiness, the transition to "let go" and rise to an energetic crescendo can hardly be stopped. When the ritual has failed to create that intimacy, your efforts can now fall flat! A misinterpretation of a group's affirmative desire and predisposition for ecstasy will prevent it from happening.

The ecstatic experience is one of the expressed ritual purposes of a devotional. Your whole ritual can be aimed at creating ecstasy to commune with named god forms or deities, or to feel connected with an aspect of the sacred nature of the universe. In these rituals, every action is developed and planned to support the ecstatic intention. For this to take place, you need several things: a group of participants ready to connect, a ritual designed to elaborate the characteristics and nature of the god form, and an ecstatic experience relevant to it.

Guiding the Crescendo

To take the energy generated within a community ritual and transform it and apply it for the best overall result is not an easy task. We've already discussed the use of a physical object or prop that is symbolically charged with the intent of the ritual and then transforms. Lighting a central fire, adding an offering to a fire, or changing lighting conditions can be a great focal point to aid participants at this time.

The plan for the group ecstatic experience can go well, but without a focus at the crescendo, and a gentle, planned method for returning to a normal state, we create a bumpy ride. The team or team leader needs to be perceived as trustworthy to manage this energetic experience. A mixed community of participants is contributing their energy from many levels of focus and understanding. Everyone needs to feel like their contributions are added to a conduit with direction, unifying the focus at its peak, and bringing us all back down.

A team-modeled act of will, gesture, or indication of thanks can signal the peak has been reached and aid people to come back from the ecstatic experience. This signal should be clearly communicated and understood by your ritual team. As exciting as this time is, your team needs to remain focused and aware of the peak being approached. Hand and arm waving or body movements can be coordinated to signify the energy peak. Sound, such as a gong or chime, is also effective as a signal. At the energy peak you can increase speed or tempo or the pitch of any vocalization you are using.

People attend community ritual with the expectation that anything they contribute energetically is used to further the intention. The best way to demonstrate that is by having a concrete focus during energy raising. Participants may not know each other or the team. By offering a prop or symbol to energize, we take away any trust issues inhibiting people. There are always people in the group who sense and direct stray energy, as your team should. As long as people feel empowered and trust their contributions are used, they will add their energy.

Ritual Integration

It is perfect! You have a whole community sincerely connected, joyfully holding hands. They might be clapping or singing with feeling, or walking, stomping, or dancing with wild abandon. The energy has peaked and you have empowered the ritual intent. Now let's just bring it all home. How do you bring your group back to earth with a feeling of accomplishment?

Once you have clearly peaked the ecstatic experience, a smooth movement to a pause for a time of calm is called for. As hard as it is to guide a community to reach for an ecstatic or energetic peak, it is just as hard to settle your community so what has been experienced can be absorbed. We don't have to just turn off the excitement we have generated like closing a spigot. Like a pot of boiling water, we can just take it off the heat and let it simmer down to a manageable level.

Whatever method you used to raise the energy can keep going, but allow it to taper off to the point where participants begin to feel what has happened. If you used movement, the action might slow or change from moving around your ritual space to happening in place. If drums are driving the ecstatic energy, arrange ahead of time for a signal to stop. With song or chant, this can be accomplished by a change of pitch or tempo or a reduction in volume down to a whisper, or all three techniques. Your ritual team will need a cue to help guide this process smoothly and together.

Participants will sense the change, and now it is up to your team to make sure they are all on the same page and understand what has happened. The easy way is to tell everyone what they have done: "We have empowered our purpose of celebrating the arrival of spring." Here is another opportunity to use the senses to communicate and do this with a prop, banner, or small drama. Use your imagination and creativity to make a more memorable choice!

Ground the Excess

If you have really generated a sense of excitement, there still may be a wonderful but distracting buzz filling their ears. Immediately assess what your participants are feeling. You can change gears and do what is called "grounding" the excess, helping people remove any distractions from continuing on to complete the ritual. There may be people who want to keep working the intention, and you can now tactfully help stop this with team modeling.

Your ritual team can lead activities similar to what you learned in attunement, but now directed at our most consistent source of stability, the earth below our feet. Have your team model assuming a slightly exaggerated comfortable and anchored stance and taking a few deep breaths. This simple action will usually completely change the atmosphere, reducing all participants' level of distraction. If this is hard for your community to do, accompany the stance with descending hand and arm movements or sounds to really demonstrate sending energy downward. In some instances, your ritual team may actually have to kneel on the ground and lower their heads to the earth. There are plenty of other options for creating this ritual transition, and knowing your community will present the best alternative. You may not have to do anything, and people will do it all on their own.

Ritual Endings

Sometimes you will need an activity to acknowledge that the ceremony is over and prepare your audience to leave ritual space. This usually happens when participants are having too good a time to want it to end. Recognizing what you have all just shared in ritual will anchor the communal experience in their memory.

Sharing food or drink is a traditional way to acknowledge your work together. This celebration of the ritual purpose fulfilled could look like:

- Passing out bread, a cracker, a cookie, something in a bite-sized piece
- Orchestrating participants feeding each other
- Participants passing by a feast table and choosing an item
- Passing around a chalice of water, juice, wine, or spirits
- Accompanying a fire offering with appropriate words
- Offering a verbal affirmation
- Distributing a gift or ritual token

In a rite of passage, this task usually falls to the ritualista facilitating the ceremony. No matter how obvious the transition or ritual purpose, your team may need to offer something that summarizes the experience. For many communities, allowing participants to have a time of sharing together, even with a song, is enough. We don't always need to be guided!

Ending a ritual can be one of the most difficult parts to master. You have seen meetings end with the shift from a group focus to an individual one. This can be very jarring. In ritual, you are transitioning from a shared sacred experience and returning back to a world of separateness. If you don't respect that boundary in how you plan your ritual ending, you risk diminishing what just happened to your community. You can use a few well-crafted words, distinct changes in tempo, or an abrupt change in focus to help prepare this transition.

You may have called many resources to help you make this ritual experience happen. In any step along the way, if you have asked natural forces, ancestors, deities, or shared powers to aid you, formalize a way to thank them. This thank-you doesn't have to be with words. It can be demonstrated with an offering: a flower or a candle, or a libation of food or drink to a body of water, the earth, or a fire. Sometimes a bow, a curtsy, or a physical flourish will fit the occasion as a thank-you.

Sometimes it happens that the "all dance" ecstatic energy raising becomes the ritual's end, and your participants disperse gradually as they are ready. That is perfectly acceptable, but you and your team should plan on staying until the last stragglers have left. Again, if you have called spiritual forces to aid or witness your rite, acknowledging that and releasing that connection must be done, even silently, during or after the ecstatic ending.

You may find yourself in a situation like one we had early on. We were completely finished with the ritual and yet no one wanted to accept it. Ritual participants stood looking at each other in our sacred space clearly waiting for more, some sign that they *had* to be done. Being unprepared, we finally said, "Okay, the ritual is over now. Thank you for coming!" That was an important lesson for us. After the ritual critique, we came up with a better solution. Now we always plan in advance for a solid ritual ending and exit.

In a ritual exit, your team models a physical leaving or deconstructing of the sacred ritual space. This could be moving out through any gate you had entered, starting a song or chant of farewell. The physical outward procession from the ritual space offers many advantages. People leave while still in the ritual mindset, and yet many will stop just outside the gate to engage in casual conversation. Individuals who are immediately moved to offer praise or criticism of the ritual will often return with you into the ritual space as you re-enter to take props down. Either way, the exit procession has cemented the ritual's end for you before these casual interactions take place. Indoors, the ritual team can form a sort of reception line to move participants through, even if you never leave the same room.

You may have further business to attend to before people actually depart. Many communities welcome a time to announce future events. Your team may want to solicit ritual comments or invite participants to fill out a feedback form. There may be a social gathering or community feast in a different location that ties in to the community. Whatever you have to do, be sure there is a clean break and at least a short pause before any "normal" announcements or interruptions take place after the ritual. Participants will be processing their experience and most will appreciate some uninterrupted time to do that.

Team leaders should thank everyone on the team privately for their service. In offering community ritual, modesty in glorifying your team contributions is appropriate. Let participants thank your team on their own. For sponsors or benefactors, a mention in any printed material is usually enough of a thank-you.

Ritual: Path of the Serpent

·················

Location: Sacred Harvest Festival, 2008
© Judith Olson Linde and Nels Linde

Ritual context

This was a celebratory ritual after a week of exploring the Fool's Journey and the many aspects of Qabalah and tarot. A slow snake puppet led a procession of 250 participants along the magical serpent's path, winding through a 100-foot long Tree of Life. All the trump personas from the Tarot Path-Working Ritual were present, reciting from *The Book of Thoth* as the procession passed by to an energetic closing ceremony.

Ritual intent

Take an experiential journey through the Tree of Life.

Ritual description

None was provided to the festivants.

Ritual setup and supplies

A Tree of Life large-scale set was created, with Kether at the central ritual fire, and Malkuth as an entry point. Sephira symbols were placed on poles and marked with torches. Path lines were marked in ribbon on the ground. PVC pipes were dug into the ground to support the snake puppet when the carrying supports were inserted to form a standing gateway.

Team members

All the tarot trump characters. Four court card characters: King of Wands, Queen of Cups, Prince of Swords, Princess of Disks. Seven volunteers to carry the snake puppet.

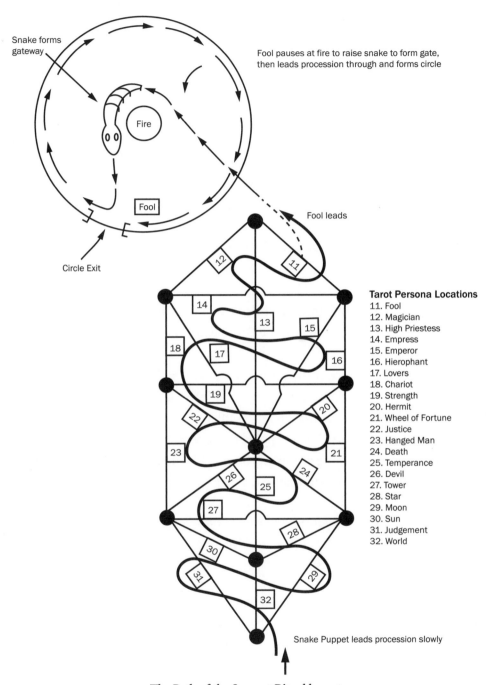

Snake forms gateway

Fool pauses at fire to raise snake to form gate, then leads procession through and forms circle

Fire

Fool

Circle Exit

Fool leads

12

11

14

13

15

18

17

16

19

20

22

23

21

26

24

25

27

28

30

31

29

32

Tarot Persona Locations
11. Fool
12. Magician
13. High Priestess
14. Empress
15. Emperor
16. Hierophant
17. Lovers
18. Chariot
19. Strength
20. Hermit
21. Wheel of Fortune
22. Justice
23. Hanged Man
24. Death
25. Temperance
26. Devil
27. Tower
28. Star
29. Moon
30. Sun
31. Judgement
32. World

Snake Puppet leads procession slowly

The Path of the Serpent Ritual layout.

Ritual script

The trump characters were at their path stations and ready. The snake-head stick puppet was mounted on two carrying poles with a couple of sections of body hoops behind. The festivants had been energized by drumming at the gathering place in preparation for the procession through the park to the Tree of Life. The snake began the slow procession along the Serpent Path.

As the participants passed them, each trump character spoke his or her *Book of Thoth* poem quote from the Tarot Path-Working Ritual (see chapter 6), describing the definition of each path. The line of festivants, led by the snake, turned left at the Fool's path. Now led by the Fool character, the serpent procession emerged at the crown. The procession headed widdershins (counterclockwise) around the central fire of the large circle area where, just past the fire, poles were in place to set up the snake head and body as a standing gateway facing the eventual exit for the ritual.

The Fool led the line of folk through the snake gateway from tail to head, and then deosil to form a large circle, to the song for the Fool's path, "The Happy Wanderer," by Florenz Friedrich Sigismund.

All sang along, as the festivants continued into the circle. The snake puppet was now laid upon the ground, its carrying poles lowered into pipes dug into the earth, and the body folded up behind it. Once the circle was filled, the Fool led the festivants on a slow inward spiral, singing, "We Are Your People," by Beverly Frederick, and clapping until all were in a tight, moving, laughing group. As the energy faded, the Fool moved dramatically to the South, focusing attention upon the King of Wands character:

King of Wands: *"I am fire of fire, and I stand in the South to close the portal between this world and that. Djinn, mighty ruler, we find a gracious host in you. With gratitude we now bid adieu."*

At the West, the Queen of Cups: *"I am water of water, and I stand in the West to close the portal between this world and that. Nixscha, mighty ruler, we find a gracious host in you. With gratitude we now bid adieu."*

At the East, the Prince of Swords: *"I am air of air, and I stand in the East to close the portal between this world and that. Paralda, mighty ruler, we find a gracious host in you. With gratitude we now bid adieu."*

And at the North, the Princess of Pentacles: *"I am earth of earth, and I stand in the North to close the portal between this world and that. Ghob, mighty ruler, we find a gracious host in you. With gratitude we now bid adieu."*

The Fool said: *"Merry meet and merry part and…"* He waved his hand, palm up, gesturing for the festivants to finish: *"Merry meet again!"* The serpent head was raised from its ground position and led all in a return procession to the gathering location.

ELEVEN

·········

Pulling It All Together

It has been a year of turmoil, sadness, and hard feelings. We found the symbol of our
rebuilding as a community in the trees that surround us: ancient burr oaks that soar a
hundred feet tall and shelter us. They are family. For a week we made leaves filled with our
hopes for the future and what now must be left behind. We enter sacred space to find a
naked web held overhead, and begin to weave it all back together. Now comes our foliage,
fathers holding children up to tie on their dreams. When all six hundred are added, we
gather beneath and look in amazement at the hundred-foot circle of our dreams, and
see the stars above us. We created this all together. We have built our future again.

Under the Canopy ritual

The differences between a community ritual that fails to meet its purpose, one that accomplishes its purpose but is forgotten in a few hours, and one that impacts a community over the long run in the future can be very small. This chapter is about taking your gift to community and ensuring it is the most effective and sacred gift of love you can offer. In almost every human interaction, emotional and subconscious response will be governed by the details of what is encountered.

Community ritual has benefits that bounce back and forth between the ritual team and participants. These only increase when an established history of community ritual develops.

Like a song, a painting, or any work of art, the development of community ritual needs sincere attention to technique to improve.

When you began the process of creating ritual, the task probably seemed insurmountable. By the time you struggle through all the planning stages it is easy to embrace a pragmatic "Get 'er done!" attitude. Never forget, you are working to inspire people, and to engage the sacred connection they have to the universe, and to foster growth in their lives. Part of your mission, whatever you bring to creating community ritual, is to make your offering the best it can be.

You have worked through this book and have some pretty clear ideas of the who, how (style), and what (the ritual purpose) you want to offer. You have written a ritual intent and an outline. You have made some notes of brainstormed ideas of actions or engagement techniques you plan to include. How do you ensure this will be a great ritual?

We always keep our written ritual intent close at hand as we develop the ritual outline. Before leaving the planning stages, we sit down with our ritual team and go over what has been included. Like a corporate mission statement, the written ritual intent is one yardstick by which our eventual success is measured.

• • • • • • • • • • • •

Exercise

To create an intense and engaging ritual, try this process. Ask your team members to close their eyes and then read the ritual intent aloud. Now, holding that purpose in mind, together look at each item in your ritual outline and ask, "How does this move our community to experience the ritual purpose?" You may also revisit the wording of your written intent during this exercise. Is it clear? Does it descriptively cover what your ritual purpose is? Is there any word or phrase in it that can be improved? Can anything be left out of the intent and have it still cover what is essential? The written intent is meant to guide the outline, not the other way around!

To make your ritual great you need to completely envision the experience. If working in a team, do this with the whole group. Start with your arrival as a participant and imagine what happens. Does someone welcome you? What do you receive? Are you introduced to anyone? What do you do while waiting? How do you know when the ritual or procession begins?

Ask these kinds of questions as you imagine encountering every portion of the ritual. Sometimes this can be done as a guided meditation, with your team taking the ritual journey as one member reads from the outline. Your goal in this process is to "see" and experience your ritual from the first moment onward as if you were a participant. As you envision it, ask yourselves, "What is missing? Is there any detail, any sensory experience that we can expand or refine that will enhance engagement with this ritual?"

Visioning as a group has distinct advantages. When you vision individually, you often insert the details that your subconscious needs to feel, what you personally expect. When you are visioning as a group, each individual should be encouraged to completely describe what they see and feel. From this process you begin to see where you can add enhancement to the effectiveness of the ritual. You can also recognize those things which are being individually added.

Once you find the parts of the ritual that can benefit from additional detail enhancements, you can brainstorm as a team to improve those individual items. For a character encounter in a path-working, you might refine each team interaction by asking: How are they costumed? What exactly do they say? With what emotion or tone do they say it? How does their body move or interact? How do they indicate the interaction is over and the participant should proceed? Usually you realize through this process that you have not really thought the ritual experience completely through. Try not to presume anything. You have so many ways of interpreting actions and expression that as a ritual team you need to go over each item thoroughly.

Every aspect of the ritual needs to be visioned. If there is a procession, who starts it? How is it organized? What kind of feel or interaction is expected to occur on the way? What happens when the ritual space is approached? You may imagine a seamless and wordless evolution where people are drawn into the procession. Left not fully designed, the reality often ends up as someone saying, "The ritual procession will start here, please line up." You default to a method that does nothing to add to the ritual intent. Your task here is to make a conscious choice to define every moment of the ritual experience that you have control of, and to design it to contribute to the ritual experience and intent.

Listen for times when you hear yourself saying, "Oh, I'll just explain to them what to do." None of us really enjoy being "told" what to do or feel, and within ritual verbal instruction creates a deadly disconnect from the intent you are building. If at any point you find yourself inclined to rely on verbal instructions, ask yourself, "Is there a way to make this experience flow and be understood with no instruction?" or "What methods or sensory input could convey what is needed better than words?" This empathetic approach will make all the difference between a ritual that engages and moves people emotionally, and one that leaves participants bored and disengaged.

Imagine that to begin a procession you have a team member walk deliberately around the gathering assemblage ringing a small table bell. She wears a smiling look of calm deliberation that clearly transmits something is about to happen. When she gets back to the exact spot where the procession is to start, there is another team member with a small drum. The bell carrier lines up behind the drummer. They both start walking in place for a few steps, until people are sure to notice them. They both wave people to them with a smile and happily but slowly start the procession. They are careful to move slowly enough that people keep up and don't form a straggled-out group.

This scenario does not necessarily move your particular ritual intention forward; it just accomplishes the start of a procession with real engagement, creating a ritual state of mind.

Ritual affords a chance to be creative in every task involved. Take the chance to do so! This visioning and refining process is used over the whole scope and outline of your ritual in order to enhance the experience.

Rehearsal

Judy: *During ritual rehearsal is where I earned the name "Mistress Judy." There would be fifteen people milling around the site, and inevitably only two of them have remembered their ritual copies. Eight of the people have minor roles as teams, each team offering a different individual experience during one part of the ritual. Three of them are choir, and the rest have major speaking parts requiring blocking or interaction with a prop. We usually have about an hour. The organizational skills required here are epic. While keeping the flow of ritual in your head—who does what, where, and how— you also have to attain and hold the complete attention of each person there. When someone tries to change or add to the script in rehearsal, you must politely but firmly say no. At this point it is too late. When nervousness starts to manifest as mundane chatter or random distraction, you must gently put an end to it and pull the attention*

back to the business at hand. You have asked for and received the time and coopera-
tion of all these people; you owe it to them to keep everyone on task. Here is where your
leadership is put to the test. Some people may see you as "mean" or "bossy," or they may
name you "mistress," and that's okay. As Ritualista, it is your job.

After your team has participated in all this planning and visualization, they will think they have it down cold. Theater teaches how crucial rehearsal is. To be natural and authentic, you have to be comfortable enough that you no longer have to think. You can't force yourself to smile or to give off a feeling of welcoming calm. To be effective, you need to rehearse enough that your true human nature comes through without conscious effort, and you are able to add all the sensory details that will make your ritual a great experience.

The biggest obstacle between you and the next level of performance is yourself. It is perfectly normal to feel stress and anxiety when in a leadership or performance role. Some ritualistas avoid the concept of rehearsal for one main reason: they are afraid. You may draw forth a whole list of excuses to avoid rehearsing; it is boring, you don't need it, you don't want to "overwork" your role and become stiff. This is giving in to anxiety. Rehearsal of the ritual offers you the best opportunities to improve your effectiveness.

If you have the luxury of arranging for your practice to take place on site, you have a great advantage. The practicalities of staging, prop placement, blocking, timing, entries, and exits can all be finalized during rehearsal. It allows you to find out who on your team can be heard and who needs to project. Your level of comfort as ritual begins will be heightened by familiarity.

When you are visualizing, brainstorming, or reading the words of a script, it all seems so clear and easy. The old joke about the difficulty of walking and chewing gum at the same time is really true. For most of us, without practice it is difficult to walk and sing, to smile and offer a blessing, to be our authentic selves and speak even a few words. The repetition of rehearsal is the tool that will help you gain these skills.

Stagecraft

"Blocking" is a theater term from the world of stage direction. Ritual space is not exactly a stage, but the principles of good stagecraft can make the difference between mediocre and great ritual.

Blocking is the pre-planning of all the physical activity on a stage. With good blocking your team knows to be in their correct places at the right times during ritual. People and props that are out of place can be disastrous and downright dangerous at times. You often need to plan for the movement of not just your team, but how all the ritual participants will enter, move from here to there while participating, and then exit or stop. For ceremonies that involve complex or timely movement of participants, we recruit friends to come to blocking rehearsal to act as intuitive moving bodies ("sheeple").[30] This advance testing of how you will get people from point A to point B can be the critical difference between a smooth transition and total chaos in the middle of your ritual!

Part of good blocking is to position the team members who are the focus so that when they move they have their backs to the audience as little as possible. They will obviously be heard better when facing their audience. The face is expressive and will communicate as much or more than any composed lines being spoken.

Blocking can be critical to efficiently work with large groups. We like to offer at least one individual experience in a ritual, and without planning, this can be very time consuming. Use blocking to devise a plan to divide your audience into many smaller groups to offer an individual experience simultaneously, and to later re-form into a large group. In the "Ritual of the 13 Moons" (chapter 5), we divided people into twelve groups and blocked a process to move each smaller group, at the sound of a gong, through twelve different stations. How do you distribute to, or gather something from, more than a hundred people in a manner efficient enough to avoid long waiting? Block out four different people to do the task simultaneously. Have a plan for how to divide the assemblage in four, and let each team member know where in the group they start and finish.

---

30   Sheeple: A humorous term invented to describe ritual extras recruited to simulate people moving as aimlessly as sheep.

Good blocking helps in establishing an invisible barrier between team members and participants when that is needed. In a theatrical-style ritual, this is essential to creating a convincing scene. This barrier can be created very subtly but also on a large scale. This separation of the audience from ritual characters gives people a sense that they are both observing and a part of the distinctly separate ritual reality you have created.

If your team is all near the center facing out, your audience will naturally create a circle as they enter. If your team is gathered in a line all facing the same direction, participants will form a group or horseshoe shape facing you. We instinctively all want to be able to see and engage.

The term "center stage" literally means the center section of the sacred space and usually the focus of the action. Using outdoor (tiki) torches and a central fire for lighting, blocking helps to test and mark the visual focal points in advance. In some cases a blocking rehearsal should involve actually placing actors' "marks" (chalk or other marking on the ground) so the places where your team can be best seen and heard are clear. Part of rehearsing then becomes going over the movement of everyone from mark to mark during the ritual.

You may think stagecraft planning and blocking rehearsal are excessive attention to detail that is unnecessary. Drop that notion! Planning the movement of your team members and everyone present is as important as any forgotten line or action in your ceremony. Those who have taken blocking for granted, especially in a daytime rehearsal, sometimes find themselves lost or tripping over each other later in the dark.

It can be difficult to wordlessly get a large group of people moving as you intend in a ritual. It can be even more difficult to get them to stop! Humans have a herd instinct just as many animals do. We are most comfortable gathered in a group, and then once moving we tend to continue unless there is strong leadership calling a halt. Blocking your participants' movement should also include planning out actions that will make them stop.

When participants are moving in a line or circle, it takes directing their attention to a leader to signal a change in movement. This can be accomplished with a sound or exaggerated motion that draws focus. A chime or gong or any sharp sound will work. Once a moving group knows and recognizes your leadership, movement can be ended easily. Plan ahead to establish yourself as leader of the herd, and you won't be caught in a perpetual-motion ritual!

Performance Tips

Many of these tips become self-evident once you gather your team and start rehearsal. These are not so much rules as things to observe and determine if they need to be noted, refined, or discussed. Each ritual is unique and will have different skills that are primary.

- Rehearse the ritual. Don't skimp or succumb to your fears—schedule and get to it!

- Keep ritual words simple! Participants will hear what we convey, not our particular words.

- Match ritual roles with team talents. Push everyone to improve their skills but from a position of basic comfort.

- Clearly define timing cues and who gives them. Do not leave cues to chance; be sure to rehearse them with your whole team!

- Speak loudly and slowly. Enunciate! Practice it. In rehearsal, have someone stand where the farthest participant will be and have them verify that everyone can be heard.

- Let actions be primary over words. When speaking, be aware of what your eyes, energy, emotions, and attitude are conveying.

- In a theatrical role, do not make eye contact with the audience unless it is part of the role and meant to be intimate. If you are acting as a mythic character, humans do not deserve eye contact!

- Take your community ritual seriously. Avoid becoming giddy when in the spotlight and translating that into silliness.

- Once the ritual starts, there is no going back and no apologies. Work past any errors or omissions without concern. Don't lose your rhythm!

- Test your props, and test them again.

- Clearly and thoroughly communicate the demands of each ritual role. When you hear yourself saying, "You know what I mean..." about a role or action, you and they probably don't!

- As a team, you are a host offering a service. Be gracious and remember the people you serve are always right.

- If you use fire or candles, plan in case they get out of control or won't light.

- If you use a campfire, always have someone assigned to be fire tender.

Special Needs

It is very important to consider those who are differently abled or who have limited mobility. There are those who may be able to walk to your ritual site but need to sit during the ritual itself, because standing for extended periods is painful. There may be people attending in wheelchairs or who need to provide care for another. The blind or hearing impaired might attend. You may not know in advance, but keeping these possibilities in mind will help you to be observant and creative. If the ritual is designed with movement as an integral part, you should allow for the possibility that not everyone can participate. You should have a contingency plan for sensory experience that includes people with major limitations.

As you gain a thorough knowledge of the community you serve, you will learn who is available to assist people with special needs. If you know people who have skills in interpreting through American Sign Language (ASL), invite them to attend your ritual and be ready to interpret if needed. As ritual becomes part of a community core, you will need to budget to provide services to broaden the ritual experience.

It is not critical that the ritual experience of a person with limits be exactly identical with the majority of ritual participants. The important thing is to demonstrate that you have considered the demands you are making of those participating in the ritual and that you are willing to accommodate those who have difficulty meeting those demands. Try to solicit people with mobility or sensory challenges to privately identify themselves at the gather point of the ritual. Knowledge is power, and armed with the knowledge of what part of your audience has limitations, you can adapt. You may want to have folks with mobility issues go first in a line or path-working, so they set the pace for the ritual and are sure to not feel left out. This can be an advantage when the inclination is for people to rush through an experience. For people who need to sit, try to incorporate a place for them near the center of your sacred space, so they are not relegated to a poor location and kept "out of the way" or behind other people. This also works well for hearing-impaired people. By placing them in the center of the action, they will be able to hear better!

We have had legally blind people participate in ritual. During a labyrinth walking ritual, we found a solution for a blind participant. An aide walked slowly with the blind person's hands on his shoulders. While they moved slower than the bulk of participants, people were happy to slip past in the walking line or be patient to accommodate this person being able to participate.

As our communities age, more of us are unable to stand for even 20 minutes. Nearly every ritual we offer has at least one person who must be able to sit at some time during the ceremony. Plan your processions to allow or provide for people to be transported. Carrying a chair along as you can walk can be difficult. Allow people to deliver their chairs in advance to the ritual area, or use a wheelbarrow, wagon, or car to transport chairs for people.

Children can be a challenge, particularly for families at night when energy levels are waning. Unless a ritual is designed specifically for adults only, we always welcome children. We encourage families to make a "ritual camp" within the sacred space when possible. This is a blanket or stroller–centered area where the whole family can keep together. If movement is involved, they can return there to meet up together. We allow people with kids to remain near the ritual exit if they choose, but we also let them know a crying or wandering child is less distracting than a yelling or stressed-out parent.

Our world is filled with limitations, the many "onlys" we encounter every day. Community ritual is a place for inclusivity, and ritualistas should make every attempt to structure their offering to be as welcoming and accessible to as many people as possible. All it usually takes is a little forethought and planning to accomplish this. The experience of being a truly inclusive event can become one of the most memorable characteristics of your ritual.

Problems and Solutions

Ritual locations all have problems, whether indoors or out. Most of the potential problems with location are resolved by an early assessment of the site. If your indoor site doesn't allow flame or is cramped, be sure to plan for that. If your outdoor site has roots and rocks, don't expect to move quickly or in low-light conditions. If there is no rain shelter, either bring a temporary shelter or make a concrete plan to decide when specifically to cancel or reschedule a weather-threatened ritual.

Ritual area lighting should never be a surprise, but it is amazing how often it arises. Be sure to test the lighting available in the location and time of day of your ritual. It is easy to add supplemental lighting indoors or out if you know you'll need it. Sometimes just adjusting ritual blocking to bring ritual actions into the light is enough to solve many problems.

Some of the most difficult problems are those that arise without warning during a ritual. It's really important to have one or two designated team members who can drop other duties to act as problem wranglers. They have to be level-headed enough to sort out when an intervention to resolve a problem is a larger disturbance than the actual effect the "problem" is creating. A participant stumbling, a sneezing attack, or a crying child are things that will usually resolve quickly by themselves or with a neighboring participant's help. As ritualists, we are often more upset and embarrassed when problems occur than the disruption to participation they objectively represent.

Problem solving in ritual is just as important a skill as ritual design. A calm, resourceful, creatively brainstorming approach to what seems insurmountable will nearly always generate the perfect solution to move your ritual on to greatness.

Publicity

How does your audience know to attend? You must wear the hat of a marketeer! Of all the tasks required for success, this one is the easiest to avoid. In some communities there are multiple events to choose from on any given weekend. Bombarded with advertisements and inducements to attend a vast array of experiences each day, the choice becomes competitive. Marketing your ritual does not degrade the sacred nature of your purpose. Think of ritual as sacred performance art; without generating some excitement to attend, it may never be appreciated and experienced. Your community needs to know what they can expect, why it is important, and how as a group and an individual they can benefit. The skills you have learned in writing a clear and positive ritual intent will be applied in your communication and promotion.

If you haven't written a larger ritual description for publication yet, it is time to do so. A ritual description is a slightly expanded intent that more completely covers the actual experiences to be encountered in the ritual. Be sure to reference all activities that your community will be concerned about, such as physical access, any substances or allergens that may be encountered, inclusivity, suitability for all ages, and meditations or devotions that may be included. Mention anything they need to bring with them or think about in advance. As with your intent statement, you won't want to disclose the complete experience. Describe it using metaphor and positive outcome verbs (will, shall, etc.). Be specific enough that your community will be excited to attend.

If you are working with an organization or community group, make a presentation of the intent and description to verify that your ideas correspond with the expectations they have for the event. A concise ritual intent and description help your team and the sponsors to be united in consolidating resources in support of the ritual and its promotion and advertising.

How to get information out to your community will be defined by the research you have already done in designing the ritual. Do they have local gathering places? Are they voracious readers? Do they participate in arts appreciation events? Are they families who attend child-centered activities? All this information can help you decide where and how to place any advertising or posters, or whether to send out targeted mailings.

In the age of immediate communication, it has become common to neglect to allow for the advance notice people still need to make plans. Your rule of thumb for most any event is to publish initial advertising 4 to 6 weeks in advance, then reinforce that with updated information 10 to 14 days in advance. Lastly, you should send out a reminder 2 or 3 days before the event.

It may be worthwhile to print and distribute information at places like coffee shops, specialty stores, or community centers. Local newspapers can be used for advertising in targeted areas. You ad may not get read unless it is prominently featured or published with a supporting article. Talk to local and neighborhood publishers; many are thrilled to find unusual content for feature stories in advance of events.

Social media has come to overtake and become a substitute for most print advertising. Creating an "event" and inviting people has practically no cost but your effort. To use this effectively you need a huge "friend" base to invite, and active users to read your invitation. It is so easy to "like" or imply attendance that the clicked response you get on social media is largely fictional. If one person out of ten who affirmed they are coming to your event actually shows up, you are doing well! Still, social media is important in spreading your announcement. If you follow it up with posts that build a sense of excitement, it can be very effective in generating a buzz that spreads widely and gains you participants.

For a ritual with an educational component in its purpose, publicity can be critical to its success. This type of ritual can be just the catalyst to shake a casually formed community onto a path of deeper involvement with each other and draw them out of their isolation. Use the power of social media to touch thousands of people quickly and get the word out. By referencing the knowledge you hope to transfer about issues and concerns we all share, you can more effectively promote this ritual purpose.

Your best publicity will come from personal contact and word of mouth. Make sure your ritual team understands how important their involvement is in gathering up a ritual audience, right from the start. A well-marketed community ritual will have an audience and a sense of excitement surrounding it long before the event itself.

Assessment and Critique

When you create community ritual, you are entering uncharted waters. Learning everything you can about it and how to improve it is critical. In the best conditions, a successful ritual will be a good experience for a third of your participants, a great one for a third, and a third will have no comment!

In spite of this, you need to gather information and sort through it to learn from the event. Information gathered immediately after ritual contains important content. Immediate reactions gathered are subjective, tainted by the surge of ecstasy and the joyous afterglow that community ritual generates, but they usually do accurately reflect our participants' subconscious response. This is not the moment to try to intellectually examine and criticize the details of what took place. Use this time to gather impressions participants are willing to share. Be sure to jot them down to be included in later ritual discussion. It is unlikely that you or your team members will hear many negative comments during the afterglow. Attendees will also be more candid if they speak to others who are not identified as presenters.

For your ritual team to really grow from the experience, schedule and publicize in advance a time to discuss and review the ritual. Including the time and place for critique in the event program, or posted somewhere near the entrance or exit, will ensure better attendance. Allow at least a day to pass so that people have some time to let the impact of the ritual be absorbed and the intellectual process of analysis take place. If you assembled your team for a singular event, including a critique process is still important for the participants' feedback and individual team members' growth.

This process can become antagonistic without several ground rules to guide the discussion. It is easy to make judgments of blame and to be shaming of individual failures when ritual truly is a team effort. To really learn from the experience, you need a safe place to share what may be hard to hear and an atmosphere that focuses on improvement rather than personal criticism.

Some rules typically used to govern critique are that everyone agrees to:

- Participate fully and stay for the whole meeting.

- Commit to both listening and speaking. Silence can be an intimidating form of criticism.

- Speak only for oneself. Do not repeat what was "heard" anonymously without owning the opinion.

- Be specific and clear. Vagueness leaves room for interpretation and confusion.

- Stay focused on what can actually be changed.

- Offer criticism with a desire to enrich and support the ritual work.

- Give specific suggestions for alternatives to replace parts that did not work.

- Listen to the complete idea being presented before formulating any response.

- Employ a "vibe watcher" to detect any dominating or destructive words or behaviors and direct the attention of the group to them before they accelerate and cause harm to the team.

As you plan and prepare for your ritual-assessment meeting, assemble all of the relevant data. Bring your financial information. Have the audience numbers and demographics you planned for and compare them to who actually attended. It can be really helpful to hand out a survey form at the ritual exit or provide a link to an online feedback survey in any ritual promotional materials.

When your meeting takes place, it is important to have an agenda to guide the discussion and a wise chairperson to keep you on track. Leaving this to chance opens the opportunity for an individual agenda to dominate. You can organize the discussion by subject areas, such as how well you accomplished the ritual intention, the strengths and weaknesses (with specific ways to improve), and the performance of the ritual team (with specific ways to improve). You can also go through the complete ritual vision outline and review every aspect.

Take complete notes of the meeting or record it. Using this process, you may come up with some alternate ritual visions that could create a whole new ritual. Save these, because all ritual ideas have value and that future ritual will benefit from them!

Ritual Tomorrow

Community ritual is an art form, a personal mode of expression that engages a large group of people together. Like any art, trends develop and wax and wane over time. As our spiritual practices, theater techniques, even electronic media, film, and video develop, new inspiration will enter and influence how we experience ritual and how it is created.

The loss of defined religious affiliations has been a major factor in empowering people to set their own course in developing meaningful ceremony. It is difficult to speculate how society will change, influencing how we will find our spiritual center as a community in the future. No doubt the diversity of our spiritual expression will demand a customized ritual, and that will have to come from the people who are inspired to serve a particular community.

What we do know is that independently created community ritual is filling a real need presently. A growing number of people recognize the spiritual nature present in themselves and want to share that with their family, friends, and neighbors. Occasionally an already existing congregation can have members step up to create what ceremony is needed. More often, people like ourselves, who have experienced and been touched deeply through ritual, decide the offering of ritual is too important to leave unfulfilled.

We (Judy and Nels) sometimes find ourselves as participants, floundering in a disorganized ceremony led by folks wandering about trying to express themselves. As painful as the learning process is to watch, we never leave a community ritual early. It always represents a sincere effort to touch and move people. There is the temptation to critique during ritual. Try to resist, and remember, it is important to acknowledge the gift presented and applaud the effort. Ritualistas today steer through uncharted waters, and certainly a few reefs will be hit along the way. We presented here many tools and collected guidance to help you avoid common mistakes. Most importantly, we hope this book empowers you to take the risky and daring step to offer a ritual. In a world where much of our lives is out of our direct control, here and now, in creating and offering our own powerfully relevant ceremonies, we can truly take the sacred back!

Ritual: Under the Canopy

· · · · · · · · · · · · · · · · ·

Location: Sacred Harvest Festival, 2011
© Judith Olson Linde and Nels Linde

Ritual context

This was the final ritual in a series. During this week of rituals, about 600 paper oak leaves were made, printed 12 per page on colored paper. There were 400 leaves on green paper to represent positive affirmations and qualities of the community. Another 200 leaves on yellow paper represented traits and issues of the community that were best washed away. Each leaf had a string hot-glued on its base to tie it onto the canopy in this ritual. All week, festivants had access to the leaves and wrote down relevant affirmations and traits to wash away.

Ritual intent

Bring the forest family of community back to our lives, and share the canopy.

Ritual description

No description was provided to participants; 8:00 p.m. gather (8:45 p.m. is full dark) and process to ritual circle.

Ritual setup and supplies

An 8-sided, 4-foot-diameter wheel was built at the ritual circle, mounted to spin horizontally on a vertical post. The post was 9 feet high and anchored 4 feet deep in the center of a large fire ring (there was a sand and steel fire shield around the pole base). Eight tie holes were drilled on the wheel edge, with 40-foot twine ropes tied through the holes. Eight 8-foot 2 x 2 posts were set around the 100-foot-diameter circumference, and a rope from the wheel was attached to each. These 2 x 2s were anchored leaning outward with a stake and rope tie, so the wheel ropes were about 5 feet high at the edge. This prop looked like a giant twine roof with 8 radial spokes of twine rope leading out to 2 x 2s from the elevated center wheel. There were also two "stop" poles in the center which when wedged into the wheel spokes could keep the wheel from spinning. Additional twine was cut into 12-foot lengths, enough for all participants.

Team members

Ritualista 1 and Ritualista 2, eight helpers at the perimeter 2 x 2s, two greeters at the gate, choir, one fire tender, two helpers at the center.

Ritual script

A procession with drumming, led by six ritual team members, moved from the Heart Chakra gathering location to the ritual site, carrying the baskets of community-written paper leaves. At the ritual gate, two greeters passed out 12-foot strings of twine, saying, "*Add your branches to the forest canopy.*"

Ritual team members guided people to walk right in and modeled how to weave the strings (the "branches") into the radial canopy ropes. This created an interwoven web (the canopy). When all had finished, Ritualista 2 rang a chime, and the team members modeled and led the participants outward to form the circle.

From the circle, Ritualista 2 said, *"Let our branches intertwine with our forest family."* Raising her arm, she intertwined her fingers with the person to her left, and modeled passing this on around the circle.

In the center, Ritualista 1 faced East: *"Carried by the wind … "*

And then turned deosil, raising his arms toward each direction in turn, saying:

(South) *"cracked open by fire … "*
(West) *"sprouted with your gentle rains … "*
(North) *"and rooted as it finds a home … "*
(back to the East) *"and it stretches to the sky."*

The two greeters started passing out the leaves.

Ritualista 1: *"You can learn a lot from trees! Many things beset a forest, our magical grove here, all of us individually, and as a community. Sun, wind, hail, lightning, yes, and even fire sweep through us."*

Ritualista 2: *"What we are offered as a forest is constant change. We can send new roots and new sprouts out."*

Ritualista 1: *"We can find new ways to mingle our roots and intertwine our branches."*

Ritualista 2: *"We can vision our grove tomorrow, and add new leaves to feed us that sunshine."*

Ritualista 1: *"We can heal the scars of broken branches, and let those parts we no longer need wither and yellow. We can empower our forest family, and send those visions to be with us always!"*

At a chime cue, eight team members came forward and modeled adding leaves on. The participants came under the canopy and tied on the 600 leaves as the choir sang this song:

"Like a Tree," by Judith Olson Linde

"Like a tree, like a tree, I want to be. Like a tree, like a tree, in harmony.
Like a tree, like a tree, reaching for the sky. Let the trees teach me the ways of the wise.
Like a tree, like a tree, you and me. Like a tree, like a tree, we're a family.
Like a tree, like a tree, reaching for the sky. Let the trees teach me the ways of the wise."
Let my roots spread out, and my limbs grow strong.
So I can offer comfort all day long.
Could our branches touch to form a canopy?
A place for all our young to truly be.

The fire tender began stoking the fire as this song wound down. Chime cue.

Ritualista 1: *"Welcome to our forest family! Let the image of this canopy sustain us until we meet in this grove again!"*

The festivants were given time to come under the woven canopy, now covered with 600 leaves, and look at it from below. Drumming and the song "I Am the Fire," by Abbi Spinner McBride, raised the energy. As this energy song began, the eight helpers removed the anchors from the 2 x 2 poles and lifted them up, raising the canopy to its full 8-foot height.

As the song continued, the eight pole holders began to walk clockwise, turning the central wheel and the canopy of leaves. When two rounds of the song had been sung, two team members at the center blocked the rotation by wedging poles into the spokes. As the eight pole holders continued to walk around the circle, the twine canopy with leaves began to wrap around the central pole. The fire tender stoked the fire at the center as the outer poles were drawn completely in, and the helpers were handed scissors to cut the twine canopy loose and add it to the fire. (See the diagram in chapter 12.) The energy and song reached a crescendo, and a drum break ended the song, followed by a time of grounding.

The ritual ended with thanking. Facing to each direction, Ritualista 1 said:
"The air that carried the seed.
The fire that cracked it open.
The water that nourished it.
The earth it took root in.
Thank the trees for guarding our sacred grove and the spirit that sustains us … Trees!"

TWELVE

....

Amazing Props and Tools

I stand in the center, slathering shortening over the four-foot poppet; two hundred people have eyes trained on me. The fire fills the wide pit and is roaring. We lay the poppet on the pentacle of heavy wire, and sing our spell to grow our community in the balance. As we gather close around it quickly heats. Pop, pop, pop, popcorn starts flying out everywhere and the people dance trying to catch it! Faces are joyous with wonder—how can this be? The corn is done popping and the wax catches flame. A fire on top of a fire starts over the poppet, a swirling vortex of flame leaping into the night. The spell is done!

STONE SOUP RITUAL (THE JIFFY POPPET RITUAL)

Great ritual can take place in an open field or a bare room indoors without a single physical object besides the ritual team and your participants. It is difficult, but it can be done! As you seek to enhance the engagement of participants, you will find the need for more. More stuff, more decorations, more sensory stimulus, more definition of your sacred space. In this chapter, we offer tools, tips, props, and tricks to add to your rituals, and to do so with the most reliable results and least amount of cost and effort. Many items will need to be mounted or positioned just right.

As a ritualista you will need your own physical toolkit as well, essential items that will be invaluable as you set up your ritual space. We include here items that you can find at thrift, surplus, hardware, or farm supply stores, items you can purchase cheaply and have on hand. A visit to your ritual location, whether indoor or outdoor, is important to assess the site, but having a trunk or tote with supplies and tools will help cover what you forget or don't notice!

For indoor rituals, most often you are limited as to what can be placed or hung without any impact on the room structure or finish. Always carry both duct tape (stronger hold) and painter's tape (non-marring removable adhesive). A two- or three-step foldable stepladder fits in a car and is invaluable in even an 8-foot-ceiling room. We carry a bag of small squeeze clamps, which can attach cloth, lights, banners, or information sheets to any surface edge. Get a package of poster putty, a pliable, sticky gum that won't mar or stain surfaces, to hang lightweight items.

....

Personal Tool Tote
Mistress Judy's ritual kit!

- Sunhat, sunglasses, sunscreen; for ritual setup, rehearsal, or performance in full sun

- Umbrella, rain poncho

- Big ball of string and a compass; useful for circle setup

- Almanac or moon phase app; useful for timing sunset and moonrise

- Farmer's (strike anywhere) matches in a zip-lock bag; these always light

- Alcohol and Epsom salts; one cup to one handful burns for about 20 minutes

- Index cards and Sharpie pen; for those who are worried about forgetting their lines

- Pitch pipe, voice recorder

- Scissors

- Flashlight

Many indoor sites won't allow an open flame, so all your plans for candles, even in a secure holder or enclosure, may be out the window! Consider picking up some tiny LED battery-operated candles. They are not a great replacement but may be the only alternative in some spaces. A few strands of string lights can be taped in place to offer a soft lighting alternative to commercial fluorescent lighting. These are available as battery-operated LED versions if electric power is limited or not in a convenient location. A couple of clamp-on lights with a spotlight bulb installed can draw the visual focus to a particular area. Need a campfire? Electric campfires and tabletop flames are available at reasonable prices. They echo the feeling of humans gathered around a fire, and some are pretty visually compelling.

Indoors, cloth coverings for room contents (or walls) may be important to simplify or reduce visual distractions. Thrift store flat bedsheets can be dyed a pleasant color, and a collection of theme-decorated cotton wall tapestries are great to carry along for last-minute coverings. If you work often indoors, it may be worth investing in a roll of photography backdrop paper. You can get large-width rolls of almost any length. With care, even paper can be rolled back up and used multiple times.

Gateways can be created with decorative additions to the actual room door. Freestanding gates need to be very secure and usually involve a wooden structure. Design something that can be disassembled with a screwdriver or with hand-tightened fittings for easy transport. A trick to make a lightweight structure more stable is to provide attachment points for several gallon jugs near the bottom. These you can fill with water or sand (and empty) at the site and cover with a decorative cloth. We have a whole tote of thrift store imitation vines, plants, and flowers. Even if a little tacky, they provide a visual reference to nature and will spruce up a room, gate, or altar. Many garden centers sell freestanding metal gate arches you can assemble on site. These are a good investment if you work indoors often.

Indoors and out, ritualistas often need one or more altars. We carry most ritual items in flat-topped totes, and these can be covered and serve as a low altar, or stacked. A good set of "TV tables" can be a thrift store purchase. They fold and are lightweight. Outdoors we sometimes rope them to a stake beneath them for more stability. The premier ritual table is the plastic folding table, about four feet by two feet. They are sturdy but can be bulky to transport. If you are handy with woodworking tools, it is useful to have one collapsible round table. Legs can be formed by interlocking plywood sheets to hold a round surface at any height you choose. It breaks down into three easy-to-carry sheets.

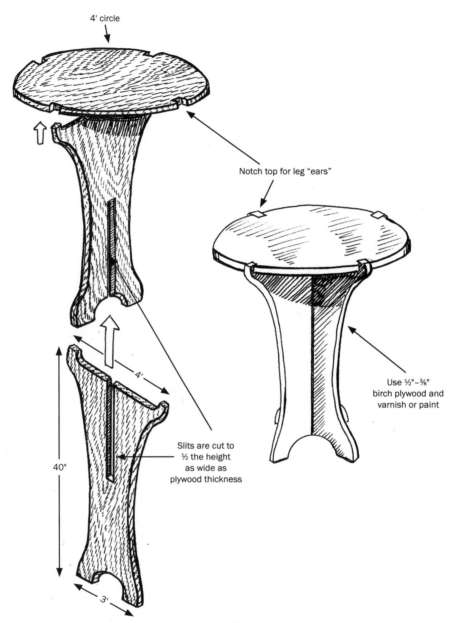

4' circle

Notch top for leg "ears"

Use ½"–⅜"
birch plywood and
varnish or paint

Slits are cut to
½ the height
as wide as
plywood thickness

4'

40"

3'

Design for a site-assembled round altar table.

Mounting Systems

We have tried many options for mounting cloth gateways and directional banners or to hang items outdoors. Wind is a powerful force, and a completely solid cloth creates strong resistance even in a light breeze. First, consider anchoring a banner only at the top. This can be visually distracting but reduces wind drag considerably. In some designs cloth can have slits cut through it to stay fixed on all sides and still allow wind to pass through. Even the sheerest of fabrics can still generate significant force on mounting systems.

By far the best mounting system is one driven into the ground. We have acquired a selection of 4-foot-tall metal T shaped farm fenceposts for creating gateways and mounting banners. These are best installed with a post-pounding tool, a heavy metal tube with side handles and one welded metal end. You just slip it over the post and lift and drop until the post is a foot or more in the ground. We use PVC pipe sized to slide over the post to reach heights up to 10 feet tall. Secure crosspieces can be added by drilling holes to receive wooden dowels, or you can use tie wire (look at a farm supply store) to mount any type of wooden piece horizontally. If transporting length is an issue, PVC pipe can be purchased in various diameter sizes that slide into each other to create a telescoping length made from several pieces. Most PVC pipe also has plastic elbow and tee fittings to build a structure if you wish. If wood (1 x 2 or 2 x 2-inch sizes) is a preferred material, we still anchor it to a metal post whenever possible. Both wood and PVC can be painted or wrapped in cloth for a more decorative look. Be sure you have permission to drive stakes or posts or do any digging outdoors. A search for underground electric or telephone lines that may not be apparent can be requested free from most utility companies and often is required by law.

A freestanding gate or hanging post can be used outdoors, but must have a secure and broad base and be heavily weighted (with water jugs) or anchored/guy-wired with rope and camping stakes or leaning support posts. This may be your only choice if you're on cement or a surface you cannot anchor or drive stakes into, but unless it is very secure, we have found this method troublesome!

Outdoors, the ritualista gains a lot of advantages setting up a ritual space. You may have a site already decorated by nature. A park, meadow, grove clearing, or desert can all provide the ritual backdrop. In urban locations you might want to visually screen offensive views, but it is far easier to choose a pleasing location right off. We have completely screened off a ritual area with secure posts and cloth banners, but if you need this level of privacy, finding a more suitable location is preferred.

Ground Marking

You may want to make markings on the ground either to define the border or walking paths of your ritual space or to create ritual art or decoration. On hard surfaces, sidewalk chalk is designed for just this purpose. We use the art of Rangoli to create thematic designs to enhance many rituals.[31] Traditionally rice flour and spices such as cumin, turmeric, cayenne, and paprika are used on smaller designs. Brightly colored powders made for this purpose are also available from ethnic Indian specialty food stores. The design is, in effect, a prayer that blesses the site as participants walk it into the earth.

Photo by Jenna Touchette

Rangoli from the 2008 Sacred Harvest Festival Ritual.

---

31   "Rangoli: Painting the Earth," www.historymuseum.ca/cmc/exhibitions/cultur/inde
    /indact4e.shtml.

For larger scale, and for any border definition, our primary material is garden lime. It is a fine white powder and cheaply available, at just a few dollars for a 50-pound bag. For colored lines we use white silica sand, which can be colored with a small amount of powdered tempera paint. These substances are nontoxic and biodegradable; however, they both contain small particles unhealthy to breathe when airborne. Use of a cloth mask is advisable while laying the powder in any quantity.

This lime-laying tool is made from a recycled screwtop plastic lemonade jar. Just duct-tape it securely to a 3-foot wooden stick a few inches off the ground, drill multiple ¼-inch holes in the bottom, and test it out to make a lime "shaker."

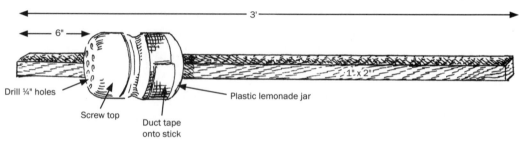

**Fill with lime and walk while tapping the stick
on the ground to make a white line.**

Clay Bead Necklace Gift

Many items for use as a ritual gift can be gathered or purchased cheaply. Creating a gift allows for the addition of words or images directly inspired by and connected to your ritual intent. Paper, wood, metal, and most craft media can be used. We have specialized in clay beads, as we have the resources to produce these, but you can contact a local pottery or ceramic shop and usually find someone excited and willing to help you with materials and firing for this project. Clay has the advantage of being directly from the earth, able to display intricate details, and easily produced using press molds.

We usually make prototypes, and from them molds, in low-temperature red clay. It is fine-grained and retains the detail. We like to keep the bead design fairly flat for ease of firing and reduced weight. Working with the wet clay, make the basic shape you desire, and using fine tools (even a toothpick), add any words or detailed images. You are making the original, so make it exactly as you want it to appear (note that it will shrink about 15 percent after drying and firing). Plan for the hanging hole in both location and direction; you want it to hang well on the neck. You can pierce the hole as you make the beads.

Once you have the original made, let it air-dry thoroughly or in a 200-degree oven overnight. Take it to a ceramic shop and ask them to fire it to "bisque" hardness. Now you need to make your actual bead molds from the original. Make half-inch slabs and cut them to the outline shape of your bead. Press the original you made into the wet clay, one for front and back if you have designs on both sides. The clay will flatten out as you press the original into it, so you may have to trim them back to size. We usually make several molds so we can pick out the best and have several people making beads. Again, air- or oven-dry these, and once dry, use a needle or other fine tool to refine any detail that has been lost. Make another trip to the ceramic shop and get your molds fired to the same hardness.

Now you are ready to press-mold the beads. Take a small amount of wet clay, about the size you want the finished bead, and roll it in your hands into a smooth globe shape. Press it between your front and back molds (or just into the front if one-sided). Holding it between the molds, run a fine-bladed knife around the edge to make your finished shape. Carefully pull apart the molds and your bead will appear!

Back of bead mold, front of bead mold, original bead for molds,
finished flame-fired bead (top left, clockwise).

Gently remove and set to dry. When the air-drying beads start to change color (about half dry), pierce the hanging hole using a tiny metal rod, plastic tube, or a drilling motion with a tiny V-shaped point. Once the beads are completely dry, use a knife to scrape off any sharp edges and around the hanging hole. Make as many as you need, and when dry, back to the ceramic store for another firing, and your beads are complete!

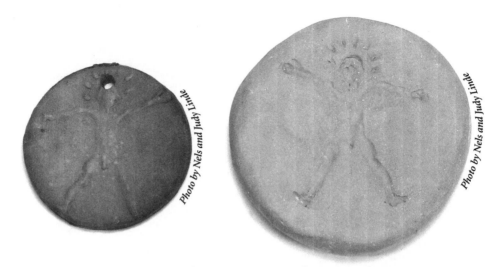

Photo by Nels and Judy Linde

Photo by Nels and Judy Linde

A simple mold made by pressing a charm into wet clay (right).
Finished Enki bead, embossed design, flame flashed (left).

For a raised, embossed-style design, you can press an existing item into the mold shape, and fire that to use as a mold to make beads directly. The bead for the Enki ritual was made by pressing a small metal charm of a human figure directly into the disk mold shape. This eliminates the step of making an original to make the mold from, but realize any words added will need to be in reverse when working directly on a bead mold.

There are air-drying and oven-fired clays available in craft stores that can be used for this same process. The result is less durable and detail is hard to incorporate, but for a small quantity of ritual gifts, it's worth a try.

We typically make all our originals and molds using a red clay for strength and detail, and then make the actual beads using a raku clay. This is a coarser low-fire clay designed to take thermal shocks. After the beads have been kiln-fired to bisque hardness, we fire them again in a ritual fire. Place a 4-inch stone in the center of your fire pit, and use wood chips (small-animal bedding) to cover a small area around it. Lean all your beads on edge radiating outward from the center stone, and cover the beads in more wood chips. Now cover it all with aluminum foil, tucking the outside edges downward to the ground. Place a barbecue grate over the top and build your ritual fire on top of that. After burning for a few hours, the coals will ignite the wood chips surrounding your beads. Starved for air by the foil barrier, the smoke created will "flash" black markings randomly on the beads, creating a fire-touched look. Play archaeologist once the fire has cooled and retrieve your beautiful beads!

Mirrored Gloves

Mirrors are a handy prop to use in ritual. They can be used to reflect light and the image of participants back to themselves. This trick makes great use of them. Buy some brown cloth gardening gloves, gather some 3- or 4-inch round mirrors, and hot-glue them to the palms of the gloves. That's it! Now your team can move or dance around participants and strategically offer a mirror for reflection.

Hourglass Timer

This is an easy-to-build, adjustable timer hourglass, large enough to be easily seen and used to regulate events that need a defined time in ritual. It is built with a few scraps of wood, some dowels, and two liter-size, heavy, clear plastic bottles. There is an openable end to add sand and in the middle between the two bottles is a slot to slide in a strip of wood to regulate flow times (various size holes in each strip).

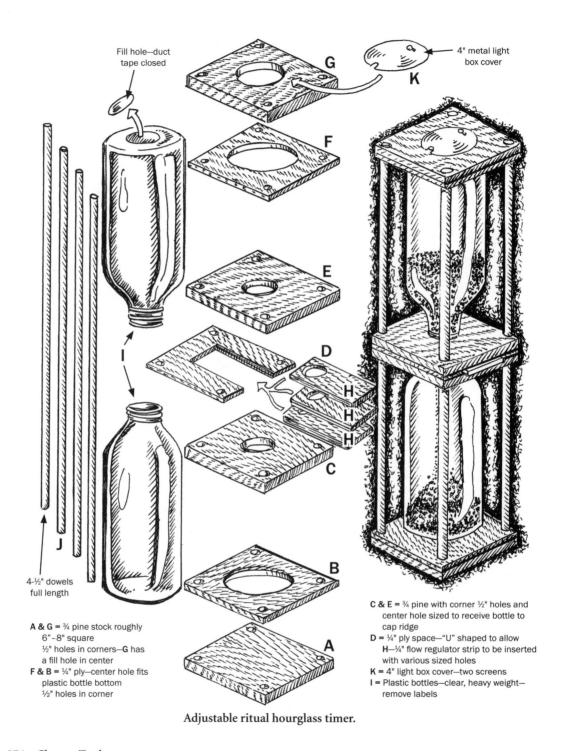

Fill hole—duct tape closed

G

4" metal light box cover

K

F

E

D

H
H
H

C

I

B

A

4-½" dowels full length

J

A & G = ¾ pine stock roughly
6"–8" square
½" holes in corners—**G** has
a fill hole in center
F & B = ¼" ply—center hole fits
plastic bottle bottom
½" holes in corner

C & E = ¾ pine with corner ½" holes and
center hole sized to receive bottle to
cap ridge
D = ¼" ply space—"U" shaped to allow
H—¼" flow regulator strip to be inserted
with various sized holes
K = 4" light box cover—two screens
I = Plastic bottles—clear, heavy weight—
remove labels

Adjustable ritual hourglass timer.

You will need to custom design this to fit your plastic bottles, so collect them first. We use sturdy flat-bottomed water bottles with a narrow top (liter soda bottles usually have a curved bottom shape and are too lightweight for sand). Then purchase four 3-foot-long half-inch dowels and gather a few square feet of ¼-inch plywood, and a few square feet of ¾-inch plywood or pine stock. Plan to cut most of your squares at least three inches larger than the diameter of your bottles; you will need room to drill half-inch holes in each of the four corners outside of the bottle diameter. Once you lay out one square with the corner holes, you can use it as a template to drill the rest. Cut three ¼-inch squares and four ¾-inch squares and get all your dowel holes drilled in the corners. Then with a circle drill bit or saber saw, cut the center holes in the squares:

- (A) ¾-inch ply, no center hole

- (B) and (F) ¼-inch ply, center hole to fit water bottle bottom diameter

- (C) and (E) ¾-inch ply, center hole to fit water bottle top, snug to stop at cap ridge

- (D) ¼-inch ply with a 2-inch slot cut to receive flow regulator strips

- (G) ¾-inch piece, 2-inch diameter fill hole. (Cut a hole in the bottom of one bottle bottom, too!)

- (H) Several ¼-inch ply strips, 2-inch wide with holes from ⅛ to ⅜ inch lined up to allow sand to pass between the bottles and regulate sand flow rate

Slide all the pieces together on the dowels as in the diagram, and once you know it all fits, glue and tack nail it all together. Fill the top bottle two-thirds full with sand through hole (G), tape the hole with duct tape, and add a 4-inch round metal electrical-box cover over the fill hole for security. Try it out and time it with different size regulator strips (H).

Infinity Step Gateway

This lightbox creates the illusion of infinite depth below you. The photo doesn't do it justice; the human eye can detect five or six layers of light rectangles receding into an immense depth!

Constructed with a wood frame of a 2 x 10-inch stock and a salvaged piece of ¾-inch-thick solid tempered glass, it can safely support a 600-pound person. Most urban areas have at least one glass manufacturer, where small reject panes can be bought and the box designed around the glass size, as we did (you cannot cut it!). The mirror is slightly angled to face a bit toward the direction of entry. This way you see the receding rectangles of lights before you are actually over them. It is powered by battery or 110-volt small LED string lights, and part of how it works is to shield them toward the glass so they are only seen reflected in the mirror.

This prop needs complete darkness to work well. Outdoors, we build a dark passageway made from a heavy tarp or black plastic thrown over a rope, with the bottom edges spread apart to form a triangular tunnel. The rope is either stretched between two tree branches or between staked poles. Add a door flap on each end to create total darkness. Indoors, a well-darkened room works fine.

The box is about a foot deep and for best effect outdoors we bury it to ground level and surround the ground around it with black cloth. A stepping stone, set back a few inches, will increase the step downward onto the glass. This is a good effect and keeps people from trying to step past the glass. Indoors, you need a small platform surrounding it with enough room to step onto and off of the lightbox. For this height you also need a short step at each end. Even when you absolutely know it is an illusion, most people have a difficult time making this "leap of faith"!

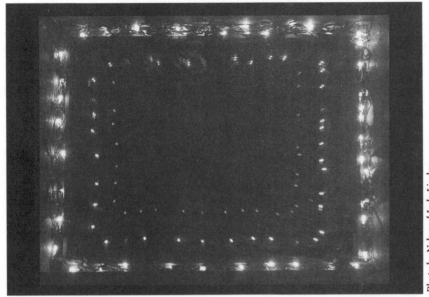

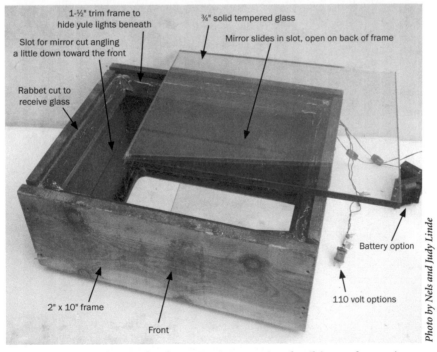

1-½" trim frame to
hide yule lights beneath

¾" solid tempered glass

Slot for mirror cut angling
a little down toward the front

Mirror slides in slot, open on back of frame

Rabbet cut to
receive glass

Battery option

2" x 10" frame

110 volt options

Front

Step into the Abyss and Infinity Box construction detail (top to bottom).

Natural Material Gateway

Grapevine and willow are present in hardwood forests and marshes across most of the United States. Wild grape is considered an invasive species, and many landowners are happy to have it harvested. Both are flexible and can be bent and wrapped to create a freestanding gateway that can accept many thematic additions and decorations for ritual.

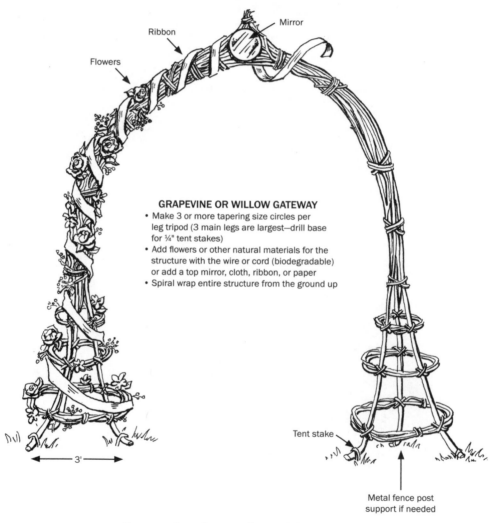

Flowers

Ribbon

Mirror

GRAPEVINE OR WILLOW GATEWAY
- Make 3 or more tapering size circles per leg tripod (3 main legs are largest—drill base for ¼" tent stakes)
- Add flowers or other natural materials for the structure with the wire or cord (biodegradable) or add a top mirror, cloth, ribbon, or paper
- Spiral wrap entire structure from the ground up

3'

Tent stake

Metal fence post support if needed

Construction of a natural material gateway.

You will need a pile of willow or grapevine in various lengths and thicknesses. Save the six heaviest and longest pieces (at least 6 to 8 feet long) to form the two tripod legs. To join pieces use either a strong biodegradable cord or tie wire. First, make six circles by bending the lighter weight material—two each of 3-foot, 2-foot, and 1-foot diameter—and tie each in several places to keep them a circle. You may need several layers so it is built like a cable circle. Then lay out your six heaviest pieces in groups of three, and create the tripod bases by joining the legs to the circles at one, two, and three feet from the bottom, so by four feet your tripod legs can join together. Stand your two tripods up and, with help in steadying them, join them to form an arch with additional overlapping pieces. If you have sturdy material and tight construction it will stand freely, but you can also add two "T" metal fence posts in the center of each leg tripod for support, or stake each leg down to aid stability. Once you have it up, wrap the entire structure with lightweight material, joining with ties as needed. Add ribbon, flowers, paper, or cloth and even add a top mirror or emblem for additional decoration.

Participant Potato Printed Gateway

You can use this design to mask acrylic panels, have ritual participants print theme images on them, then reveal a hidden design underneath and transform the panels into a ritual exit gateway.

We purchased two 2 x 6-foot pieces of acrylic. These worked great because the size was right for creating male and female outlines, and because acrylic comes with a clear plastic protective sheeting, perfect for creating a stencil mask. Secure enough 2 x 2-inch stock to create frames for your acrylic. Make the frames so the inside dimension is about a half-inch smaller than the acrylic. A saw kerf cut down this surface allows the acrylic to slide in and be held securely as the frame is assembled. On each long side outer edge are mounted two pipe straps to fit half-inch pipe.

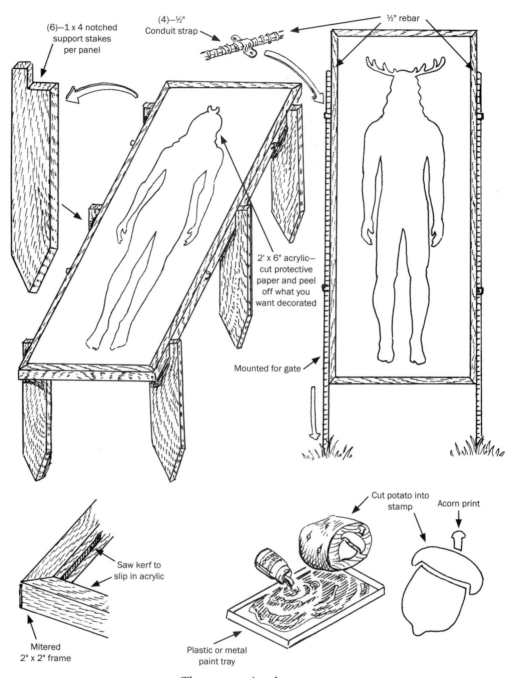

(6)—1 x 4 notched support stakes per panel

(4)—½" Conduit strap

½" rebar

2' x 6" acrylic— cut protective paper and peel off what you want decorated

Mounted for gate

Saw kerf to slip in acrylic

Mitered 2" x 2" frame

Cut potato into stamp

Acorn print

Plastic or metal paint tray

The potato printed gateway.

To make the frames into outdoor work tables, we cut six 1 x 4-inch stakes with a notch near the top to support the frame while participants printed the acrylic. Two 6-foot pieces of half-inch rebar were driven into the ground, ready to receive and support each panel frame vertically when slid down through the pipe straps. We placed the two frames about four feet apart so printing helpers could stand between them holding the paint trays and potato print blocks. You can install the rebar posts at the ends of the panels just in advance so they are in place ready to make the gateway but not in the way of the ritual.

We carefully cut male and female outlines on the acrylic coating with a razor knife and peeled off the portion within the outline. Participants used half potatoes with designs cut into them to print over the whole acrylic surface, unable to see the stencil. As the ritual progressed and the paint dried, the stencil was carefully removed from around the shapes, revealing them as the printed surface. At the ritual ending, we raised the panels to vertical, slid them onto the rebar posts, and removed the support stakes to form an exit gate.

Gong Gateway

You can use two PVC pipe frames to suspend steel pipes cut to a pentatonic scale as a sound gateway to enter a ritual. Hank Knaepple designed and built this one. Once you have a bass note pipe cut, you can get other notes close in length and then fine-tune them. Use Internet resources for length proportions of wind chimes, or if you have an engineer in the team use the Fourier theorem [32] to compute them.

---

32   S. Scott Moor, "Designing a Wind Chime," http://leehite.org/documents/Wind_Chimes _Student_Project_S_Scott_Moor.pdfs.

Photo by Nels and Judy Linde

Gong Gateway on display.

Use 3-inch PVC pipe to build two support structures: two 8-foot legs are joined with a 6-foot crosspiece with elbow fittings and slid onto heavy "T" fence posts to support each bank of pipe gongs. You can add angled support ropes anchored to side stakes for additional stability if needed. For the best sound, suspend the pipe gongs from a rope that crosses the pipe diameter through holes drilled about a quarter of the way down from the top. To stabilize the pipes from excessive swinging while being played, stretch a light cord twice between the frame legs, weaving it alternately between the pipes near their bottom. Play them with a rubber mallet!

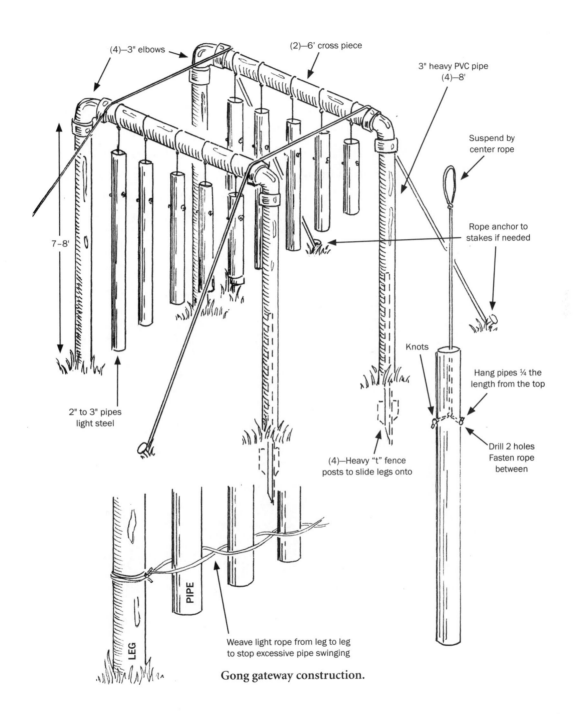

(4)—3" elbows

(2)—6' cross piece

3" heavy PVC pipe
(4)—8'

Suspend by
center rope

Rope anchor to
stakes if needed

7–8'

2" to 3" pipes
light steel

Knots

Hang pipes ¼ the
length from the top

Drill 2 holes
Fasten rope
between

(4)—Heavy "t" fence
posts to slide legs onto

LEG

PIPE

Weave light rope from leg to leg
to stop excessive pipe swinging

Gong gateway construction.

Sheer Flags/Path Gateways

Create colorful sheer fabric flags that double as path-working gateways when mounted on rebar support poles. These large sheer flags moving, almost floating, around and over participants can be a great tool during energy raising. We have found these quick to install and remove as gateways, and versatile for many purposes. Eight-foot-tall, half-inch rebar is easily driven into the ground and removed. These have a welded bump (or a wrap of tape or wire will work) an inch from the top to catch and support a 1 x 2-inch crosspiece drilled with a ⅝-inch hole. Use an 8-foot 1 x 2-inch pine board for the flag handle, and a crosspiece and staple through a strip of light cardboard to affix the sheer fabric.

Sheer fabric gateway and removable flag.

Wheel Rope Canopy

Initially developed and offered around the world by the EarthSpirit Community,[33] "web weaving" rituals use a pole with many strings stretched from the top to the ground, creating the spokes of a web for participants to weave prayers into. This derived variation used a 4-foot wheel mounted to spin atop an 8-foot-tall four-by-four with twine spokes connected to perimeter poles, creating an 80-foot-in-diameter canopy. The perimeter poles were lowered so participants could weave a web of horizontal twine and then tie their leaf-shaped wishes to it. Lifting the perimeter poles, the canopy could be raised to eight feet so participants could fully walk under it. By walking the perimeter poles in a circle, the whole web rotated above participants, and then by stopping the wheel rotation, the whole web was drawn into a central fire and offered as an energy raising.

The wheel part of this prop can be built many ways, but integral to how it spins is a metal rebar point mounted into the end of the support 4 x 4-inch pole. Building the wheel around a 1-foot threaded pipe allows for a flange on one end to mount to the wood, and a cap on the other end gives a rounded surface under the cap for the point to rotate upon. The wheel adds a dramatic touch, a giant canopy rotating above the participants, but the same canopy effect can be achieved with a stationary center pole, just without the rotation. To have a fire surrounding the central pole, we sunk it four feet into the ground and then shielded the first three feet aboveground by putting a piece of 8-inch stovepipe around the pole and filling it with sand.

---

33   The EarthSpirit Community, www.earthspirit.com.

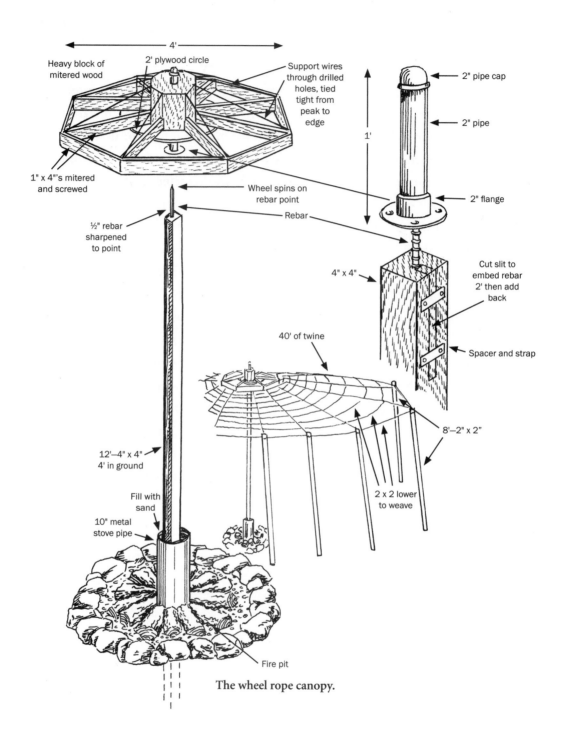

4'

Heavy block of mitered wood

2' plywood circle

Support wires through drilled holes, tied tight from peak to edge

2" pipe cap

2" pipe

1'

2" flange

1" x 4"'s mitered and screwed

Wheel spins on rebar point

Rebar

½" rebar sharpened to point

4" x 4"

Cut slit to embed rebar 2' then add back

40' of twine

Spacer and strap

8'–2" x 2"

12'–4" x 4" 4' in ground

Fill with sand

2 x 2 lower to weave

10" metal stove pipe

Fire pit

The wheel rope canopy.

Popcorn Poppet

This is a design for a poppet figure in which participants add popcorn. It was then laid over a fire for a tasty energy raising!

An inch-thick beeswax poppet shape was cast onto a 4-foot sheetmetal circle. This sheet was reinforced with a pentacle of tack-welded ¼-inch steel rod on the underside. We used wet clay lined with aluminum foil to make a 1-inch raised outline of the shape on the support sheet to pour the beeswax into, and then removed the clay, leaving a aluminum foil edge. After pouring in the beeswax and letting it harden, we drilled hundreds of ¾-inch holes into the poppet.

To install the support circle and poppet over the fire, we drove five heavy metal fence posts evenly spaced around a 4-foot fire pit. Between them we stretched heavy wire forming a pentacle, just above the large fire. Participants added popcorn kernels to the poppet holes, and then the top was slathered in shortening. With a full-width raging fire just below the support wire, the poppet was added, and within a minute, popcorn explosion! An experiential energy raising that can be adapted for any image design.

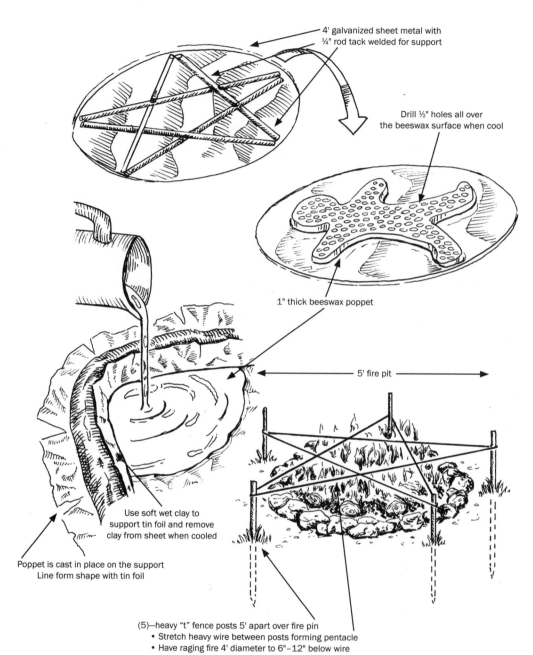

4' galvanized sheet metal with
¼" rod tack welded for support

Drill ½" holes all over
the beeswax surface when cool

1" thick beeswax poppet

5' fire pit

Use soft wet clay to
support tin foil and remove
clay from sheet when cooled

Poppet is cast in place on the support
Line form shape with tin foil

(5)—heavy "t" fence posts 5' apart over fire pin
• Stretch heavy wire between posts forming pentacle
• Have raging fire 4' diameter to 6"–12" below wire
• Fill poppet holes with popcorn and shortening
• Place pan with poppet on wire over fire

The Jiffy Poppet.

Snake Walking Puppet

This is a large multiple-person walking snake puppet with glowing eyes. The technique can create whatever length puppet you need: a dragon, peacock, dragonfly, etc. Papier-mâché can work for the head, but it is more fragile to carry.

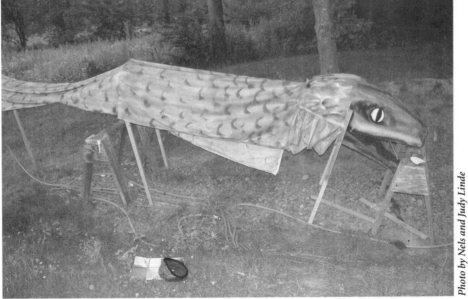

Constructing the snake head, the muslin-covered snake head, and the completed snake walking puppet with tail and supports (left to right, top to bottom).

We used a lightweight plywood base structure, adding shaping with heavy wire supports to create the finished shape. Muslin was then stretched tight over the form and stapled. Latex paint further stretched and hardened the fabric. We added a spring-loaded lower jaw with a tire inner tube rubber tongue that bounced as we walked. The glowing eyes were two battery-operated closet dome lights masked with black electrical tape. A sturdy 2 x 2-inch removable walking handle was added to each side, steadied by a half-inch plywood brace. These two carrying handles could be dropped into two 7-foot by 3-inch PVC pipes (mounted over "T" fence posts) to form a gateway. The same design brace and double handles had a curve of heavy wire arching the top to support the body cloth, and ties were sewn into the cloth. The tail was supported by a single 2 x 2 with a circle of heavy wire to give it shape.

Photo from Harmony Tribe Photo Archives

Dancing behind a soft-look cloth shadow screen.

Shadow Screen

Create a display screen to perform behind and create a shadow display for your audience. The concept can be used indoors with a projector screen lit from behind. Your ritual dramas will be enhanced when you display just the shadows of the characters, using the imagination.

For a large outdoor screen, we used 4-inch PVC pipe and fittings. Two 7-or 8-foot pieces make the height, and 8-or 10-foot pieces make the top and bottom width. Join as shown with elbows at the top and "T" fitting at the bottom, and secure with duct tape. Cover it with a large white cotton sheet to give softened shadows (as in the photo). Translucent white greenhouse-cover plastic will give very sharp, crisp shadows. Duct tape your covering tightly to the PVC frame and slide the whole frame down upon heavy "T" fence posts. A portable halogen shop light works best for illumination, but even a clip-on type reflector light mounted on a chair back will work.

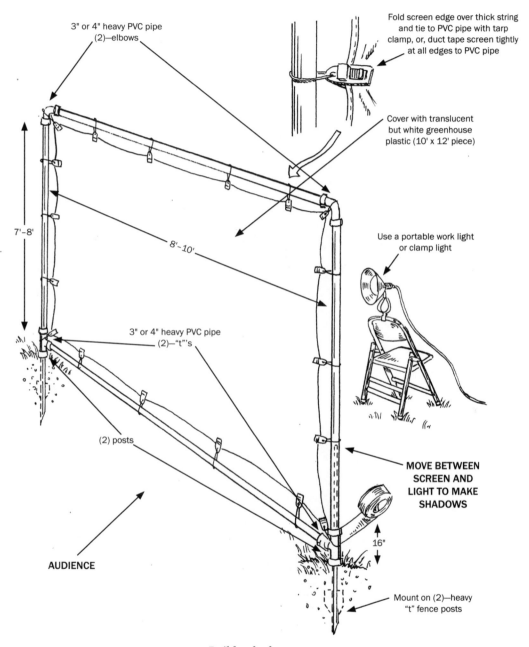

3" or 4" heavy PVC pipe
(2)—elbows

Fold screen edge over thick string
and tie to PVC pipe with tarp
clamp, or, duct tape screen tightly
at all edges to PVC pipe

Cover with translucent
but white greenhouse
plastic (10' x 12' piece)

Use a portable work light
or clamp light

7'-8'

8'-10'

3" or 4" heavy PVC pipe
(2)—"t"'s

(2) posts

MOVE BETWEEN
SCREEN AND
LIGHT TO MAKE
SHADOWS

16"

AUDIENCE

Mount on (2)—heavy
"t" fence posts

Build a shadow screen.

Magic Fire Starter

This is an easy-to-build-and-test device to make a fire appear to start spontaneously. The design is a completely hidden outdoor foot switch and safe ignition system. The timing must be intuitively guessed, aided by testing. It takes 20 to 30 seconds for ignition once the switch is tripped, allowing time to move away from the fire and switch area.

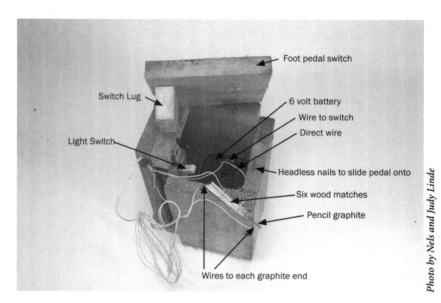

Foot pedal switch

Switch Lug

6 volt battery

Wire to switch

Direct wire

Light Switch

Headless nails to slide pedal onto

Six wood matches

Pencil graphite

Wires to each graphite end

Photo by Nels and Judy Linde

The magic remote fire starter (detail in top photo).

Photo by Nels and Judy Linde

A small wooden box is built with scrap lumber just large enough to accommodate a square 12-volt battery and a household light switch. The box lid is designed with a piece that, when stepped on, flips the switch. Dig a post hole (8-inch diameter) deep enough to hold the top of the box at the base of the existing grass sod bottom, then remove any excess dirt and cover the lid with the removed sod from digging the hole. Remove any excess dirt, and with a hatchet cut a gash trench 1 inch deep along a 10- to 15-foot path from the box to the fire center. Light-gauge "doorbell" type two-strand wire is placed and covered in the trench.

One wire runs directly from the positive battery post to one end of the igniter. The second wire connects the negative battery post, through the switch, and onto the other end of the igniter. To build the igniter, remove the lead from a pencil about three inches long, and carefully wrap each bare wire end tightly around each end of the graphite. Then take about six stick matches and twister-seal them with the heads tightly pressed surrounding the center of the graphite rod. When the electricity is passed through the graphite, it quickly heats until the matches catch fire. Once the switch is completely concealed underground, I mark it with a small colorful tack or golf tee, so I can easily find it in ritual. Understand, you do all this in private, and do not allow participants or ritual team members to wander around the fire area once it is laid.

For the fire to start quickly, use more matches, finely shredded newspaper, and finely split pine or cedar kindling to make a "nest" for the igniter. We put a small pine stake in the center and clothespin the igniter up a bit so air is readily available and the kindling is lightly surrounding it on all sides and above. Using bone-dry wood, continue to lay a sound log cabin or tipi-style campfire structure around your ignition "nest" to completely conceal it, but loose enough to not restrict air into the igniter. In ritual, hit the switch and intuit and count in your mind to know exactly when to turn the focus to the fire lighting!

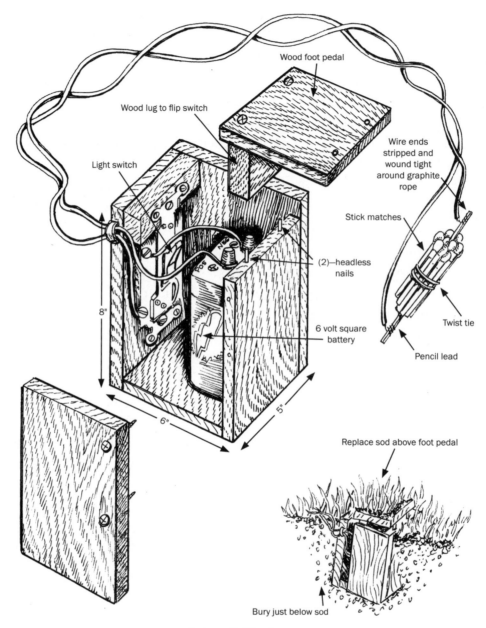

Wood foot pedal

Wood lug to flip switch

Light switch

Wire ends
stripped and
wound tight
around graphite
rope

Stick matches

(2)—headless
nails

Twist tie

6 volt square
battery

Pencil lead

8"

5"

6"

Replace sod above foot pedal

Bury just below sod

Automatic Fire Starter.

The True Mirror

We see ourselves as a reflection daily in our mirrors, but how can we see ourselves truly as others see us? We all have imperfections and asymmetry in our faces, one ear lower than the other or a smile lifted on one side. When we see a double-reflected image, we may not even recognize ourselves!

This true mirror uses acrylic mirrors and is designed for two people at a time to use, one on each side. For it to work you must be directly at eye level, have the perpendicular mirrors placed at precisely 90 degrees, and look at it from a position 45 degrees out from the mirror intersection, directly into the intersection. The mirror reflects our split face to the opposite side of a flat reflection so we see ourselves as we appear to others. Lettering reflected appears normal, not mirror-reversed. We are so used to looking in mirrors that if we move our hand to touch our right ear or face we are shocked to see our left reflected hand do the touching (as it would appear for someone looking right at us)!

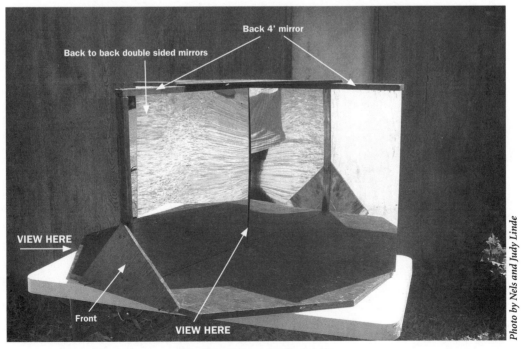

The True Mirror (with detail).

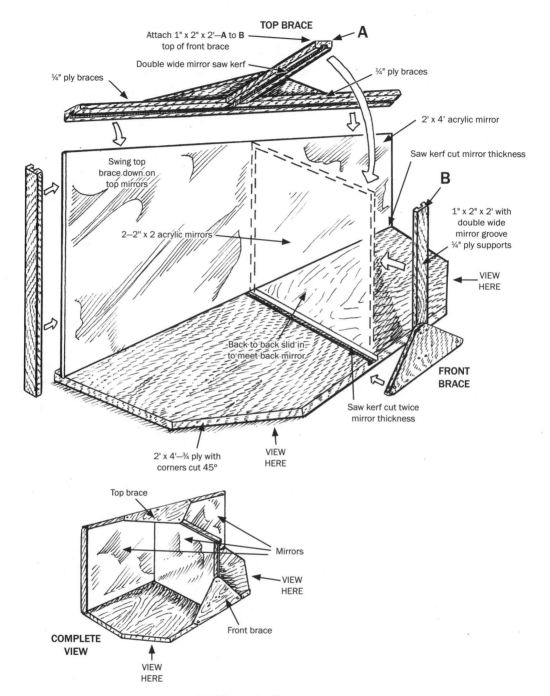

TOP BRACE

Attach 1" x 2" x 2'—**A** to **B**
top of front brace

A

Double wide mirror saw kerf

¼" ply braces

¼" ply braces

2' x 4' acrylic mirror

Saw kerf cut mirror thickness

B

Swing top
brace down on
top mirrors

1" x 2" x 2' with
double wide
mirror groove
¼" ply supports

2—2" x 2 acrylic mirrors

VIEW
HERE

Back to back slid in
to meet back mirror

FRONT
BRACE

Saw kerf cut twice
mirror thickness

2' x 4'—¾ ply with
corners cut 45°

VIEW
HERE

Top brace

Mirrors

VIEW
HERE

**COMPLETE
VIEW**

Front brace

VIEW
HERE

Building a double true mirror.

This double true mirror is built to break down and store away, and to be as lightweight as possible. The base is of ¾-inch plywood cut 24 x 48 inches long. One corner of each base end is cut at a 45-degree angle, and that is where participants will look into the mirror from. A 48-inch saw kerf cut ⅛-inch deep runs down one edge to receive the single 2 x 4-foot acrylic mirror along the back. A 24-inch saw kerf, equal to two mirror thicknesses, is cut ⅛-inch deep, dividing the base into two 2 x 2-foot squares (with one corner angled at the viewing corner). The front brace and top brace are similarly kerf cut and made to be perpendicular with triangles of ¼-inch plywood as support. To assemble, place the base on a tall 4-foot draped table, set in the mirrors, and hold them in place as the top and front braces are added and connected at the front top corner, holding the mirrors tightly together and perpendicular in each direction.

Photo by Nels and Judy Linde

Nels trying to touch the right side of his face as seen in the mirror.

Fire Effigy Figure

We have built more than 25 of these over the years, and you can use the same principles to build one on a smaller scale. It starts with two large poles of green-cut poplar laid in an "X" with the top ends on sawhorses. Securely screw and wire all the framing together. Add a pelvis just below the crosspoint and a collarbone piece above it using more poplar. Add fingers using deck screws to make hands on the top ends and wrap the arms with evergreen trimmings to fill them out. The head form is a globe made of wild grapevine, mounted on a pole and fastened to the collarbone and the main "X" crosspoint. To reduce ladder time, wrap the chest with grapevine and stuff it full of small dried brush before you are ready to lift the structure. Dig two post holes 3 to 4 feet deep with room for a "kick board"—a board inserted in each leg hole to keep the legs from sliding past the hole as you lift.

Photo by Nels and Judy Linde

The fire effigy frame built on the ground.

Raising the roughed-in fire effigy frame.

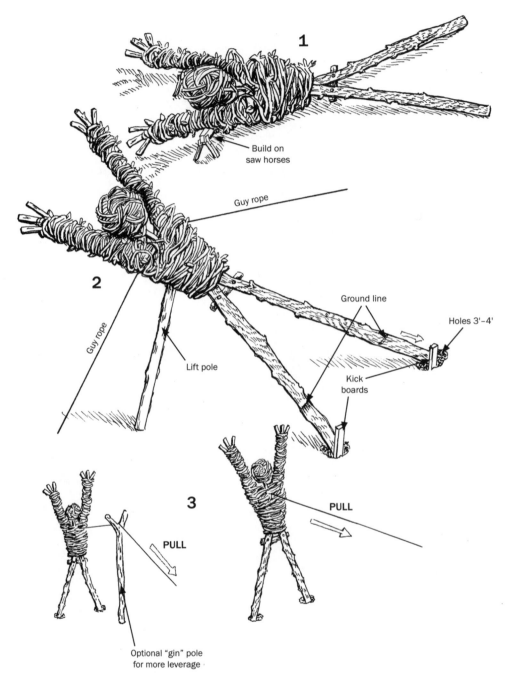

1

Build on
saw horses

Guy rope

2

Guy rope

Lift pole

Ground line

Holes 3'–4'

Kick
boards

3

PULL

PULL

Optional "gin" pole
for more leverage

Building a large-scale fire effigy.

For these large effigies we use a tractor loader to raise it, but you can use muscle and get the chest end lifted as high up as you can reach, and then brace it in place with a "V"-topped pole lodged into the chest. We have people holding guy ropes to keep it steady as the tractor (or car, or muscle) gets on the other end and, with a rope tied to the collarbone, pulls it the rest of the way until it drops in the post holes. For more leverage for lifting the structure to vertical, you can use a "gin" pole, a tripod-anchored derrick pole with a pulley or a block and tackle on top. Now pull out the kick boards and tamp the legs in place, filling their holes with stones and dirt. Add sticks surrounding the leg until they each become a cone of brush. Once that is done, it should be sturdy enough to lean a ladder on. From there it's all "more sticks!" as you fill it out using ladders, wrapping occasionally with wire as needed, until you like the form. We spend a whole day just finishing the face and covering the whole skin with corn husks, wrapping occasionally with twine. Light with a torch, and stand back!

Ritual: Stone Soup

·················

Location: Sacred Harvest Festival, 2005
© Judith Olson Linde and Nels Linde

Ritual intent

Community magic lays the seed for future growth. Raise the power, be reborn, and feed the self.

Ritual description

Our community magic lays the seed for future growth. What do we offer, what can we bring? What do you have? When we build together, we reap the rewards. Raise the power, be reborn, plant the seed, and feed the self.

Ritual context

This ritual's opening was used for several rituals offered over a week's time with the unifying theme "Folk Magick." This had the effect of creating a unifying element between the rituals and evoking the feelings experienced in the previous one. It also had the advantage of allowing us to put increased effort into refining one good opening, and then having it ready for the next ritual in advance. It allowed participants to focus on the rite knowing already how the space is made sacred. The entire series of rituals was written in rhyme.

Ritual setup and supplies

At the circle center was a fire with five metal fence posts around it. Heavy wire was stretched taut between the five posts in a pentacle shape just above the fire. On one side of the fire was a large cast-iron cauldron, with a smaller one (filled with vegetable soup) inside it, lidded and covered with a cloth. On the other side of the fire waited a 4-foot beeswax poppet, supported by a sheet-metal circle with metal carrying poles. The beeswax poppet was an inch thick and covered with ¾-inch drilled holes to the base. (See chapter 12 for details on making this poppet.) At the gate was an array of baskets, each holding a different item participants could choose to add to the "soup." These items were symbolic of energies that benefit a community, such as toy soldiers for protection, seeds for new growth, feathers for freedom or dreams taking flight, play money for financial support, safety pins for safety, keys for new opportunities, and paper clips for organization.

Team members

Ritualista, 4 elementals, 12 ritual helpers, Bard storyteller. The ritual team in the opening was dressed in flowing skirts or baggy pants and all had folk-style head scarves.

Ritual script

The song for the procession to the ritual area gate was "Behold (There Is Magic)" by Abbi Spinner McBride. A core of 12 team members led the procession in a "spirit canoe" formed by six pairs standing shoulder to shoulder with their inside hand on the inside shoulder of the person in front of them. Their outside hands became paddles for the canoe, swung back in cadence to the festivants' clapping and drumbeats, and in time with the song.

At the gate, the spirit canoe folk took up the baskets of symbolic items. Two team members smudging at the gate acted as regulators into the circle. The Ritualista whispered to each as they approached the baskets: "*If you could contribute anything freely to your community, what would it be? First you must take it!*" Festivants chose what items to take and entered the ritual area.

Standard folk ritual opening

The festivants entered through the gate and formed a circle. Four elemental team members wandered around outside the circle as if no one was there. They carried a potato fork (N), broom (E), scythe (W), and staff (S). Entering the circle, they took their respective places in front of altars facing into the circle. The Ritualista entered the circle with a rhyming chant:

"In a clearing on a moonlit [cloudy, twilight] night, illuminated by firelight,
Assembled here we circle round, to see what blessings can be found
In the company of other folk, and what magic we may invoke."

The Ritualista paused at each direction and signaled with a tambourine, saying a simple rhyming call:

(East) *"Where the moon rises and dawn breaks the day, on scented breeze newness wafting our way."*

(South) *"To the South lie the sands of fire, choices made, the loin's desire."*

(West) *"In the West the misty shore, rainbow's end, the ocean's roar."*

(North) *"To the North the mountains of stone, caves of my ancestors, antler, bone."*

As the Ritualista mentioned each direction, each elemental team member turned to their altar, lit their candle, blew a kiss to their direction, and then turned back toward the inside of the circle. Rotating slowly in the center with her arms out, the Ritualista continued:

"The Lord and the Lady are present here too, and spirit, as always, within each of you."

The Ritualista now pointed out the cauldron near the fire:

"This empty pot will feed no kin, without your gift we can't begin.
Can you offer a smile, an open door? We build with trust, love at the core.
We learn from those who came before."

Team member regulators were at each altar. The Bard began the folk story of Stone Soup (see chapter 3), with four pauses included in his tale. At each pause, an elemental team member brought the festivants in his or her quarter into the circle, beginning with the North–East group (the people between the North altar and the East altar). The festivants traveled by the cauldron and added their objects. As they passed to return to their place in the circle, their elemental team member gave each a few popcorn kernels and asked this question:

"What seeds can you plant to ensure that our community grows?"

The story ended after the last quarter (West to North section) of festivants added their contributions. The team members then moved to the cauldron, and as the soup was transformed, the Ritualista said:

"From what we contribute, with value unknown,
a hearty broth of strength has grown."

The soup cauldron was lifted out of the bigger cauldron and taken around the circle. The thick soup, still warm, was distributed to each participant in tiny paper cups. When the soup givers were about a quarter of the way around, the Ritualista called for everyone's attention and said:

"How can we ensure this bounty for tomorrow?
A sense of belonging, from which our children can borrow.
For continued growth, you must plant your seeds,
and harvest your intent with deeds."

The poppet, on its support circle, was carried around the circle by two team members as festivants poked popcorn into the drilled holes in the beeswax. The fire tender kept stoking to make the central fire roar. When the poppet had completed the circle, it was carried to the center near the fire. A team member seductively smeared Crisco all over the poppet by hand, and then it was laid on the wire pentacle over the fire to be "popped."

The Ritualista said:
*"With the sweetness of magic, with fire transformed,
join power and hands! Make our image reborn!"*

Drumming and the song "We Are Your People," by Beverly Frederick, began, and the team members gathered in the circle to dance around the fire as the popcorn began to pop. The song faded away as the drumming and dancing overtook the participants and the poppet burst into flames. The Ritualista clanged the Stone Soup kettle to signal the circle's close. The elementals closed the circle, extinguishing their candles as the song returned for a final energy raising, and the Ritualista bowed to the center. The spirit canoe re-formed and led the group to the exit gate and back to the gathering spot.

THIRTEEN

....

Adapting Ritual to Scale

It is nearly dark, and in fifteen minutes more than eight hundred people have moved through the labyrinth, singing in turn the three parts of a glorious song celebrating the time of growth. They have formed a layered circle a hundred feet around, and our team comes to the center to face them for the final rounds. With a hand-and-drum signal, the final verse begins, and on the last word, "Moon," the team all sweep their outstretched arms out, and all eight hundred singers stop on a dime! We gather the participants inward and bless our sunflower seed gift and the wishes collected over a week, now part of the shining sunflower raised over the fire. The Ritualista circles it with her oak staff focused upon it, calling all to empower the wishes and memories that they may grow in the coming year. With a sharp grounding thud, she plunges her staff to the earth and the fire erupts! Drumming and dance fill the night.

CELEBRATE THE FULLNESS RITUAL

You may have the opportunity to take a ritual you have written or offered and rework it for a larger or smaller audience. Many of the methods covered in this book for creating effective ritual in groups can be applied and adapted for use in smaller groups or extremely large groups of 500 or more. Most of the rituals included were designed for between 100 and 200 people. At that size you can include a path-working or other experience that offers an intimate interaction with each person in some form. It still requires careful planning to execute well. When you expand your audience above 200 there are significant changes and adaptations that must be made to create something that will flow well and not last for hours! Adapting a medium-size ritual for a smaller audience is much easier.

Scaling Down

The ritual described in the introduction of this book, "The Union of the Elements," was originally an arc of three separate rituals that we combined for a smaller audience. Each part was essential to include to make the whole complete. The first two rituals each contained a personal interaction with a different prop, which were then combined into one for the final ritual. With a smaller audience, we were able to join these experiences together and embrace all three.

When scaling down an existing ritual outline, consider it an opportunity to refine the details of your ritual. It is just as satisfying to create an excellent experience for 25 people as it is for several hundred, and it is a chance to reach to the essence of your ritual intention. Assess what elements were fundamental and most effective in the larger version and vision how you can add more depth. When time concerns are reduced, you can do more one-to-one interaction with each participant.

Plan to keep your sacred space small so each person can see and be aware of the action, and of each other. If you used a swift gateway entry process, consider including a challenge or blessing relevant to the intention. Make every portion a time for personal interaction with your team. If you have included a path-working, you can double the intensity by adding sounds or smells to whispered words or actions. You will need strong modeling by your team to get a song or chant going, but you should have extra time at the ritual gathering to make sure everyone is familiar with the tune or words.

The most difficult part will be energy raising, as in a smaller group people tend to be more inhibited about moving or singing loudly. Have a plan to stimulate involvement by using your team to draw people out and closer to the center. We all feel freer in a tightly knit crowd and not being observed as the center of attention. Allow time at the ritual ending for all the participants to connect with each other. Here a slow spiral dance works well so participants have the time to look directly into each other's eyes.

Scaling Up

Scaling up is harder than scaling down and requires consideration of more factors. What worked well for 50 people may be a disaster for 200. Take the time to look at each portion of your outline and vision the effects of increased numbers at each point. Wherever people are restricted in their passage, there is the potential it will become a "choke" point that causes waiting and disengagement. Anything that you are handing out or any activity that is individually experienced will need more time to complete and more team involvement.

••••••••••••

EXAMPLE

The "Gratitude" ritual in chapter 2 worked great for about 120 participants. To revise the script and team roles for 400 participants, here are some changes we would consider:

- Create two identical paths of five veils each, and have one whisperer say all the lines at each veil, keeping the team number the same.

- Send four to six participants at a time down each path as a group.

- Have both paths join at the sixth veil and deities.

- Assign ten whisperers double duty upon entering the circle. Five would assist the deity pair with multiple bowls of grapes and handing them out. Spread the other five whisperers around the center of the circle and have them each recite the spoken lines in turn (spoken by Ritualista 1 and Ritualista 2 originally) facing outward toward the participants as the grapes are passed out.

- Keep the spiral dance at the ending, but lead it much slower for a large group.

With these changes, essentially the same ritual could be expanded in size, staying within the same basic time frame with the same size ritual team, and providing two paths, five extra veil gateways, and a lot more grapes to distribute!

Processions

Once a ritual gets over a couple hundred people, you must apply some special techniques to accommodate a gate entry. The group could be broken into several processions designed to take different routes and speeds to arrive with staggered timing at the ritual site. When a very large procession is arriving at the same time, it may be necessary to have multiple entry gates, like highway toll booths. Use multiple entry gateways that either all provide the same experience or offer varying experience if you have a large enough ritual team to support them. Your participants will naturally gravitate to the shortest line, keeping any waiting times minimal. Having your procession move right into sacred space avoids any gateway slowdown, but you will still need a team of greeters to guide people to suitable placement.

Often a large procession will arrive all at once to the ritual site. Use two people holding a 4 x 10-foot veil to slow them into manageable groups by lifting the veil to float like a parachute until a dozen or so pass under and then dropping the veil to halt entry for a time. This can also be a method to offer a smaller group path-working as part of the entry process.

Create Layers

In large rituals (300-plus), a gateway can be used to break participants entering en masse into individuals, pairs, or more manageable groups of 5 to 15 people. Plan for a team of guides to aid the process. A hundred people will form a single-layer circle nearly a hundred feet across. When a ritual exceeds 150, use gracious guides to help divide the circle into several layers (at least one extra layer per hundred people). Use your modeling skills with sweeping hand and arm motions to alternate layers left or right of a dividing guide to fill the space. You might even add floor marking tape (outside, use garden lime) for white lines that visually direct people to form multiple layers. This is not the time to start barking crowd-control orders; plan ahead to make it as silent and painless a process as possible! You may want to direct people of shorter stature, those with children, those with chairs, or limited mobility people into the inner ring. This ensures more will be able to see and hear. Prepare your team with instructions to adapt to participants' responses. If someone does not wish to go where directed, as a gracious host you must honor their choice.

In the "Ritual of the 13 Moons" we needed to provide 12 different experiences that participants would rotate through. We developed an entry process where we counted participants as they entered and formed a large circle. We used guides to divide and then lead them into 12 individual circles to receive each experience as a smaller group of about 12 people. A ritualista then used our hourglass prop to determine a set time for the experience to be completed and sounded a gong. A guide led each group to form the next experiential circle in the series. After 12 gongs, all 150 people had had the same 12 experiences.

Limit Waiting

We all hate to wait in line, and in a ritual it can destroy any engagement you have built or hope to maintain. When a ritual audience exceeds 300, the ritualista is wise to exclude experiences that are designed for an individual.

....

EXAMPLE

A 20-second experience will take an hour and 40 minutes for 300 individuals to pass through—and likely much longer!

1 experience every 20 seconds = 3 per minute = 100 minutes for 300 people

Add four more people offering the experience and take people in pairs:

- 4 experience stations, taking 2 people at a time
- 8 experiences every 20 seconds = 24 per minute = 12–13 minutes for 300 people!

Practice any limited group experience you plan and time how long it takes. Multiply by the projected audience (divided by small group size) and add a generous cushion to fully realize how long this requires your participants to wait and stay engaged. A reasonable guideline is to have two to four people offering the same experience for every hundred people you expect in your audience. Remember, people will wait, both for the experience and also for the balance of the audience to complete theirs. Don't be afraid to offer some intimate interactions, but apply these design principles to mitigate any waiting time.

Provide for a participatory or entertaining activity during a wait time. We have a few strong singers to lead people in song or chant at either or both ends of a choke point. Understand this only works for about 30 minutes, at which point you lose both the lead voices and the engagement. We have also used a jester character, drumming, fire spinners, or a child-friendly activity to keep waiting people engaged. Keep any time-passing activity related to your intent, so those who are waiting stay in ritual mode. A ritual can sometimes be designed so once the waiting is passed, participants enter sacred space and then join right in an ongoing activity, eliminating an after-wait.

In large-scale ritual, whatever intimate experience is offered must be worth waiting for. Vision what you wish to offer and design it to work effectively for a small group instead of an individual. If you're including a blessing or offering a bit of food or libation, plan to have multiple team members provide the service. Establish dividing reference points so each server will know where in the group they start, and where they will meet those already served. Here directional altars or other marked reference points can help, as well as having some costuming that denotes team members for an easy visual reference of their location.

Assign team members to critical roles in minimizing waiting. Have a person who regulates the entry into any choke point. People can be so polite that they slow a process down, or tire of waiting and crowd an intimate experience. Have a team member assigned as a handler to monitor path-working and help solve problems. One person can't see the whole process, and without someone who can travel the whole path at the first sign of a slowdown and alleviate problems, they will continue and worsen. Most of your team will be occupied creating an experience and not be able to help. If a participant is really slow, whether in thoroughness or limited mobility, we often make sure they are first or last in a line. The handler could empower others to pass slow participants rather than wait. They may also advise team members on the path ahead to simplify the experience if it is too time-consuming.

Be Effective

In a large-scale ritual, you need to be realistic and sensitive to your team members' endurance, commitment, and abilities. It can be difficult to keep the team energized when they are performing a lengthy duty. It is just as important that they stay engaged, offering their authentic self, and don't succumb to fatigue or skimp under pressure. It is easy to say, "Just say this line to the next 200 people who pass by you," but doing that effectively may not be possible for many of your team.

In a 100-foot-diameter circle, every speaking person must project their words. All the great words you wrote will be wasted if they can't be heard. Make it a top requirement for speaking roles, and test their abilities in rehearsal with someone listening 100 feet away. Even then most people will naturally become quiet when put in the spotlight. Have a team member assigned for each speaker to focus on across the space while speaking and a hand signal to direct them to increase their volume. Blocking exactly where each role player should stand can be critical in large ritual. Have ritualistas speak across the center of the space—for instance, from the North if speaking to the South direction. A team member located in the center may need to rotate slowly as they project for most of their words to be heard. Practice this in rehearsal! In very large rituals (over 500), the background crowd noise is difficult to overcome when speaking. In rituals of this size, consider employing several unison speakers to either simultaneously speak from different areas or form a speaking chorus to deliver key lines. This takes practice and rehearsal so the words are clear and the message overcomes any group dissonance. If you enter the ritual and find people too spread out to hear, warmly invite them closer "so you can see them," rather than give a harsh verbal direction to move in. Consider every other solution before resorting to electronic methods of amplification. We've witnessed its use a few times, but never effectively.

A rehearsal, and maybe several, is vital when offering a large ritual. Despite all your visioning, it is the place where the reality of what you have planned really confronts you. This is the time to assess where any problems might occur, and to change the ritual outline or details to prevent them. It should be clear who is directing the rehearsal, and they should give strong leadership to listen, pay attention, and limit any distractions during rehearsal. Usually you will be the ritualista who takes this role and can make any final decisions and adjustments.

Practice all the lines and blocking of the speakers and any entrances and exits. You may find areas that are just too complex or beyond the scope of your team. Now is the time to simplify—better to have a smooth delivery than an awkward but grand plan. Make sure everyone is familiar with any cues, what sound or event triggers the next, and whom to look to for leadership during each part. Check your ritual stage during rehearsal for any lighting or visibility issues or any sensory distraction that may intrude later. Moving a prop, altar, or ritualista's position can make a world of difference.

If you haven't worked with your team on general presentation before rehearsal, you need to spend some time cheerleading their own engagement in their role. Stress the importance of being sincere and welcoming in every interaction during ritual. This will be more important than any "mistake" they might make. You will probably have many specialist team members who may just help with an entry, or a song, or one speaking part. They all need to know at least the overall ritual outline, signals, and cues, and whom to look for when they need guidance. You need them to understand they should join in with any team modeling, even if they are instructed to become a participant once their role is complete.

When a large group enters a sacred space unimpeded, there may be an aimless sort of milling about trying to find their proper place while waiting for everyone else to arrive. Have silent greeters who use gentle sound and motion with modeling to guide them to their places, not a verbal commanding tone.

As we mentioned before, getting a large group to begin moving is difficult and getting them to stop can be even harder! A clearly costumed leader can get movement started by exaggerated modeling after a sound (chime or gong) signal to draw attention. The same process will usually work to stop a moving mass, but it may be harder to get their attention. If the movement is part of an energy-raising action, follow the energy raising. Do not attempt to meddle with the movement even if your leadership mind says it needs to stop. Ride that energetic wave. Until fatigue is sensed and growing among the participants, adapt your plans to allow it to continue. Participants are engaged and invested at this time, so feel the joy of success and be patient!

Songs and Chants

Several hundred people singing or chanting in unison is an amazing addition to a ritual. Limit your ritual to songs or chants that are easily learned, and tunes that don't demand a great vocal range. Be sure to go over the song thoroughly, rehearsing at your gathering location prior to beginning, and have the lyrics printed and available. A song or chant that is adapted to use a call-and-response method is effective to garner involvement in a crowd. Be creative and add hand, arm, or body movements to energize participation.

The ritual included with this chapter used a three-part song that was the heart of the ritual, but to use something this complex in a ritual for 800-plus people took a lot of preparation and planning. First, we had the luxury of a morning gathering for several days prior to the ritual, during which we spent a few minutes every day teaching each part to participants. We had six to eight people with strong voices to begin and lead each part in the ritual, who had rehearsed separately all week. We provided the lyrics by printing them out in bold marker on muslin tabards worn by all our singers. That way the words were visibly reinforced for participants as they passed by.

Ending an engaged group song or chant is often accomplished with a gong or strong visual signal for the group to pay attention. In this ritual, the group passed through the simple labyrinth and moved out to form a multilayered circle, all singing the last part. At this point all of our singers came to the center and faced outward to the crowd. As the final verse repetitions approached, Judy held up her hand with three fingers up, and counted them down until the final verse. The drum accompaniment stopped for the last verse, and at the end of the last phrase all the singers flashed their arms rapidly out from their chest to fully extended and down. All 800 people stopped singing at the same moment. This crisp ending was as energetic as the voices in unison!

Ritual: Celebrate the Fullness (for 150 Participants)

. . . .

Location: Sacred Harvest Festival, 2007
© Judith Olson Linde and Nels Linde

Ritual context

When we offered this ritual for about 150 people, it was so powerful that we found the ending was not strong enough—no one wanted it to be over at this point! We decided that, given the opportunity, we would strengthen the ending. We were offered the opportunity to adapt this ritual for about 800 people at Pagan Spirit Gathering in 2012. (See the following ritual.) The three-part song incorporated in the ritual, "Dark of the Moon," by Karen Beth, is used with permission and has been recorded by Libana.[34] These are the lyrics:

Part 1: *Dark night, starry night, new beginnings. Dark night, starry night, will come to be.*

Part 2: *Dark of the moon, new beginnings. Plant a seed. Dark of the moon, come tonight.*

Part 3: *Dark of the moon, new beginnings. Dark of the moon, plant a seed tonight. Dark of the moon, what we envision will come to be by the full moonlight.*

Ritual intent

Celebrate the gifts of Divinity. Fill your vessel and those of our community.

Ritual description

This ritual is all movement and song. Plant the spiritual seeds for the coming year and touch the healing waters. Process from the Heart Chakra (gathering place).

Ritual setup and supplies

A central fire was lit at the ritual circle. A gravity-powered, hand-filled fountain was set up to the left of the labyrinth entrance and covered to hide it. A simple labyrinth of three circles winding to the central circle and fire was laid out with lines of barn lime. At the center

---

34   Listen to it at www.libana.com/listen_to_libana/s/dark_of_the_moon.

fire were three people in chairs with baskets of planting soil and little cups. A smudger and a team member handing out sunflower seeds were at the labyrinth entrance gate.

The Fountain

This was a large, primitive, fired-clay mask. It was designed to mount on two rebar poles in the ground. Behind the forehead was a small bucket with a drain hole with tubing to allow a trickle of water out the mouth. Colored twine hair hid the back and on the ground below was a decorative basket-bucket to catch the excess water. A team member with a small pitcher poured water into the head/top bucket, causing a stream of water to run out the mouth. The surplus was collected and used again from the bottom bucket, creating a continuous streaming fountain.

This used an approximate 60-foot circle, laid out with 6-foot-wide paths marked in white lime. The procession entered and encountered:

- [S1] = Four singers offering the first set of lyrics (all singers faced the procession and began singing as they were reached)

- [S2] = Four singers offering the second set of lyrics

- [S3] = Four singers offering the third set of lyrics

- [C] = Three people handing out cups filled with soil, one to each participant

- [F] = A person handing out a sunflower seed to plant in their cup

- [M] = The fountain maiden continuously filling the fountain to water each cup

Team members

Ritualista, smudger, seed giver, three soil givers, maiden at the fountain. Twelve singers spread out along the pathway. Four are singing each verse while holding placards with the words of each. Two wranglers, one at the center, one at the exit just past the fountain.

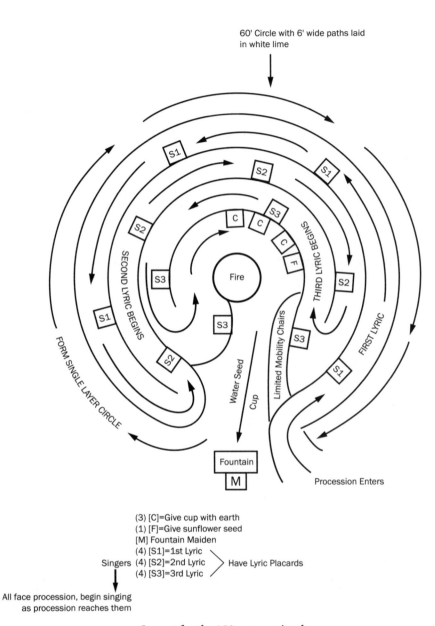

60' Circle with 6' wide paths laid in white lime

FORM SINGLE LAYER CIRCLE

SECOND LYRIC BEGINS

THIRD LYRIC BEGINS

FIRST LYRIC

Fire

Water Seed

Cup

Limited Mobility Chairs

Fountain

M

Procession Enters

(3) [C]=Give cup with earth
(1) [F]=Give sunflower seed
[M] Fountain Maiden
(4) [S1]=1st Lyric
Singers (4) [S2]=2nd Lyric ⟩ Have Lyric Placards
(4) [S3]=3rd Lyric

All face procession, begin singing
as procession reaches them

Layout for the 150-person ritual.

Ritual script

As the procession reached the entry gate, a wafting smudge and a seed were given. Participants were guided into the labyrinth by the Ritualista, past the first four singers, and counterclockwise into the outer circle to part 1 of the song. After completing the circumference back to the exit alley, participants reversed clockwise into the middle inner circle, where the next four singers started part 2 of the song. As participants reached the exit alley again, they reversed counterclockwise into the inner circle as the next four singers began part 3 of the song. The Ritualista took the whole labyrinth line around the fire into the center, where each festivant was given a cup of soil (and another seed if they dropped theirs) and shown by demonstration to plant it.

Still singing part 3 of the song, they were then led out the exit alley past the now unveiled and flowing fountain to water their seed. The line turned clockwise and re-formed outside the former outer circle that was now slowly moving into the center. This new circle held all the participants by the time it returned to the fountain. All were singing: *"Dark of the moon, new beginnings, dark of the moon, plant a seed tonight…"*

Once all had re-formed the outer circle, a three-beat drum cue was given, and the whole ritual team slowly gathered and walked to the center as the song slowed into a crescendo end. *"So mote it be!"* *"Merry meet, merry part, and merry meet again!"*

Ritual: Celebrate the Fullness (Adapted for 800 Participants)

· · · · · · · · · · · · · · · · ·

Location: Pagan Spirit Gathering, 2012
© Judith Olson Linde and Nels Linde

Ritual context

Adaptation for Pagan Spirit Gathering (PSG). Requests included the integration of a burnable prop, the inclusion of several honored guests as principal speaking parts, a time for Selena Fox to speak, and a change from the gift of a cup with watered earth and a seed, to energized seeds in a bag to take home and plant. The ritual should end with the burning of the prop and an energy raising. The ritual process was adapted to accommodate 800 people and to flow smoothly without any backup or waiting. The ending was modified to end with a powerful celebration on the last night of the festival. The ritual was produced without a hitch and was completed in about 40 minutes!

Ritual intent

Celebrate the gifts of Divinity. Manifest your wishes for our tribal community in the coming year. Receive and nurture the seed of your PSG experience to empower a new beginning for yourself under the new moon.

Ritual description

This ritual incorporates movement and song. Receive the spiritual seeds for the coming year. We encourage limited mobility people to arrive at the ritual circle 15 minutes early to secure participatory seating, or just join in the procession! A sacred space will be prepared for your arrival. Children are most welcome!

Program invitation

We'll be teaching the song and creating a sunflower composed of our wishes for the coming year for our tribe, beginning at Tuesday's New Moon morning meeting. We need many voices and much help to support this ritual! Please stop by the Hawkdancing booth anytime to contribute to the ritual, work on the song, or add your wishes!

The three-part song incorporated in the ritual, "Dark of the Moon," by Karen Beth, is used with permission and has been recorded by Libana.[35]

Advance participant preparation

The prop was a 4-foot-diameter sunflower design cut from ¼-inch plywood. It had small petals cut on the edges and a small stem to affix to a 2 x 4 for placement atop the central bonfire. The center 40-inch circle had 800 ¼-inch holes drilled in a double helix pattern on the sunflower. It was painted on both sides with green petals and a spiraling yellow, orange, and red center. Each morning for the five days before the ritual, the sunflower was taken to the morning meeting, where festival participants were encouraged to write on 4-inch squares of tissue paper (yellow, orange, and red) their wishes for themselves and the community, which they wanted to grow and bloom in the coming year. Each wish was rolled into a tube and inserted through a hole in the sunflower, and both ends were fluffed so it remained in place. This completed sunflower with wishes was used to decorate the final fire of the gathering. On Saturday morning, the ritual day, the early arrival of limited

---

35   Listen to it at www.libana.com/listen_to_libana/s/dark_of_the_moon.

mobility people at the procession was explained. The three separate verses of the song "Dark of the Moon" were taught in preparation at three separate meetings.

Photo from Harmony Tribe Photo Archives

Nels helps festivants insert written wishes into the sunflower prop.

Ritual setup and supplies

The final fire with the sunflower prop was laid at the ritual circle. A simple labyrinth pathway (12 feet wide, marked with lime) wound from the entryway into the central fire. All along this path's boundaries, and marking the turns of the path inward, stood 18 song leaders, each wearing a muslin chest tabard with the song part lyrics written on them. These lead singers worked on one of the three song parts all week, so that six for each verse could be spread around the three continuous winding concentric paths leading inward.

At the center fire, the path was split around the fire and then opened to a wide path leading directly out to the circle edge. Six "toll booth"-style lanes were on the entrance side of the fire, leading outward. Each lane had two people in a line offering a small bag and sunflower seeds. These were staggered so, like at a toll booth, as people reached this point they could easily see which had the shortest line and move to that lane. At the circle edge (next to the entrance) were limited mobility people in chairs directing people deosil as they passed through to form a multilayered circle after they exited the labyrinth.

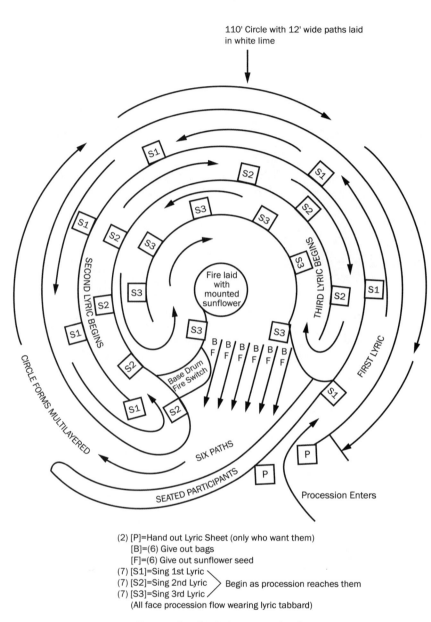

110' Circle with 12' wide paths laid in white lime

S1
S2
S1
S3
S2
S1
S2
S3
S3
SECOND LYRIC BEGINS
S3
S2
THIRD LYRIC BEGINS
S3
Fire laid with mounted sunflower
S1
S3
S2
S1
S1
FIRST LYRIC
CIRCLE FORMS MULTILAYERED
S2
S3
B/F B/F B/F B/F B/F B/F
S3
Base Drum Fire Switch
S1
S2
S1
P
SIX PATHS
P
SEATED PARTICIPANTS
Procession Enters

(2) [P]=Hand out Lyric Sheet (only who want them)
    [B]=(6) Give out bags
    [F]=(6) Give out sunflower seed
(7) [S1]=Sing 1st Lyric
(7) [S2]=Sing 2nd Lyric } Begin as procession reaches them
(7) [S3]=Sing 3rd Lyric
    (All face procession flow wearing lyric tabbard)

Layout for the 800-person ritual.

This used an approximately 110-foot circle, laid out with 12-foot-wide paths marked in white lime. The procession entered and encountered:

- [P] = Two people offering printed lyric sheets if desired
- [S1] = Six singers offering the first set of lyrics (all singers faced the procession, wearing a tabard with their lyric, and began singing as they were reached)
- [S2] = Six singers offering the second set of lyrics
- [S3] = Six singers offering the third set of lyrics
- [B] = Six people handing out a small drawstring bag, one to each participant
- [F] = Six people handing them a sunflower seed to put in their bag

Supplies for 1,000:

- 400 pounds fine garden lime (eight 50-pound bags) for labyrinth marking
- 1,000 small drawstring bags
- Bowl of water and a green branch for circle casting
- 1,000+ sunflower seeds in six containers
- 600+ 4-inch squares of yellow, orange, and red tissue paper
- plywood sunflower with mounting pole
- 200 printed lyric sheets (eight per page on 25 pages); only hand out to those who want them
- Tools: hatchet, post-hole digger, fire kit, three lime shakers, rope, hammer, screwdriver

Ritual team

Ritualista 1, Ritualista 2, four guest directional callers, Selena Fox, 18 ritual singers, 12 aides distributing seeds and bags, drumbeat player, two greeters, several wranglers.

Ritual script

All ritual players and limited mobility folks were called to the circle 15 minutes before the procession start. All 18 ritual singers were in place, as were the 12 aides handing out sunflower seeds and small drawstring bags in the toll booths and those seated at the exit. Many with limited mobility or folks in chairs can be incorporated here! Seated helpers were given tasks and set up.

As the camp procession took place, a simple, silent circle blessing with water by Ritualista 2 and a sacred space casting by Ritualista 1 were made for the assembled team awaiting the procession arrival. The guest directional callers silently called the quarters in their own way.

The procession began and wound through the whole camp with this chant and alternating drumbeat:

Sing tonight [boom—boom] Plant a seed [boom—boom] Dream tonight [boom— boom] Come tonight [boom—boom]

A lead caller shouted the upcoming words during the double drumbeat so the procession could join in as an echo.

The procession reached the labyrinth gate, the procession stopped, and the drums were silenced. A lone voice started the first song part, then a bass drum gave support with a slow walking beat. The labyrinth walk began (four to six people wide) with the second song repetition. Two people were seated at the entrance to hand out lyrics to those who wanted to carry one (optional). The path looped back the opposite way at the entry and toll booth exit path three times.

The 18 lead singers wearing lyric placards were stationed at the turns and along each path. As the path completed a circumference and reversed inward, the festivants were led by the singers to change to the next part of the song's round, and then again for the third part of the round. This third part of the round was maintained until all festivants exited through the toll booth lanes.

At the circle edge, people in chairs directed the exiting procession deosil to form the circle. As the assemblage all passed by, deeper into the labyrinth, the supporting singers turned to support the next part of the song round. When their part of the labyrinth emptied, they joined in the procession toward the center, emptying the circle.

As the last people left the toll booths, all inner-circle aides and singers followed, bringing all supplies out to the circle edge. All were singing: *"Dark of the moon, new beginnings, dark of the moon, plant a seed tonight…"* When everyone had exited, the song ending was cued by the lead singers backing into the circle facing outward into the circle of participants. Ritualista 1 held up three fingers, signifying three song verses left, then two, then as the bass drumbeat stopped Ritualista 1 held up one finger. As the last verse ended, the 18 lead singers swung their arms from the waist outward as the final phrase *"dark of the moon"* was emphasized. All 800 people stopped on cue!

The lead singers moved to join the participants, and Ritualista 1 said, *"Please step in closer, so we can all hear each other."* The lead singers motioned for the circle of people to step in closer to meet them. The circle was tightened. The four quarter callers stepped in and voiced their words facing the direction of their call to be heard across the circle. They were offered these words to use or could speak in their own words, their choice:

In the West facing East: *"We thank the East and ask the blessings of sweet air upon this symbol and our future and for attending this rite."*

In the North facing South: *"We thank the South and ask the blessings of transforming fire upon this symbol and our future and for attending this rite."*

In the East facing West: *"We thank the West and ask the blessings of healing water upon this symbol and our future and for attending this rite."*

In the South facing North: *"We thank the North and ask the blessings of rich earth upon this symbol and our future and for attending this rite."*

They rejoined the circle when finished.

Selena Fox, Ritualista 1 (Judy), and Ritualista 2 (Nels) all entered the center of the circle. All words were delivered facing outward and VERY loud!

Selena Fox, holding up a bag and a seed:
"We hold a symbol of our experience this week and of our tribe and spirit over the ages. It is the seed of what is to grow for us in the coming year. Nurture this gift and take it home to keep as a symbol, or to plant, or to offer under the approaching full moon."

Ritualista 2, focusing on the center fire:
"We call on our tribal spirit to bless this flower, as we send it forth to empower our wishes and our future. We thank Spirit, grateful for that feeling of community that sustains us through the times of struggle and pain."

Ritualista 1, circling the fire with her staff focused on the sunflower prop:
"As this rite comes to an end and we prepare to celebrate, let us each take a moment to focus on memories of the week, memories of joy, friendship, fellowship. Moments of promise, wonder, or renewal. And know that these memories will sustain us through the coming year until we meet here once again. For each of us, may our intent take root, grow, flourish, and blossom, with the aid of the waxing moon. So mote it be!"

Ritualista 2 had moved to the bass drum to trip the fire-starting switch (laid underground) when Ritualista 1 finished. As Ritualista 1 stomped her staff to the earth, the fire erupted. Ritualista 2 started a drumbeat and the singers led participants in a 20-minute dance around the fire as the sunflower wishes were burned and empowered. All the energies were thanked and released silently as the circle emptied.

Dark of the Moon Lyrics:

part 1   [:Dark night, starry night, new be—ginnings;
                  Dark night, starry night, will come to be:]

part 2   [:Dark of the moon, new be—ginnings, plant a seed:
                  Dark of the mo—ooon, come tonight:]

part 3   Dark of the [:Moon, new beginnings, dark of
                the moon plant a seed tonight,
                Dark of the moon what we envision
                will come to be in the full moonlight.
                Dark of the:]

Bibliography

Dolores Ashcroft-Nowicki, *The Shining Paths: An Experiential Journey through the Tree of Life* (The Aquarian Press, 1983; 2nd ed., Loughborough, UK: Thoth Publications, 1997)

Joseph Campbell, *The Hero with a Thousand Faces* (Novato, CA: New World Library, 3rd edition, 2008)

Joseph Campbell, *The Power of Myth* (New York: Anchor, 1991)

Aleister Crowley, *The Book of Thoth*, Ordo Templi Orientis

Barbara Ehrenreich, *Dancing in the Streets: A History of Collective Joy* (New York: Picador, 2006)

Donna Rosenberg, *Folklore, Myth, and Legends: A World Perspective* (Columbus, OH: Glencoe/McGraw-Hill, 2001)

David Salisbury, *Teen Spirit Wicca* (Soul Rocks Books, 2014)

Malidoma Patrice Somé, *Ritual: Power, Healing, and Community* (London: Penguin Books, 1997)

Patricia Telesco, *Spinning Spells, Weaving Wonders* (Berkeley: Crossing Press, 1996)

Ritual Books and Inspiration

Renee Beck and Sydney Barbara Metrick, *The Art of Ritual* (Berkeley: Apocryphile Press, 2009)

Isaac Bonewits, *Neopagan Rites: A Guide to Creating Public Rituals That Work* (Woodbury, MN: Llewellyn Publications, 2007)

Ivo Domínguez, Jr., *Casting Sacred Space: The Core of All Magickal Work* (Newburyport, MA: Weiser Books, 2012)

Amber K and Azrael Arynn K, *RitualCraft: Creating Rites for Transformation and Celebration* (Woodbury, MN: Llewellyn Publications, 2006)

Deborah Lipp, *The Elements of Ritual: Air, Fire, Water & Earth in the Wiccan Circle* (St. Paul: Llewellyn Publications, 2003)

Malidoma Patrice Somé, *Of Water and the Spirit: Ritual, Magic and Initiation in the Life of an African Shaman* (London: Penguin Books, 1995)

Starhawk, M. Macha NightMare, and the Reclaiming Collective, *The Pagan Book of Living and Dying: Practical Rituals, Prayers, Blessings, and Meditations on Crossing Over* (New York: HarperCollins and HarperSanFrancisco, 1997)

Oberon Zell-Ravenheart and Morning Glory Zell-Ravenheart, *Creating Circles and Ceremonies* (Wayne, NJ: New Page Books, 2013)

Songs and Chants: Where to Find Them

Edith Fowke and Joe Glazer, *Songs of Work and Protest: 100 Favorite Songs of American Workers Complete with Music and Historical Notes* (Mineola, NY: Dover Publications, 1973)

Hugin the Bard, *A Bard's Book of Pagan Songs: Stories and Music from the Celtic World* (St. Paul, MN: Llewellyn Publications, 2002)

Kate Marks, *Circle of Song: Songs, Chants, and Dances for Ritual and Celebration* (Full Circle Press, 1994)

The following Internet song and chant resources were all accessed in December 2015:
Ár nDraíocht Féin: A Druid Fellowship (ADF) songs and chants:
www.adf.org/rituals/chants-and-songs.html

Beth's Pagan Chant Page
www.soulrebels.com/beth/chants.html

Cern's Pagan Songbook Online
www.cernowain.com/pagansongbook/psb.html

The Chant Archive
www.chantarchive.com

EarthSpirit Community Pagan Chant Library
www.earthspirit.com/mtongue/chtlib/chtlifr.html

En-Chant-Ment
    www.en-chant-ment.ca/chants.html

Expanding Inward Chants
    www.expandinginward.com/chants

Fire Circle Chants
    www.firecirclechants.com

Pagan Chants of the Month archive page, by Ivo Domínguez, Jr.
    www.seeliecourt.net/panpipe/oldchan.html

Pagan and Wiccan Songs and Chants
    www.sanfords.net/Pagan_Humor_and_Thoughts/chants.htm

Reclaiming Tradition Chants
    www.cernowain.com/pagansongbook/reclaiming/chants1.htm
    www.cernowain.com/pagansongbook/reclaiming/chants2.htm

Selected Pagan Dirges and Songs from *The Pagan Book of Living and Dying*,
    by Starhawk, M. Macha NightMare, and the Reclaiming Collective
    www.cernowain.com/pagansongbook/reclaiming/dirges.html

VegasVortex, Chants We Sing
    vegasvortex.com/pages/chants

Index

devotional, 19, 57, 68, 89–91, 159, 167, 208, 209, 233

drumming, 29, 35, 99, 132, 139, 170, 229, 240, 259, 261, 305, 307, 312

E
....

ecstatic, 31, 55, 57, 91, 92, 211, 232–234, 236

effigy, 2, 17, 23, 28, 298–300

elder, 38, 61, 148

elemental, 3, 7, 8, 11, 12, 29, 96, 97, 114, 163, 181, 220, 222, 224–227, 303, 304

elements, 1, 6, 9, 11, 24, 38, 39, 56, 62, 63, 65, 69, 95, 97, 108, 112, 114, 149, 160, 308

empowerment, 35, 60, 66, 165, 230–232

energy raising, 114, 116, 181–183, 189, 232, 234, 236, 284, 285, 287, 305, 308, 314, 319

Enki, 10, 155, 159, 166–173, 207, 212, 272

environmental, 34, 35

evocation, 207, 208

experiential, 24, 56, 57, 66, 80, 136, 145, 238, 287, 311

F
....

facilitator, 183

feast, 46, 113, 114, 218, 236, 237

fellowship, 35, 80, 81, 92, 167, 211, 230, 326

festival, 2–4, 6, 33, 46, 63, 65, 68, 110, 114, 117, 140, 193–195, 221, 229, 238, 258, 268, 301, 316, 319, 320

folktale, 60

G
....

gateway, 81, 115, 133, 137–139, 157, 159, 178, 209, 218, 222, 227, 238, 240, 276, 278–284, 290, 308, 310

gathering, 2, 3, 47, 74, 101, 117, 131–133, 135, 139, 160, 166, 172, 181, 182, 195, 201, 207, 230, 232, 237, 240, 241, 246, 254, 255, 259, 305, 308, 315, 316, 319, 320

god form, 90–92, 207, 233

Goddess, 10, 12, 14, 20, 25, 70, 127, 149, 152, 167, 175, 204, 207, 208, 224

gong gate, 218, 219

greeter, 44, 131, 132, 222, 224

ground, 8, 52, 69, 72, 117, 140, 157, 164, 179, 191, 198, 199, 205, 218, 235, 238, 240, 241, 249, 256, 267–269, 273, 276, 281, 284, 285, 298, 317

guardian, 45, 125, 142, 147, 157, 162, 163, 168, 169

guide, 11, 23, 24, 26, 44, 59, 63, 69, 106, 109, 113, 120, 167, 170, 172, 183, 197, 205, 230, 233, 234, 244, 256, 257, 310, 311, 314

guided meditation, 66, 107, 204–206, 218, 245

H
....

handler, 42, 162, 312

healing, 20, 34, 59, 87–89, 98, 99, 125, 126, 170, 198, 227, 316, 325

Hecate, 24, 26, 28, 29

I
....

Icarus, 8, 61, 63

illusion, 138, 149, 150, 152, 157, 219, 276

incantation, 20, 163, 207

incense, 3, 83, 118, 119, 134, 160, 199, 207, 214

initiation, 85, 145

inspiration, 4, 32, 54, 57–59, 61, 68, 91, 107, 221, 230, 257

intimacy, 21, 45, 55, 56, 80–82, 155, 156, 158, 160–163, 165, 233

invisible guides, 45, 137

invocation, 166, 171, 207, 208

L
....

leadership, 1, 4, 19, 40, 41, 88, 125, 166, 247, 249, 313, 314

LED, 3, 14, 26, 47, 52, 99, 107, 116, 121, 123, 128, 133, 144, 157, 196, 199, 200, 203, 224–226, 229, 230, 233, 238, 240, 241, 258, 259, 265, 276, 302, 305, 311, 319, 324, 326

lighting, 178, 179, 184, 204, 230, 233, 249, 253, 265, 293, 314

limited mobility, 36, 135, 251, 311, 312, 320, 321, 324

liturgy, 17

M
....

magic, 2, 3, 6, 9, 11, 14, 20, 49, 58, 96, 117, 119–121, 123–129, 179, 184, 191, 192, 203, 215, 224, 227, 231, 292, 301–303, 305

meditation, 35, 66, 91, 107, 123, 124, 128, 140, 142, 144, 187, 204–206, 218, 245

memorization, 4, 183–185

metaphor, 61, 113, 184, 209, 254

Minotaur, 53, 54, 62, 63, 69, 70, 72–74, 231

mirrors, 38, 150, 178, 219, 220, 273, 295, 297

modeling, 45, 134, 161, 164, 170, 187, 189, 211, 232, 235, 308, 310, 314

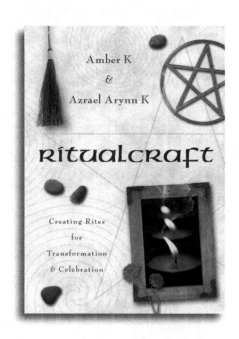

RitualCraft
Creating Rites for Transformation and Celebration
AMBER K & AZRAEL ARYNN K

You can change yourself and your world with effective, focused rituals. This book by renowned Witches Amber K and Azrael Arynn K shows you how to craft powerful and meaningful rituals for your life, your family, and your spiritual community.

The authors share their vast knowledge of ritual planning and performance, providing a framework for creating your own successful rituals. They illustrate the principles of ritual crafting with stories from their own experiences as they explore a variety of topics including rites of passage, esbats and sabbats, seasonal celebrations, rites for personal transformation, and rituals done simply for the fun of it.

You'll find information on all aspects of ritual including correspondences, timing, environment, attitude, music, meditation, altars, tools, costumes, and safety. This comprehensive book also offers worksheets, outlines, suggested themes, sample rituals, and a guide to teaching others.

Whether you're a beginner or seasoned practitioner, this comprehensive guide will help you take your own Witchcraft to new levels of significance, celebration, and personal transformation.

978-1-56718-009-1, 624 pp., 7 x 10   **$29.95**

A GUIDE TO CREATING
PUBLIC RITUALS THAT WORK

Isaac Bonewits

Neopagan Rites
A Guide to Creating Public Rituals That Work
Isaac Bonewits

Practical and engaging, this guide represents the best practices from Isaac Bonewits' over thirty-five years of experience creating, attending, and leading public ceremonies as a Neopagan priest and magician. Ideal for Earth-centered spiritual movements and other liberal religious traditions, *Neopagan Rites* explains how to design powerful and effective rites of worship for small groups or large crowds.

With his trademark humor and candor, Bonewits covers every important aspect of creating and performing a public ritual that inspires and unifies the participants, and fulfills its intended purpose. You'll learn how to:

- Determine the purpose of your ritual
- Create a basic ritual format that can be customized for different events
- Choose the optimal time and location for your event
- Enhance your ceremony with music, singing, poetry, and dance
- Add visual drama with costumes and altar decorations
- Include people with special needs in your ceremony
- Raise, channel, and send energy to your ritual's deity or cause

978-0-7387-1199-7, 240 pp., 6 x 9   **$15.95**